QUEER VIRGINIA

NEW STORIES IN THE OLD DOMINION

QUEER

VIRGINIA

Edited by

CHARLES H. FORD & JEFFREY L. LITTLEJOHN

UNIVERSITY OF VIRGINIA PRESS

Charlottesville and London

The University of Virginia Press is situated on the traditional lands of the Monacan Nation, and the Commonwealth of Virginia was and is home to many other Indigenous people. We pay our respect to all of them, past and present. We also honor the enslaved African and African American people who built the University of Virginia, and we recognize their descendants. We commit to fostering voices from these communities through our publications and to deepening our collective understanding of their histories and contributions.

University of Virginia Press
© 2025 by the Rector and Visitors of the University of Virginia
All rights reserved
Printed in the United States of America on acid-free paper

First published 2025

1 3 5 7 9 8 6 4 2

LIBRARY OF CONGRESS CATALOGING-IN-PUBLICATION DATA

Names: Ford, Charles Howard, editor. | Littlejohn, Jeffrey L., editor.
Title: Queer Virginia : new stories in the Old Dominion /
edited by Charles H. Ford and Jeffrey L. Littlejohn.
Description: Charlottesville : University of Virginia Press, 2025. |
Includes bibliographical references and index.
Identifiers: LCCN 2024058199 (print) | LCCN 2024058200 (ebook) | ISBN 9780813953267
(hardback ; alk. paper) | ISBN 9780813953274 (paperback ; alk. paper) | ISBN 9780813953281 (ebook)
Subjects: LCSH: Sexual minorities—Virginia—History. | Sexual minorities—Virginia—
Social conditions. | LCGFT: Essays. Classification: LCC HQ73.3.U62 V57 2025 (print) |
LCC HQ73.3.U62 (ebook) | DDC 306.7609755—dc23/eng/20250120
LC record available at https://lccn.loc.gov/2024058199
LC ebook record available at https://lccn.loc.gov/2024058200

Cover art: A Map of the State of Virginia, Philadelphia (H.S. Tanner and
E.B. Dawson, 1827). (Library of Congress, Geography and Map Division)
Cover design: Cecilia Sorochin

CONTENTS

A NOTE ON TERMINOLOGY

This anthology uses the adjective "queer" as the increasingly standard umbrella term to describe people whose sexuality, gender, or gender identity differ from cultural norms in the past or present. The term "queer" began as a vulgar epithet for same-sex behaviors and crossdressing in the late-nineteenth century. It was an especially cruel schoolyard taunt for those children who had no idea what it meant. Academics and activists then reclaimed the word "queer" beginning in the 1980s, as they searched for a comprehensive unifier for a diverse and fragmented movement. The "alphabet soup" of identities represented by the initialism LGBT (lesbian, gay, bisexual, transgender) was becoming increasingly unwieldy and confusing as more letters were added in the twenty-first century. A single adjective or noun seemed more appropriate and persuasive for an increasingly sympathetic general audience who engaged in and supported queer rights. While the reclaiming of the word "queer" was happening, queer theory emerged in the academy during the late 1980s, legitimizing and privileging outsider perspectives on familiar topics. This anthology is certainly within that now thirty-year-old tradition, even if, as local histories, its essays add more detail to the abstract strokes of theory, further grounding the subjects of the discipline and making them even more credible to a public who may still see queer communities as brand new or media-created.

For the coining of the term "queer theory," see Teresa de Laurentis, "Queer Theory: Lesbian and Gay Sexualities, An Introduction," *Differences: A*

Journal of Feminist Cultural Studies 3.2 (1991), iii–xvi. For more recent refinements of queer nomenclature and identities, see Cynthia Weber, "From Queer to Queer IR," *International Studies Review* 16.4 (December 2014), 596–601; Christian D. Chan and Lionel C. Howard, "When Queerness Meets Intersectional Thinking: Revolutionizing Parallels, Histories, and Contestations," *Journal of Homosexuality,* 67.3 (2020), 346–66.

QUEER VIRGINIA

QUEERING VIRGINIA HISTORY

Today, most queer histories of the United States remain focused on the pioneering efforts and landmark events that took place in large metropolitan areas such as New York City, Chicago, and San Francisco. The Stonewall Rebellion of 1969 provides the line between the oppression of the closet and the emergence of liberation, while San Francisco's Castro neighborhood stands as a model community that fostered an oasis of freedom in the 1970s. The American South only occasionally makes an appearance in these narratives and exhibitions in part because it lagged behind in political and cultural acceptance of queer identities and culture.

At the same time, a generation of detailed research on queer cultures outside of the big cities has helped to add to this persistent narrative. At the turn of this century, John Howard's *Men Like That: A Southern Queer History* revealed the existence and importance of homosexual men in the most unlikely of places: rural and small-town Mississippi. Around the same time, James T. Sears showed the vibrancy of liberation activism in the urban South, illustrating, among other things, the vigor of the Unitarian Church in Norfolk and its efforts to build community and visibility. A decade or so later, Brock Thompson wrote a personal historical narrative about his state of Arkansas, finding once again queer spaces and communities in places one would never guess. The inclusivity of these histories has gone far beyond the experiences of cisgender white men. In the late 2010s, Jaime Harker looked at women's liberation and gay liberation literature written by Southern authors, while cultural theorist C. Riley Snorton has traced the inherent intersectionality of Black and transgender identities in the American South and beyond from slavery through the present day. Finally, two significant monographs on different parts of Florida have set the standard for connecting local queer history with familiar national developments. Jerry T. (Jay) Watkins III, a contributor to this collection, has examined the LGBTQ dimensions shaping tourism in the Sunshine State's northern panhandle after World War II. Similarly, Julio Capó Jr. has connected local queer history with broad national themes such as the frontier, popular culture, and urban planning in his magisterial look at Miami before World War II. Accordingly, this collection of local studies from queer Virginia builds upon this growing oeuvre, offering a crucial enhancement and expansion of what it meant to be "queer" in the United States in the twentieth and early twenty-first centuries.[1]

Other sources of our inspiration and guidance must include E. Patrick Johnson's *Sweet Tea* and *Black. Queer. Southern. Women.* in their use of oral and personal-experience narratives to celebrate and demonstrate the nuanced diversities of queer cultures and mores. G. Samantha Rosenthal, another contributor to this collection, also has been a pioneer in connecting familiar themes of twentieth-century American history, such as urban blight and renewal, with experiences and stories from local queer people on the margins, who usually are found nowhere in scholarly monographs.[2]

While spotlighting the preservation of difference, the essays in this collection certainly see the simultaneous queer desire to conform or to work within the system. Essays in this volume have benefited from recent insights about the "politics of respectability," a term which emerged from the work of Evelyn Brooks Higginbotham on African American women leaders of the Gilded Age and Progressive Era. In her book *Righteous Discontent*, Higginbotham describes the politics of respectability as a strategy for social and political mobility employed by members of marginalized groups who abandon controversial aspects of their identities in an effort to assimilate or acquire power. This type of politics helped the more connected and mainstream in queer cultures to be accepted, but it certainly left out more androgynous, less gender-convergent people. In reference to Virginia in particular, the work of Megan Taylor Shockley helped the coeditors trace and clarify the reasons for the recent legal and political triumphs for queer cultures in the Commonwealth by deploying this lens of the politics of respectability. In contrast, white working-class lesbian Sharon Bottoms, who was portrayed as less than respectable, lost legal custody of her own child in the 1990s. In reaction to this widely known setback, activists chose their litigants to be middle-class and professional, helping all Virginians to secure basic rights in this century unexpectedly, as our first chapter shows.[3]

While reflecting trends within queer history, this collection adds to the field of Virginia history. Popular knowledge of the history of Virginia usually begins with the English settlement at Jamestown and ends with Robert E. Lee's surrender at Appomattox. The state's prized reputation as the birthplace of key founding fathers and the "mother of presidents" has always focused on the eighteenth and nineteenth centuries. Only recently has twentieth-century Virginia received attention as scholars have examined the struggle for African American civil rights and the meaning of liberty in the modern United States. This anthology extends that inclusion to local queer history.[4]

In the collection's first essay, we examine the entrenched opposition to same-sex relationships in Virginia and show how members of the LGBTQ community fought against and ultimately overcame such opposition. Beginning with evidence from the colonial, revolutionary, and antebellum periods, the chapter argues that Virginia's prohibitions against same-sex relationships evolved over time, becoming more restrictive as each decade passed. By the twentieth century, Virginians had enacted laws to prohibit sodomy, to sterilize the "unfit," and to prevent the spread of "obscene" materials. LGBTQ activists fought against such discrimination, and, by the end of the twentieth century, ministers in the Unitarian Church, United Church of Christ, and Metropolitan Community Church were offering spiritual sanction to same-sex couples. In response, Virginians outlawed same-sex marriage in a 2006 constitutional amendment. Most importantly, this overview explores the sudden cultural, political, and legal changes that led to the 2014 federal court opinion *Bostic v. Schaefer,* allowing same-sex marriage in Virginia. Despite entrenched oppression that took centuries to develop, court cases brought by impeccably respectable plaintiffs relied upon the Fourteenth Amendment to dispose of the legal discrimination that seemed so formidable just a few years before.

In the second essay, historian Amy Bertsch examines the ways in which Hannah Nokes, a Black transgender woman, presented herself to the public in the 1930s. Bertsch's essay opens with Nokes appearing as a witness in the well-known capital murder case of George Crawford, a Black man accused of killing two white women in Loudoun County, Virginia. Charles Hamilton Houston, the famed attorney with the National Association for the Advancement of Colored People (NAACP), defended Crawford by challenging Virginia's use of all-white jury pools. Bertsch's analysis reads across the grain, however, and focuses on the way that lawyers, jurors, and newspaper reporters perceived Nokes during her time in court. In fact, Bertsch's research shows that Nokes was viewed as a curiosity, but that she overcame discriminatory treatment and remained in the public eye, even appearing in a favorable spotlight in *Rural Electrification News* during the New Deal.

In the next essay, G. Samantha Rosenthal moves the narrative to western Virginia, where she examine the community of African American transgender women who engaged in sex work around Salem Avenue and Market Street in downtown Roanoke during the 1970s and 1980s. Rosenthal argues that sex work provided many transgender residents of Roanoke an opportunity to earn money and to build community, just as the city launched an effort to shut down sex work and "revitalize" the urban core. As a result, Rosenthal's essay shows that Black trans women acting as sex workers played a central role in the city's modern history, despite the fact that many in the cisgender community wanted to outlaw and erase the trans people in their midst.

Next, Jerry (Jay) Watkins examines the recent partnership between Diversity Richmond and the William and Mary LGBTQ Research Project, which together have collected oral histories from community elders and produced a complementary digital archive and exhibition for the public. This essay highlights the struggles that the two groups encountered as they contended with the for-profit demands of twenty-first century capitalism. In the old capital of the Confederacy, efforts to create diverse spaces and exhibits have been complicated by gentrification and tokenization of LGBTQ community members. Watkins argues that, in such an environment, Diversity Richmond should be seen as one element in an extensive network of organizations and activists working to create a space for queer Richmonders, rather than a single and monolithic center of "queer Richmond."

In chapter five, Senlin Means traces the emergence and impact of the HIV/AIDS epidemic in Charlottesville, a city best-known for hosting the state's flagship university, through the experiential lens of local queer activists and leaders. Through this often-poignant journey, Charlottesville's clubs, bars, and AIDS service organizations come alive, as the epidemic proved to be both a crucible and turning point in the ongoing struggles for legal equality and cultural inclusion. The local angle of this piece underscores the grave significance of this catastrophe, which is usually set in a metropolitan or "big-city" context.

Cathleen Rhodes then presents a history of the Hershee Bar, a long-standing lesbian bar that operated in a working-class neighborhood of Norfolk for decades before closing in recent years. Rhodes argues that the typical explanations—the use of dating apps, increasing acceptance in mainstream spaces, and changes in entertainment habits that come with committed relationships—provide only a simplistic explanation of what has happened to lesbian bars in the twenty-first century. In a detailed examination of local community efforts to keep the Hershee Bar open, Rhodes shows how city leadership refused to acknowledge the cultural and historical importance of the lesbian bar to its community. As Norfolk's leaders proposed that the bar simply move locations during the era of urban removal and renewal, they missed the emotional connections that many felt to the physical space. Indeed, when the bar that was open continuously for thirty-five years closed, it left a vacuum that seems to many impossible to fill.

In the final essay, we examine three prominent controversies that divided the residents of Norfolk, Portsmouth, Chesapeake, Suffolk, and Virginia Beach during the era of Gay Liberation. Our analysis begins with a review of the police raids that took place at local bars in the 1970s, highlighting in particular the harassment of law-abiding gay customers at Norfolk's Cue Club, Pantry, and other gay bars by the Virginia Alcohol Beverage Control Authority (VABC). Next, the essay turns to the emergence and distribution of queer publications in the 1970s, including Norfolk's Unitarian-Universalist Gay Caucus newsletter and eventual newspaper *Our Own Community Press*, which offered a voice and community-building nexus for gays and lesbians in the area. Conservative Christians and opponents of homosexuality in Hampton Roads viewed *Our Own Community Press* and other gay newspapers as instruments of deviant behavior and demanded that they be removed from public libraries in the early 1980s. As this debate raged, a screening of Frank Ripploh's controversial film *Taxi Zum Klo* in Norfolk in 1982 kicked off another fight. The film, a dark comedy about a Berlin school teacher who lived different public and private lives, proved too sexually explicit for local officials. Authorities actually seized the film after it was shown at the Naro Expanded Cinema in Norfolk's Ghent neighborhood, even though the movie soon achieved a cult status among queer and allied audiences who considered its treatment of gay culture and sexuality groundbreaking. By examining these three controversies, this chapter highlights the uneven and ambiguous nature of perceived progress in the 1970s and 1980s.

The hidden history revealed in these essays provide new lenses on seemingly familiar topics such as the New Deal, First Amendment rights, urban renewal and gentrification, the HIV/AIDS epidemic, and the judicial use of the Fourteenth Amendment. In particular, urban renewal and gentrification are frequently presented positively in relation to the preservation efforts of elite white gay men, but here the destructive consequences to queer cultures are clearly documented. The expansion of individual freedoms after World War II certainly benefited from national leaders and organizations, but it is always important to recognize, as we do here, the local people who secured civil liberties and marriage equality. Finally, the perseverance and creativity of queer Virginians in response to less-than-welcoming contexts is shown throughout the collection, indicating that widespread prejudice and oppressive laws could not stop people from being who they were.

NOTES

1. John Howard, *Men Like That: A Southern Queer History* (Chicago: University of Chicago Press, 1999); James T. Sears, *Rebels, Rubyfruit, and Rhinestones: Queering Space in the Stonewall South* (New Brunswick, New Jersey: Rutgers University Press, 2001); Brock Thompson, *Un-Natural State: Arkansas and the Queer South* (Fayetteville: University of Arkansas Press, 2010); Jaime Harker, *The Lesbian South: Southern Feminists, the Women in Print Movement, and the Queer Literary Canon* (Chapel Hill: University of North Carolina Press, 2018); C. Riley Snorton, *Black on Both Sides: A Racial History of Trans Identity* (Minneapolis: University of Minnesota Press, 2017); C. Riley Snorton, *Nobody Is Supposed to Know: Black Sexuality on the Down Low* (Minneapolis: University of Minnesota Press, 2014); Jerry T. Watkins III, *Queering the Redneck Riviera: Sexuality and the Rise of Florida Tourism* (Gainesville: University of Florida Press, 2018); Julio

Capo Jr., *Welcome to Fairyland: Queer Miami before 1940* (Chapel Hill: University of North Carolina Press, 2017). For a more comprehensive context for local southern stories, see Don Romesburg, *The Routledge History of Queer America* (New York: Routledge, 2018).

2. E. Patrick Johnson, *Sweet Tea: Black Gay Men of the South* (Chapel Hill: University of North Carolina Press, 2008); E Patrick Johnson, *Black. Queer. Southern. Women.: An Oral History* (Chapel Hill: University of North Carolina Press, 2018); G. Samantha Rosenthal, *Living Queer History: Remembrance and Belonging in a Southern City* (Chapel Hill, University of North Carolina Press, 2021).

3. Evelyn Brooks Higginbotham, *Righteous Discontent: The Women's Movement in the Black Baptist Church, 1880–1920* (Cambridge, Massachusetts: Harvard University Press, 1993); Megan Taylor Shockley, "Sharon Bottoms and Linda Kaufman: Legal Rights and Lesbian Mothers," in *Virginia Women: Their Lives and Times, Vol. 2*, edited by Cynthia A. Kierner and Sandra Gioia Treadway (Athens: University of Georgia Press, 2016), 354–76.

4. For an excellent example of a more inclusive and comprehensive look at Virginia history, see Peter Wallenstein, *Cradle of America: A History of Virginia*, 2nd edition (Lawrence, Kansas: University Press of Kansas, 2014).

FROM SODOMY LAWS TO SAME-SEX MARRIAGE

———

Discrimination and LGBTQ Activism in Virginia

JEFFREY L. LITTLEJOHN AND CHARLES H. FORD

n February 2014, U.S. District Court Judge Arenda Wright Allen issued a landmark decision in the Virginia same-sex marriage case *Bostic v. Rainey*.[1] Finding for the petitioners, Timothy Bostic and Tony London, a gay couple seeking to marry in Norfolk, Judge Wright Allen declared that all of Virginia's statutes and constitutional provisions outlawing same-sex marriage were void because they violated the equal protection clause of the U.S. Constitution's Fourteenth Amendment. In July 2014, the Fourth Circuit Court of Appeals upheld Wright Allen's decision, while restyling the case *Bostic v. Schaefer*.[2] The U.S. Supreme Court followed suit three months later, denying *certiorari* in the case and effectively overturning all Virginia laws banning same-sex marriage.[3] The high court's ruling also ended stays on same-sex marriage cases in Indiana, Oklahoma, Utah, and Wisconsin, while making it likely that same-sex marriage would expand into Colorado, Wyoming, Kansas, West Virginia, North Carolina, and South Carolina as well.[4] In fact, the *Bostic* decision set the stage for the U.S. Supreme Court's later ruling in *Obergefell v. Hodges*, which legalized same-sex marriage throughout the United States in June 2015.[5]

This chapter examines the entrenched opposition to same-sex relationships that existed in Virginia and then shows how members of the LGBTQ community fought and ultimately overcame such opposition. Beginning with evidence from the colonial, revolutionary, and antebellum periods, it argues that Virginia's prohibitions against same-sex relationships evolved over time, becoming more restrictive as each decade passed. By the twentieth century, Virginians had enacted laws to prohibit sodomy, to sterilize the "unfit," and to prevent the spread of "obscene" materials. These laws, backed by Christian moralizing and pseudo-scientific theories, served to stigmatize people increasingly known as "homosexuals," much as segregation and disenfranchisement had served to isolate and suppress the state's Black community. In fact, Virginians proved particularly aggressive in the targeting of gay, lesbian, and queer members of their communities, although the historiography on such matters remains almost nonexistent. While scholars like Peter Wallenstein, J. Douglas Smith, Pippa Holloway, and Lisa Dorr have published excellent studies on politics, culture, and law in Virginia, only one similar book by Gregory Samantha Rosenthal currently examines the discrimination against and activism by members of the LGBTQ community.[6]

Although gay, lesbian, and queer Virginians became more open during the last quarter of the twentieth century, same-sex relationships remained legally and culturally taboo in the state. The AIDS epidemic, the rise of political conservatism, and the expansion of Christian evangelicalism made matters worse. Yet there were glimmers of hope during the 1970s. For example, ministers in the Unitarian Church, United Church of Christ (UCC), and Metropolitan Community Church (MCC) began performing same-sex marriage ceremonies. These efforts to grant spiritual recognition to same-sex marriages did not, as of yet, carry any legal sanction. But, as LGBTQ activists challenged state laws and customs, the U.S. Supreme Court came to their aid. In 2003, the justices issued their historic decision in *Lawrence v. Texas* (2003), overturning state sodomy laws and making it possible for same-sex couples to pursue legal sanction for their marriages. In response, the majority of Virginia's voters decided in 2006 to outlaw same-sex marriage by constitutional amendment. This move, in turn, sparked a revitalized campaign to legalize same-sex marriage through the courts and the court of public opinion.

At the close of this overview, we pay special attention to the arguments in support of same-sex marriage, the entrenched opposition to such marriages, and the ways in which cultural, political, and legal changes created a new environment supportive of same-sex marriage during the second decade of the twenty-first century. In particular, this essay argues that LGBTQ activists adopted a form of respectability politics to push their cause forward. Early same-sex marriage efforts that had originated from the grassroots or from advocacy organizations were often limited by the marginal positions their clients, attorneys, and leaders held in the broader community. In the face of continuing opposition and oppression, advocates for same-sex marriage turned to a focus on upper-middle class, well-educated, white couples who would legitimize and "sell" the idea of same-sex marriage to Virginians.

For centuries, sodomy laws in Anglo-American culture prevented any discussion of same-sex marriage in England, its colonies, or, later, in the state of Virginia. In 1533, for example, the English Parliament under Henry VIII established the first civil sodomy law in England. Based on an ancient understanding of Judeo-Christian prohibitions against sodomy and "unnatural acts," the new legal code—called the Buggery Act—outlawed anal penetration and bestiality. In doing so, the act moved the issue of sodomy from ecclesiastical courts to state courts, and, along with the 1534 Act of Supremacy, it may have been part of Henry's larger effort to strip power from the church and redirect it to the state. According to the British Library, the "act did not explicitly target sex between men," because it also applied to sodomy between men and women and to bestiality. "Convictions between men for sodomy" were, however, "by far the most common and well publicised." Such convictions were considered felonies and were punishable by death.[7]

When the Virginia Company of London established Jamestown, the first permanent English settlement in North America, the leaders of the new Virginia colony outlawed sodomy in the *Lawes Divine, Morall and Martiall* (1610). The architect of the new legal code, Governor Thomas Gates, had arrived in the colony shortly after the deadly winter of 1609–10, better known as the Starving Times. In a desperate attempt to save the ninety or so settlers still living at Jamestown and Point Comfort, Gates established strict religious, political, and military rules. Among these was a declaration that "no man shal commit the horrible, and detestable sinnes of Sodomie upon pain of death."[8] This statement, the first antisodomy rule in England's North American colonies, established a precedent that would be followed in other colonies as well.

Virginia's English leaders did not stop there, however. In November 1624, a nineteen-year-old cabin boy named William Couse accused Captain Richard Cornish, the master of a merchant ship called the *Ambrose,* of forcibly sodomizing him. As a result, Cornish "may have been tried summarily before the governor or, more likely, the governor and Council. He was convicted and executed on an unrecorded date, probably not long after . . . January 3, 1625."[9] Edmund Morgan, the eminent historian of colonial and revolutionary Virginia, was one of the first scholars to discuss the Cornish case, but when he addressed it in *American Slavery, American Freedom,* Morgan focused on the savage punishment of two servants who criticized Cornish's execution rather than on the sexual nature of the crime. One of the critics, a sailor named Edward Nevell, lost both of his ears and had to serve the colony for a year because he insulted the governor. Another critic, Thomas Hatch, was sentenced to whipping, the loss of one ear, and an additional seven-year term of service for his criticism of the governor.[10]

A short time later, in 1629, Virginia's leaders faced another seeming violation of the colony's social order. At that time, residents of the tiny James River settlement of Warraskoyak were preoccupied with the sexual identity of indentured servant Thomas Hall, or Thomasine, who had changed gender with different jobs and sexual partners. Hall's case landed in Jamestown's

Portrait of Thomas/ine
Hall by Ren Tolson.

Quarter Court, which ruled that Hall was both a man and a woman. The court sentenced Hall to wear both male and female clothes in order to provoke public ridicule, but it seems unlikely that this accomplished the court's goal.[11]

Virginia's early efforts to control the gender identity and sexual behaviors of the colony's settlers continued throughout the seventeenth and eighteenth centuries. As the laws governing racial slavery became harsher so too did rules governing sexual relations, bastardy, and sodomy. Although Governor Thomas Jefferson made reforming Virginia's penal code a priority in 1779, during the American Revolution, he deemed sodomy as one of those awful behaviors that should still be harshly punished. Indeed, Jefferson's reform committee recommended castration for men and nose mutilation for women convicted of the crime. The legislature never passed these suggestions, however, and when the state approved its first sodomy law in 1792, the crime remained a capital offense. Between 1819 and 1848, the state reduced the maximum penalty for free people who engaged in sodomy to five years. The penalty for enslaved African Americans remained the same as it had always been, however: death without the benefit of clergy. Finally, in 1860, the legal code was updated to provide the same five-year maximum sentence for free and enslaved alike.[12]

Sodomy laws were not the only legal statutes that the Virginia leaders used to target people engaging in same-sex relationships. In fact, Virginia's 1860 legal code provided a list of crimes under the heading "offences against morality and decency." These crimes included adultery; fornication; lewd and lascivious cohabitation; racial intermarriage; the maintenance of a house of prostitution; and the printing, publishing, or selling of any obscene book, picture, or description that would corrupt the morality of youth. The 1860 legal code provided these crimes, which were considered immoral and destructive, immediately before its prohibition on sodomy. In this sense, then, the prohibition on fornication, racial intermarriage, prostitution, obscenity, and sodomy were all considered part of the same code against unnatural behaviors.[13]

During the decades after the U.S. Civil War, profound changes took place in Virginia, including the end of African American slavery, the enactment of Jim Crow segregation, and the emergence of a modern political state. The era's white conservative leaders celebrated Virginia's Revolutionary and Confederate heroes, while simultaneously trying to accommodate new ideas and technologies. Among these new ideas was the concept that homosexuals and heterosexuals were "distinct categories of people."[14] In fact, physicians and psychiatrists increasingly described homosexuality as a "disease, defect, or disorder,"[15] and thus provided "a powerful source of legitimation to anti-homosexual sentiment."[16] As a result, historian Gregory Samantha Rosenthal argues, Virginia's law enforcement officers felt free to use vagrancy and disorderly conduct laws to target gay, lesbian, and queer people who violated the standards of heteronormative behavior.[17]

Legislators gave the police even more tools of control during the 1910s and 1920s. Although Virginia remained a rural, agricultural state, novel technologies like radio and film began to reshape popular culture in cities like Norfolk, Richmond, and Roanoke. As a result, legislative leaders sought to control what they saw as illegitimate or immoral materials. In fact, the Virginia's General Assembly created its own "State Board of Censors, charged with preventing films from being shown in the state that were 'obscene, indecent, immoral, [or] inhuman.'"[18] As historian Pippa Holloway has shown, lawmakers followed these obscenity codes in 1924 with new laws on sodomy, interracial marriage, and the sterilization of "mental defectives." These bills codified popular and discriminatory views about gay, lesbian, and queer people, as well as African Americans and the intellectually disabled.[19] But state leaders were not done yet. In 1934, the Virginia Alcohol Control Board issued regulations, shortly after the repeal of national Prohibition, that prevented bars and other establishments from serving alcohol to homosexuals. This regulation served to effectively outlaw gay bars as places of community building and dating activity, and many gay, lesbian, and queer people were harassed by police or prosecuted for violating the ABC code if they challenged it.[20]

World War II and the Cold War accelerated discrimination against gay, lesbian, and queer people in Virginia. For the first time, the armed forces explicitly barred gay men and lesbians from military service, although many did serve while keeping their sexuality private.[21] Then, after the war, as historian David K. Johnson has shown, the federal government engaged in a top-down campaign of political repression to purge homosexuals from U.S. government jobs in a "Lavender Scare" that ruined the lives and careers of hundreds of men and women. In Virginia, the state even enacted a psychopathic offender law in 1950 that allowed for the mental examination of persons committing crimes that revealed a "sexual abnormality." Although the term remained undefined, the 1950 law helped to consolidate the public perception that gay, lesbian, and queer people were, in fact, criminal by nature.[22]

Virginia's modern LGBTQ rights movement began in the 1960s and 1970s in response to generations of discrimination, harassment, and violence. Inspired by activists like Frank Kameny, the founder of the nation's first gay rights organization, the Mattachine Society of Washington, DC, Virginia's gay leaders began to organize at the local level. In Richmond, for example, Gonzalo "Tony" Segura attempted to establish a local branch of the Mattachine Society, but he was forced instead to spend much of his time challenging the alcohol control code that barred the sale of alcohol to homosexuals. In March 1969, in fact, protests by gay activists led to the closure of two Richmond bars—Renee's and Rathskeller's—that catered to gays. The controversy surrounding the bars foreshadowed what was to happen at the Stonewall Inn in New York City only a few months later.[23] During the Stonewall Uprising in the summer of 1969, gay, lesbian, and queer people protested against police harassment at bars and other community spots in the country's largest city, drawing national attention to a recurring problem that members of the gay community faced.[24]

As queer activists participated in the Stonewall Uprising, they received support from an unlikely quarter: the U.S. Supreme Court. Between 1965 and 1973, the high court issued three landmark decisions that established the extensive marriage and reproductive rights adults in the U.S. enjoyed. In the first case, *Griswold v. Connecticut* (1965), the Court overturned state restrictions on contraception and ruled that a marital right to privacy allowed couples to use contraception to prevent pregnancy within the confines of marriage. Then, two years later, the justices ruled in *Loving v. Virginia* (1967) that the state's statutory prohibition on interracial marriage was unconstitutional because it violated the Fourteenth Amendment's equal protection clause. And, finally, the court ruled in *Roe v. Wade* (1973), that abortion was legal under the "right to privacy" that was inherent in the due process clause of the Fourteenth Amendment. Taken together, these decisions reshaped American legal culture and established a new political landscape in which lesbian and gay activists might launch a successful assault on the discriminatory laws that continued to limit their rights and personhood.[25]

Soon after the Supreme Court issued its decision in *Roe v. Wade*, Dr. Bruce Voeller, a founding member of the National Gay Task Force, joined with other strategists in a meeting with Supreme Court justice William O. Douglas. As the most liberal member of the court, Douglas told the activists he believed a constitutional case against sodomy laws in the U.S. might be successful if litigants could show that they realistically feared prosecution for a sex crime, even though they lived otherwise lawful lives. As a result, the activists found an anonymous plaintiff in Richmond, Virginia, who had been prosecuted under the state's sodomy law, and Voeller's partner, "who had ancestors on both sides of his family dating back to the establishment of the state's first white settlement in Jamestown in 1607," became a second plaintiff.[26]

To argue the case, the National Gay Task Force turned to Philip Hirschkop, a well-known Virginia attorney with the American Civil Liberties Union (ACLU) who had worked on *Loving v. Virginia*. Hirschkop organized a class action suit to challenge Virginia's sodomy law and argued that "the right to privacy recognized in *Roe* and its progeny protected the sexual behavior of consenting adults."[27] A three judge panel heard the case—*Doe v. Commonwealth's Attorney for the City of Richmond* (1975)—at the Eastern District Court of Virginia. Writing for the 2–1 majority, Judge Albert Bryan ruled that sodomy had long been banned by societies across the world and that even the biblical book of Leviticus contained a prohibition against the act. Virginia's law did not violate the U.S. Constitution, Bryan said, because it was "simply directed to the suppression of crime, whether committed in public or in private." Indeed, Bryan said, there was no bar to criminal penalties for sodomy "since it is obviously no portion of marriage, home or family life."[28]

Judge Robert Merhige wrote a heated dissent in the case, finding that the state of Virginia had offered "no evidence . . . that homosexuality causes society any significant harm." Indeed, he said, the state had made no effort "to establish either a rational basis or a compelling state interest" to justify its law against sodomy. The "sole basis" for the outlawing of homosexuality, Merhige said, was "what the majority refers to as the promotion of morality and decency." This was simply inappropriate. As Merhige argued, his fellow judges had "misinterpreted the issue—the issue centers not around morality and decency, but the constitutional right of privacy."[29]

Following the decision by the three-judge panel of the Eastern District Court, the plaintiffs in *Doe v. Commonwealth's Attorney* appealed their case directly to the U.S. Supreme Court. In a one-sentence ruling in 1976, without hearing oral arguments in the case, the high court simply confirmed the district court's decision. As a result, sodomy laws in Virginia and other states remained in place. The constitutional issue was settled, at least for the time being. States continued to have the right to outlaw sodomy and to arrest, imprison, and fine people who engaged in intimate same-sex relationships of any kind or duration.[30]

Despite the Supreme Court's decision in *Doe v. Commonwealth's Attorney*, gay activists in Virginia continued their struggle for acceptance and inclusion. For example, Leonard Matlovich, a decorated Vietnam veteran from Georgia, served at Langley Air Force Base in Hampton when he appeared on the cover of *Time Magazine* on September 8, 1975, declaring, "I am a homosexual." Matlovich's courage and simple eloquence made him an international icon of

Leonard Matlovich. (Leonard Matlovich Papers, Gay, Lesbian, Bisexual, Transgender Historical Society)

gay liberation and put the military—a large employer in Virginia during the Cold War—on notice that LGBTQ sailors, soldiers, and support staff wanted to serve their nation just like other patriotic members of the community.[31]

Matlovich's public statement helped to inspire a group of gay and lesbian activists in Norfolk who founded a social and political group at the city's Unitarian Universalist church. The group called itself the Unitarian-Universalist Gay Caucus (UUGC) and began publishing a newspaper called *Our Own Community Press* in September 1976. The initial issues of the paper discussed social get-togethers, as well as the UUGC's desire to establish telephone counseling, a venereal disease clinic, and free legal aid for members of the lesbian, gay, and queer community.[32] Over the course of several months, the paper grew from a one-page newsletter of three brief columns to a four-page paper including local news, poetry, and classified advertisements. By October 1977, *Our Own* had grown to eight pages with a monthly events calendar and book reviews on important new works relating to LGBTQ rights and related issues.[33]

The Unitarian Universalist Association (UUA) provided the gay caucus in Norfolk with important backing and legitimacy. In fact, the UUA had been the first national Christian denomination in the United States to recognize the rights of gays and lesbians. Organized in 1961, when two eighteenth-century liberal protestant denominations merged, the Unitarian Universalists quickly spoke up in defense of gay rights. In 1970, the organization issued its first major resolution on sexual orientation, which opposed discrimination against homosexuals and bisexuals. Then, in 1975, the UUA created its own Office of Lesbian and Gay Concerns to address religious, legal, and social matters of particular importance to gays and lesbians. In 1977, for example, the UUGC in Norfolk reported that the group had sent "letters to the Virginia ABC Board, the General Assembly, and the *Virginian-Pilot* concerning rights of gay people in the state." The group also encouraged members and concerned allies to write to Congress in support of the National Gay Civil Rights Bill (H.P. 451) to "eliminate discrimination on the basis of sexual/affectional preferences."[34]

Most evangelical Christian groups in the United States took a different stance on homosexuality. In Florida, for example, Anita Bryant, a former beauty queen, Christian singer, and outspoken anti-gay crusader, established the "Save Our Children" organization to push a homophobic agenda that challenged municipal and statewide bills to prohibit discrimination against gay, lesbian, and queer people. As historian Michael Bronski has argued, many social historians view the "success of Save Our Children . . . as the beginning of the rise of the religious right."[35] Indeed, Bryant received considerable support from two of Virginia's most conservative religious figures, Pat Robertson of Virginia Beach, founder of the Christian Broadcasting Network and Regent University, and Jerry Falwell of Lynchburg, founder of the megachurch Thomas Road Baptist, Liberty University, and the Moral Majority. Together, Bryant, Robertson, and Falwell condemned gays and lesbians, arguing that they lived an unnatural, predatory lifestyle. In fact, Bryant said, "As a mother, I know that homosexuals cannot biologically reproduce children; therefore, they must recruit our children."[36] Citing this argument time and again, Bryant developed a powerful rhetorical strategy that enabled social conservatives to raise money and advocate for "family values." In 1981, for example, Falwell echoed Bryant's campaign language, telling followers: "Please remember, homosexuals don't reproduce! They recruit! And they are out after my children and your children."[37] As a result, the religious right made the struggle against gay and lesbian liberation one of its principal priorities and pushed states to pass laws that "affected a range of family issues, such as banning lesbians and gay men from adopting children or becoming foster parents."[38]

The Unitarian Universalist Gay Caucus in Norfolk did not simply back down to Bryant and her supporters. In June 1977, when she spoke at the city's Scope auditorium, more than 350 protesters marched outside the building. Gay activists and their allies also formed the Norfolk Coalition for Human Rights and received support from the American Civil Liberties Union and the National Ecumenical Coalition from Washington, DC.[39] Together, these groups "spoke out against the 'biased persecution and intolerance for the gay minority' expressed by Anita Bryant and others." They also decried "the false propaganda using a religious basis for persecution (which) strikes at the very foundation of the basic tenet of the Unitarian Universalist Association, to seek the truth and support the worth of all humans."[40]

On July 4, 1981, an Associated Press article appeared in the *Richmond Times-Dispatch* announcing that a rare cancer had been found in twenty-six homosexual men. Citing evidence from the Centers for Disease Control (CDC), the article said that over the previous thirty months, "20 homosexual men in New York City and six in California were found to have Kaposi's sarcoma, an often fatal form of cancer."[41] Although this diagnosis failed to capture the gravity of the moment, the words in this story provided Virginians with the first hint of the HIV/AIDS pandemic to come. Between 1981 and 2007, "AIDS would claim the lives of 583,298 women, men, and children in the United States and 2.1 million worldwide."[42] The disease, spread through bodily fluids such as semen or blood, was initially associated with gay men. As a result, it was used to further stigmatize homosexuals and pass explicit laws to discriminate against them in housing, insurance, and health care. The Reverend Jerry Falwell, from his influential pulpit in Lynchburg, Virginia, repeatedly cast AIDS as divine retribution for both the sinful behavior of homosexual men and the increasing societal acceptance or indifference to such behavior.[43] This hateful, destructive language meant a great deal coming from the cofounder of the Moral Majority, and it signaled a larger movement against members of the LGBTQ community by groups like the American Family Association, the Family Research Council, and Focus on the Family.[44] Some scholars have even argued that Falwell's outspoken homophobia contributed to President Ronald Reagan's lackadaisical response to the AIDS crisis, which one historian has called "willful negligence."[45]

In Virginia, gay and lesbian activists took matters into their own hands. For example, led by psychiatrist Dr. Robert F. Scott and bar owner Tony Pritchard, a group made up of businesspeople, attorneys, and church leaders formed the Tidewater AIDS Community Taskforce (TACT) in Norfolk in 1983. This organization sponsored an AIDS helpline and HIV testing, while also providing information about job security, insurance coverage, and HIV prevention. AIDS housing groups in a variety of cities also raised funds and worked to find low-priced apartments for victims of the AIDS epidemic. In the midst of the AIDS crisis, churches across Virginia also assisted with clothing drives, fundraisers, and spiritual support. The Metropolitan Community Church was a direct supporter of TACT, in particular, and offered office space and much-needed emotional and spiritual sustenance.[46]

At the same time, the Unitarian Universalist Association "became the first large [Christian] denomination to affirm religious celebrations of the union of gay or lesbian couples." In June 1984, over a thousand delegates at the international General Assembly of the UUA voted on a resolution to affirm "the growing practices of some of its ministers of conducting services of union of gay and lesbian couples," and it urged "member societies to support their ministers in this important aspect of our movement's ministry to the gay and lesbian community." By the time the resolution passed on June 28, 1984, the Rev. Gary Gullun, minister of the Unitarian Church in Norfolk, had performed "over a dozen" exchanges of vows.[47]

Despite the work of Gullun and other progressive ministers, the atmosphere around conducting holy unions for same-sex couples in Virginia remained toxic in the late twentieth century. Even Earl Jones, the owner of Virginia Beach's Outright Books—one of the first openly gay spaces outside of a bar in Hampton Roads—felt it prudent to have his commitment to his partner publicly acknowledged via a mass ceremony done on the steps of the Internal Revenue Service (IRS) during the national March on Washington, DC, in April 1993. Jones had been with his partner, Kevin Metz, for seven years and had considered local options. But the communal context of the march in the relatively freer air of the federal capital seemed to have more impact and meaning for Jones and Metz. As Jones stated in the local community paper, "I liked what the whole symbolism was."[48]

Conservative religious groups viewed these courageous acts of affirmation and defiance—whether done in a large public group or privately within the milieu of liberal Protestantism—with complete disdain. In fact, between 1974 and 2009, anti-gay activists passed more than a hundred bills through local, state, and national governments to challenge the rights of queer people.[49] Many of the bills focused on family matters, like adoption, parenting, and marriage, and the courts almost always supported measures passed by lawmakers. In January 1993, for example, a Virginia grandmother, Kay Bottoms, filed for custody of her grandson Tyler Doustou in juvenile court. Bottoms argued that her daughter, Sharon, had been a poor mother to two-year-old Tyler and that her lesbian lifestyle endangered the child. Virginia Circuit Court judge Buford Parsons ruled in favor of the grandmother, stating bluntly that Sharon's "conduct is illegal . . . in the Commonwealth of Virginia." Continuing, the judge declared that "it is the opinion of this Court that [the mother's] conduct is immoral" and "renders her an unfit parent." The Virginia Supreme Court upheld Parson's decision, suggesting that the mother's lesbianism would subject her child to social pressure and disrupt his relationship with schoolmates.[50]

The legality of same-sex marriage first became a public issue in the early 1990s, when three same-sex couples sued Hawaii's director of health to force the state to issue them marriage licenses. Although a trial court dismissed the couples' suit, they quickly appealed their case to the state supreme court. In 1993, the justices ruled that Hawaii's denial of marriage licenses to same-sex couples violated the equal protection rights provided in the state constitution. As a result, the state supreme court returned the case to the trial court for reconsideration. Before the case could be retried, however, the state legislature passed a 1994 law that defined marriage as an institution between "one man and one woman." Then, four years later, voters in Hawaii approved an amendment to the state constitution that gave the legislature the right to limit marriage to different-sex couples. As a result, the Supreme Court of Hawaii ruled that the legislative statute and constitutional amendment meant that same-sex marriage was no longer an equal protection issue, and the case was dismissed in December 1999.[51]

As the Hawaii case worked its way through the judicial system, social conservatives in the United States Congress introduced the Defense of Marriage Act (DOMA) in May 1996. The act established the federal definition of marriage as the union of one man and one woman, and it prohibited same-sex couples from receiving tax, social security, or pension benefits as married couples.[52] In addition, the act said that each state could refuse to recognize same-sex marriages granted in other states. Meanwhile, at the local level, twenty-three states, including Virginia, passed prohibitions on same-sex marriage between 1996 and 1997.[53]

Virginia's story is, in fact, very similar to the narrative in other states. In 1997, for example, the General Assembly amended the state code to define marriage as the union between one man and one woman. Lawmakers additionally stated that "a marriage between persons of the same sex is prohibited." This ban also applied to unions from other states or countries. Legislators provided specifically that "any marriage entered by persons of the same sex in another state or jurisdiction shall be void in all respects in Virginia and any contractual rights created by such marriage shall be void and unenforceable."[54]

These limitations on marriage became increasingly controversial in the new century. After Massachusetts became the first state in the country to legalize same-sex marriage in 2004, legislators in Virginia decided that they must add additional protections to state law. As a result, social conservatives in the General Assembly proposed and passed House Joint Resolutions 91 and 187, which were intended to amend the Virginia Constitution, defining marriage as an institution between one man and one woman. As required by state law for changes to the constitution, the proposals were reintroduced and passed again in 2006 under a newly elected state legislature. On November 7, 2006, 57 percent of Virginia voters ratified the constitutional amendment.[55] The majority was smaller than expected, but having discrimination permanently enshrined in the state constitution seemed to sustain heteronormative hegemony for the long-term future.

In response, LGBTQ activists at the local, state, and national levels soon began to challenge same-sex marriage restrictions as a violation of their equal protection rights guaranteed by the Fourteenth Amendment to the

Tim Bostic and Tony London.

U.S. Constitution. They complained that the denial of the marriage right prevented them from important property, tax, health, insurance, and childcare rights, while also challenging their love for one another and undermining their full citizenship rights. As these arguments gained support across the country, two sets of Virginia litigants emerged to contest the state's prohibition on same-sex marriage. The first set of petitioners surfaced when Timothy Bostic and Tony London, a well-connected and prominent same-sex couple from Norfolk, sought a marriage certificate from their local circuit court clerk. After being denied a license due to their status as a same-sex couple, Bostic and London filed a federal lawsuit against Governor Bob McDonnell, Attorney General Ken Cuccinelli, and Norfolk Circuit Court Clerk George E. Schaefer. A short time later, a second well-positioned and long-term same-sex couple from Chesterfield County, Mary Townley and Carol Schall, joined the lawsuit, which was amended to add State Registrar of Vital Records Janet M. Rainey as the primary defendant. At the same time, the two couples announced that they would be represented by Theodore "Ted" B. Olson and David Boies, the well-credentialed and high-profile team that had successfully challenged California's Proposition 8, a similar law that banned same-sex marriage, before the U.S. Supreme Court.[56]

As this initial set of litigants emerged to challenge Virginia's statutory and constitutional law, two other same-sex couples formed a second set of petitioners in the Shenandoah Valley. There, Joanne Harris, Jessica Duff, Christy Berghoff, and Victoria Kidd filed a lawsuit in U.S. district court in Harrisonburg. Represented by the American Civil Liberties Union of Virginia, Lambda Legal, and the firm Jenner and Block, this group successfully sought class-action status before U.S. District Court Judge Michael Urbanski, who extended the scope of the case to include all same-sex couples who could not marry in Virginia.

As these two groups of litigants pursued their cases against Virginia, the state's political and legal leaders changed. In January 2014, the new attorney general, Mark R. Herring, announced that he believed Virginia's marriage amendment was unconstitutional and that he would side with the plaintiffs in *Bostic v. Rainey* rather than defend the ban in court. This was especially remarkable given that Herring had supported the 2006 constitutional amendment. At the same time, Rainey announced that she, as the registrar of vital records, would likewise abandon her prior defense of Virginia's marriage laws.[57]

Following these transformative developments, Judge Arenda Wright Allen heard two hours of oral arguments in *Bostic v. Rainey* on February 4, 2014. Attorneys Ted Olson and David Boies argued that Virginia's same-sex marriage ban violated the Equal Protection Clause of the U.S. Constitution and reduced same-sex couples to "second-class" citizenship. On the other hand, attorneys defending the statutory and constitutional law of Virginia countered that marriage had traditionally been recognized as a union between one man and one woman, and that changes to this vital institution would weaken society and endanger children. Nine days later, Judge Wright Allen found for Bostic, London, Townley, and Schall. She ruled, specifically, that Virginia's marriage laws violated the Fourteenth Amendment's Equal Protection Clause and, thus, prohibited same-sex couples from enjoying their full rights. Wright Allen issued a stay of her ruling until the Fourth U.S. Circuit Court of Appeals could hear the case. Ultimately, that court and the U.S. Supreme Court verified Wright Allen's decision and legalized same-sex marriage in Virginia.[58]

Judge Wright Allen's decision provoked little controversy because Virginia's establishment, including its attorney general, had come to see same-sex marriage as worthy of constitutional protection. This change of heart came suddenly and showed the effectiveness and prescience of activist organizations that chose the mainstreaming of queer difference over other more radical options. Virginia itself had changed—going from the most stalwart pillar of the Reagan Revolution to helping elect the first African American president in 2008, who had campaigned on the audacity of change. Giving official sanction to relationships that had previously been seen as criminal or psychopathic was just one of the reforms that came out of this period, but it certainly was the most unexpected, given the depth and longevity of the legal and cultural legacy of oppression that had begun centuries before.

NOTES

Charles H. Ford wishes to thank the Board of Directors of Hampton Roads Pride for their significant support of his local queer history projects, including this edited collection. He also wishes to thank his colleagues and students in the Department of History and Interdisciplinary Studies at Norfolk State University for their inspiration and assistance. Jeffrey L. Littlejohn wishes to thank his parents, Ronnie and Patty, as well as his colleagues for their steadfast support of his local "hidden" history projects and initiatives.

1. *Bostic v. Rainey,* 970 F. Supp. 2d 456 (E.D. Va. 2014).
2. *Bostic v. Schaefer,* No. 14–1167 (4th Cir. 2014).
3. Markus Schmidt, "Court Says Gay Marriages in Va. Could Begin Next Week," *Richmond Times-Dispatch,* August 13, 2014; U.S. Supreme Court Order Denying Certiorari, List of Orders, October 6, 2014, 39.
4. Schmidt, "Court Says Gay Marriages."
5. *Obergefell v. Hodges,* 576 U.S. 644.
6. Peter Wallenstein, *Blue Laws and Black Codes: Conflict, Courts, and Change in Twentieth-Century Virginia* (Charlottesville: University of Virginia Press, 2004); J. Douglas Smith, *Managing White Supremacy: Race, Politics, and Citizenship in Jim Crow Virginia* (Chapel Hill: University of North Carolina Press, 2002); Pippa Holloway, *Sexuality, Politics, and Social Control in Virginia, 1920–1945* (Chapel Hill: University of North Carolina Press, 2006); Lisa Lindquist Dorr, *White Women, Rape, and the Power of Race in Virginia, 1900–1960* (North Carolina Press, 2004); G. Samantha Rosenthal, *Living Queer History: Remembrance and Belonging in a Southern City* (Chapel Hill: University of North Carolina Press, 2021).
7. British Library, "The Buggery Act 1533," https://www.bl.uk/collection-items /the-buggery-act-1533, accessed August 2021. See also William Eskridge Jr., "Law and the Construction of the Closet: American Regulation of Same-Sex Intimacy, 1880–1946," *Iowa Law Review,* vol. 82 (1996–97): 1007–36.
8. William Strachey, *For The Colony in Virginea Britannia. Lawes Divine, Morall and Martiall, &c. Alget qui non Ardet. Res nostrae subinde non sunt, quales quis optaret, sed quales esse possunt* (London: Walter Barre, 1612). The law was enacted May 24, 1610.
9. John M. Murrin, "Cornish, Richard alias Richard Williams (d. after January 3, 1625)," *Encyclopedia Virginia,* https://encyclopediavirginia.org/entries/cornish -richard-alias-richard-williams-d-after-january-3-1625; H. R. McIlwaine, ed., *Minutes of the Council and General Court of Colonial Virginia, 1622–1632, 1670–1676* (Richmond: Colonial Press, 1924), 34, 42, 78, 81, 83, 85.
10. Edmund S. Morgan, *American Slavery, American Freedom* (New York: W. W. Norton & Co., 1975), 125.
11. McIlwaine, *Minutes of the Council and General Court of Colonial Virginia,* 194–95.

12. George Painter, "The Sensibilities of Our Forefathers: The History of Sodomy Laws in the United States—Virginia," https://www.glapn.org/sodomylaws /sensibilities/virginia.htm.

13. "Chapter 196: Of Offences Against Morality and Decency," in *The Code of Virginia, Second Edition, Including Legislation to the Year 1860* (Richmond: Ritchie, Dunnavant & Co.), 803–5. For more information about early same-sex marriage issues, see Rachel Hope Cleves, "'What, Another Female Husband?': The Prehistory of Same-Sex Marriage in America," *Journal of American History,* vol. 101, no. 4 (March 2015): 1055–81.

14. During the nineteenth century, important linguistic and conceptual changes emerged regarding same-sex relationships. During the period, two European reformers, Karl Maria Kertbeny and Karl Ulrichs, wrote separately about same-sex behavior and its meaning. Drawing on examples from antiquity and the Renaissance, they argued that there were robust, centuries-old traditions of same-sex relationships in the West. As historian Michael Bronski has shown, the two authors made "a case for both the naturalness of same-sex desire and the reformation of laws that criminalized homosexual behavior." In fact, Kertbeny actually invented the word "homosexual" in 1869 in order to "construct a narrative around a person defined by his or her same-sex desires and actions." Michael Bronski, *A Queer History of the United States* (Boston: Beacon Press, 2011), xv–xvii.

15. Catherine E. Stetson, et. al., "Brief of *Amici Curiae* Historians of Antigay Discrimination in Support of Plaintiffs-Appellees," *Bostic v. Schaefer,* April 18, 2014.

16. George Chauncey, *Why Marriage: The History Shaping Today's Debate Over Gay Equality* (New York: Basic Books, 2004), 10.

17. "Dr. Hawthorne Is Heard," *Daily Times* (Richmond, Virginia), October 24, 1902; G. Samantha Rosenthal, *Living Queer History: Remembrance and Belonging in a Southern City* (Chapel Hill: University of North Carolina Press, 2021), 27.

18. Pippa Holloway, *Sexuality, Politics, and Social Control in Virginia, 1920–1945* (Chapel Hill: University of North Carolina Press, 2006), 1.

19. Ibid, 1–2.

20. Rosenthal, *Living Queer History,* 39; "The French Quarter Café," *Alexandria Times,* July 2, 2020.

21. Allan Berube, *Coming Out Under Fire: The History of Gay Men and Women in World War II* (New York: Free Press, 1990), 2, 8–18, 121–48; Leisa D. Meyer, *Creating GI Jane: Sexuality and Power in the Women's Army Corps during World War II* (New York: Columbia University Press, 1996), 169–78; Margot Canaday,

The Straight State: Sexuality and Citizenship in Twentieth-Century America (Princeton: Princeton University Press, 2009), 140–47.

22. David K. Johnson, *The Lavender Scare: The Cold War Persecution of Gays and Lesbians in the Federal Government* (Chicago: University of Chicago Press, 2004).
23. Beth Marschak and Alex Lorch, *Lesbian and Gay Richmond* (Charleston, South Carolina: Arcadia Publishing, 2008), 7. See also Franklin E. Kameny, "State ABC Board's Action Criticized," *Richmond Times-Dispatch*, April 26, 1969.
24. Bronski, *A Queer History of the United States*, 209–19; Patricia A. Cain, "Litigating for Lesbian and Gay Rights: A Legal History," Virginia Law Review, vol. 79, no. 7 (Oct 1993): 1551–1641;
25. Jason Pierceson, Courts, Liberalism, and Rights: Gay Law and Politics in the United States and Canada (Philadelphia: Temple University Press, 2005).
26. Randy Shilts, *Conduct Unbecoming: Lesbians and Gays in the U.S. Military* (New York: St. Martin's Griffin), 283.
27. Mary Ziegler, "Perceiving Orientation: Defining Sexuality After Obergefell," *Duke Journal of Gender Law and Policy*, vol. 23 (2016): 234.
28. *Doe v. Commonwealth's Attorney for the City of Richmond*, 403 F. Supp. 1199 (E.D. Va. 1975), 1200–1202.
29. Ibid., 1203–1205.
30. *Doe v. Commonwealth's Attorney for the City of Richmond*, 425 U.S. 901 (1976). See also, Bob Woodward and Scott Armstrong, *The Brethren: Inside the Supreme Court* (New York: Avon, 1981), 505.
31. "The Sexes: The Sergeant v. the Air Force," *Time Magazine*, vol. 106, no. 10, September 8, 1975.
32. Information on *Our Own Community Press* is taken from the Old Dominion University Libraries Digital Collections page, https://olddomuni.access.preservica.com.
33. Every edition of *Our Own Community Press* is available online at the Old Dominion University Libraries Digital Collection, https://olddomuni.access.preservica.com.
34. "A Lot to Show for Six Months," *Our Own Community Press*, February 1977, 1; "Congress Faces 'Gay Bill' Again," *Our Own Community Press*, March 1977, 2.
35. Bronski, *A Queer History of the United States*, 221.
36. Anita Bryant, quoted in Bronski, *A Queer History of the United States*, 222.
37. Jerry Falwell, quoted at https://www.pbs.org/outofthepast/past/p5/1977.html.
38. Bronski, *A Queer History of the United States*, 223.
39. "Anita Brings Anti-Gay Crusade to Va.," *Bee* (Danville, Virginia), June 9, 1977; "Gays to Stage Anti-Anita Bryant Rally," *Richmond Times-Dispatch*, June 2, 1977.

40. Jim Early, "Unitarians Affirm Services of Union for Gay and Lesbian Couples," *Our Own Community Press*, August 1984.

41. "Rare Cancer Is Found in 26 Homosexual Men," *Richmond Times-Dispatch*, July 4, 1981.

42. Bronski, *A Queer History of the United States*, 224.

43. Mark R. Kowalski, "Religious Constructions of the AIDS Crisis," *Sociological Analysis* 51.1 (1990): 93. See also "AIDS," *Times* (Shreveport, Louisiana), July 14, 1983.

44. For the vitriolic rhetoric here coming in part from Virginia, see John Manuel Andriote, *Victory Deferred: How AIDS Changed Gay Life in America* (Chicago: University of Chicago Press, 1999), 68–69.

45. Bronski, *A Queer History of the United States*, 225.

46. Mark Hiers, "The Tidewater AIDS Crisis Task Force: Who We Are—Where We're Going," *Our Own Community Press*, August 1985.

47. Early, "Unitarians Affirm Services of Union for Gay and Lesbian Couples."

48. John Freeman, "Modern Romance: Holy Union Showcases Gay Couple's Commitment," *Our Own Community Press*, January 1994.

49. Stetson, et. al., "Brief of *Amici Curiae* Historians of Antigay Discrimination."

50. *Bottoms v. Bottoms*, 457 S.E.2d 102, 109 (Va. 1995).

51. Chauncey, *Why Marriage*, 125–26.

52. Ibid.

53. The American Bar Association, "An Analysis of the Law Regarding Same-Sex Marriage, Civil Unions, and Domestic Partnerships," 2005, 13.

54. Joan Edwards Tupponce, "Walk up Aisle Requires Many Steps," *Richmond Times-Dispatch*, January 20, 1998.

55. Tony Gabriele, "Marriage Amendment Passes," *Daily Press* (Newport News, Virginia), November 8, 2006.

56. "Timeline on Same-Sex Marriage and Virgina," *Richmond Times-Dispatch*, February 16, 2014.

57. Ibid.

58. *Bostic v. Rainey*, 970 F. Supp. 2d 456 (E.D. Va. 2014); *Bostic v. Schaefer*, No. 14-1167 (4th Cir. 2014).

BEYOND "RED WIGGED BOY-GIRL"

Perceptions of a Black Transgender Woman in
Northern Virginia before Queer Liberation

AMY BERTSCH

The capital murder case of George Crawford, an African American man accused of killing two white women in Loudoun County in 1932, captured national headlines when civil rights attorney Charles Hamilton Houston challenged Virginia's all-white jury pools.[1] As news wires, Washington, DC, papers, and the Black press covered the trial, some reporters noted that one witness for the prosecution had "masqueraded as a woman."[2]

When Hammond Nokes appeared in court wearing a green satin dress, velvet hat, and beaded necklace, the *Afro-American* observed that this "mysterious witness" had a "muscular neck," "closely-cropped beard," and "husky masculine voice."[3] Another article from the *Afro-American* dedicated to the backstory of "this queer individual" explained that Nokes's mother had raised her child as a girl.[4] While that account cannot be substantiated and news coverage during the Crawford trial rightly focused on the issue of lily-white juror rolls, the life of Hammond Nokes, a transgender African American woman, deserves more attention than a sensational sidebar. She also deserves to be called by her chosen name of Hannah, and going forward, the name "Hammond" will only be used when quoting others.[5]

But as newspaper reporters then were challenged to present an accurate and balanced portrait of Hannah Nokes, we are confronted with difficult questions in considering her story and her place in trans history. At a minimum, her story builds upon steadily expanding scholarship that shows gender variance has long existed and adds to our understanding of the complex history that is our queer past.

Several leading historians use "trans" to refer to any individual moving away from the gender assigned to them at birth, with Susan Stryker applying it to "people who cross over (*trans-*) the boundaries constructed by their culture to define and contain that gender."[6] Others have reinforced this concept while also emphasizing the existence of trans people in the past, with Emily Skidmore observing that although the term "transgender is modern, people have moved from one gender to another for a very long time."[7] Jesse Bayker supports this view of transgender history, explaining that it "really is about personal reinvention, transformation, and the possibilities for people to change their identities."[8]

"Trans" also serves as a lens to examine conventions and customs associated with gender variance. In *Arresting Dress: Cross-Dressing, Law, and Fascination in Nineteenth-Century San Francisco,* Clare Sears applied a "trans-ing" analysis to study the practices associated with cross-dressing rather than a focus on the cross-dressing individual.[9] More recently in their study, *Female Husbands: A Trans History,* Jen Manion thoughtfully chose "trans" as a verb, as in "transing" and "transed gender," to show change as an ongoing process rather than a basic switch between two genders. Manion's approach also allows historians to signify a "process or practice without claiming to understand what it meant to that person or asserting any kind of fixed identity on them."[10]

However, it is C. Riley Snorton's consideration of both gender and race while challenging the "dominant logic of identity" that is most significant to this essay. In *Black on Both Sides: A Racial History of Trans Identity,* Snorton views trans as an analytical tool to examine change, observing that "'trans' is more about a movement with no clear origin and no point of arrival."[11] But Snorton also recognizes the significance of race and particularly how "blackness is transected by embodied procedures that fall under the sign of gender." This approach is especially useful when exploring the life and perceptions of Hannah Nokes.

Before queer liberation, individuals who we recognize today as transgender existed and were known in their families and communities, but their experiences and identities as transgender people are largely unrecognized and unrecorded. As historians find their stories, we face multiple challenges of how to document and share them, even those from the relatively recent twentieth century. Do we avoid ascribing anachronistic terms like "transgender" to describe gender nonconforming individuals from the past, as Kim Gallon has in her examinations of Black female impersonators?[12] Genny Beemyn discourages its use, believing the "best we can do as historians is to acknowledge individuals whose actions would seem to indicate that they might be what we could call 'transgender' or 'transsexual' today without necessarily referring to them as such."[13] Beemyn, Snorton, and Skidmore also recognize the need for more profiles of trans people of color from the past, and in this case, the life and visibility of Hannah Nokes certainly add to that knowledge.[14]

In his examination of news coverage of Black transgender individuals in the mid-twentieth century, Snorton deliberately omits the names they were given at birth and details about how each "came to identify as differently gendered." Snorton writes that studying these media accounts is "not merely a matter of excavating forgotten narratives, or of offering up presence over absence." Rather Snorton recognizes the "potential of shadows to refigure trans historiography." Drawing upon newspaper accounts of his subjects, Snorton writes, "Positioned in the shadows of History, perhaps existing there even in their moments of notoriety, they lay the groundwork for understanding trans/gender embodiment," even with accounts that are "biased and partial, structured by the contemporaneous modes of thought that engendered a figure 'newsworthy.'"[15]

In her studies of Black newspaper coverage of African American female impersonators, Gallon finds their appearance in the press and their interactions with Black institutions indicate that "gender nonconforming and homosexual expression are not simply a sideshow of African American history but an integral part of the story."[16] Gallon's work, in particular, also provides compelling context for the *Afro-American*'s coverage of Hannah Nokes's court appearance, especially when considering the work of "pansy beat" reporter Ralph Matthews who "reported on a general range of topics and events relating to gender-nonconforming dress and homosexuality among black men."[17]

The vocabulary newspapers printed to describe Hannah Nokes in the 1930s reveals how she presented herself while demonstrating the press's inability to simply label her. Now, nearly a century later, we are cautioned against using the term "transgender" to describe her. What should become clear in this profile, however, is that Nokes identified as female, lived as a woman, and was accepted by her family as such. Although she could have lived in relative anonymity in a city, like nearby Washington, DC, she remained in her rural community. In doing so, Nokes challenged social and cultural norms of the period and built a life for herself that even lawyers and journalists were forced to acknowledge. As such, her story offers a powerful example of trans visibility decades before queer liberation, something that is even more significant considering she faced the additional burden of racial oppression.

Hannah Nokes was born in 1898 near Sterling, Virginia, to parents who were not married to each other.[18] Initially she used her mother's last name of Johnson but later went by her father's last name, Nokes.[19] As an adult, Hannah Nokes lived along Dranesville Road, across the Loudoun County line in Fairfax County and just outside of the town limits of Herndon.[20] Nokes was in certain ways a woman of her time, taking in boarders, doing laundry, and working as a domestic for white families to earn a living like many other Black women in the Jim Crow South did.

In January 1932, George Crawford spent a night at Hannah Nokes's home. He had been walking along Leesburg Pike, a major thoroughfare, with another man when he encountered a white teenage boy, Robert Hughes, on horseback. Crawford asked the Hughes boy if he knew of a place where they could stay, so Hughes had them follow him to Nokes's home where Hughes asked Nokes if the two men could spend the night. Crawford and the other man did spend that night at her home and then left the following morning. As he left, Crawford indicated that he would repay Nokes for his breakfast and jotted down her name and address in a small notebook.[21]

A couple days later, Agnes Ilsley and her housekeeper were found murdered in Middleburg, about twenty-five miles west of the Nokes home. Ilsley's car was missing, and when it was recovered in Alexandria a few days later, police found a note inside with Hannah Nokes's name written as "Mr Nock" and her address recorded as "Box 87, herdon Va."[22] Police and prosecutors quickly identified Crawford as their suspect and presented their evidence to a grand jury. Crawford was indicted for the murders and eventually arrested in

Massachusetts. But because of Charles Houston's challenge to the all-white grand jury as well as other concerns, such as protecting Crawford from a possible lynching, the trial did not take place until December of the following year, almost two years after the murders.

Hannah Nokes was not a witness to the actual crime. Prosecutors called her to testify to establish that Crawford had been in the general area in the days leading up to the murders. Her nephew, Rastus Nokes, had also been at her house when Crawford visited, and Rastus Nokes testified that he heard Crawford ask for the address and saw him write it down in a small book.

Media interest in the case was high, initially because of the nature of the crimes, but also because Houston, who had taken the case at the request of the National Association for the Advancement of Colored People (NAACP), had argued that African Americans were unfairly excluded from Virginia's lily-white juror rolls.[23] At the time of the trial, Houston and his co-counsel had captured headlines as the first all African American legal team in a major trial in the South.[24] Reporters from the local and Washington, DC, papers, news wires, and at least three Black newspapers—the *Afro-American*, the *Richmond Planet*, and the *Norfolk Journal and Guide*—covered the trial. Their reporting provides various descriptions of and perspectives on Hannah Nokes's appearance in court, with the *Afro-American* devoting the most newsprint to her and, curiously, the Leesburg-based *Loudoun Times-Mirror* not mentioning her appearance at all.

Wire stories in mainstream newspapers, like the *Baltimore Sun* and the *Boston Globe*, comprise the majority of the print coverage across the country.[25] The Associated Press (AP) story presents Hannah as a man, identifying her as "Hammond Nokes, Negro, of Herndon," using male pronouns and providing no description of her clothing or physical appearance. Readers of the AP account would have no indication that this witness had presented as female.

While its trial coverage was more detailed, the Washington *Evening Star* similarly did not report on Hannah Nokes's physical appearance or gender identity in either of the two articles in which she and Rastus were mentioned. The *Evening Star* reported that "Commonwealth's Attorney John Galleher had put on the stand Hammond and Rastus Nokes, who said Crawford and another colored man stayed at their place near Herndon on January 11," and in a second article described Hannah and Rastus Nokes as "colored residents of the section near Herndon" who had testified about Crawford's visit.[26]

But several newspapers did report on Hannah Nokes's gender nonconformity, some in a straightforward manner and others with attempts to explain her clothing and appearance as odd but not necessarily offensive or perverse. The *Alexandria Gazette*, a daily paper, published a wire story from the International News Service that referred to Nokes as "a colored farmer." It then matter-of-factly reported that "Nokes, who dresses as a woman, caused a stir in the courtroom as he took the stand and identified Crawford as coming to his home that day and leaving the next morning."[27]

Other articles in white newspapers, including the *Washington Post* and the *Washington Daily News*, reported on Hannah Nokes's clothing and physical appearance but also used specific words to explicitly portray her as peculiar. In the *Post*, Frank Getty introduced Nokes as an "eccentric Negro" before writing, "Nokes, who amused the courtroom with his woman's attire, was one of a dozen Negroes and whites who swore to having seen Crawford" in the weeks leading up to the murders.[28] Writing for the *Daily News*, Martha Strayer, while mistakenly reporting that Hannah Nokes lived in Loudoun, also described Nokes's peculiarity and her connection to the case. Strayer reported, "At the house of Loudoun County's unique colored man who dresses like a woman, Hammond Iokes (sic), where Crawford spent a night on his last trip to Middleburg before the murder, the accused man made one of those promises to pay."[29]

Based in Strasburg, about fifty miles from Leesburg, the *Northern Virginia Daily* provided the most detailed account of Hannah Nokes's appearance among the non-Black newspapers. Under the sub-headline of "'Landlord' Testifies," the *Northern Virginia Daily* wrote:

> Adding a somewhat grotesque touch to the court scene was the appearance of the queer person who conducted the house on the road to Middleburg at which Crawford is alleged to have written the memorandum referred to above. Hammond Nokes, Negro man about thirty-five years old, who wears women's clothing, identified Crawford as one of the two men who spent the night at his house two days before the crime was committed. Crawford is alleged to have written Nokes' name and mail box number down so that he could mail him the money for his lodging and meals. Nokes is said to wear women's apparel all the time and does cooking, washing and ironing for a living.[30]

Considering that both murder victims had been bludgeoned to death, this account seems particularly extreme in describing Nokes's appearance as "adding a somewhat grotesque touch."

The article also covered Houston's cross-examination of Nokes's nephew, but the writer may have taken some liberties with this published account: "Rastus Nokes, nephew of Hammond Nokes, said he saw the two men at Hammond Nokes' house on Sunday night before the murders and saw him write the box number in a memorandum book the next morning before leaving for Middleburg. Dr. Charles H. Houston, chief of defense counsel, asked the witness if Hammond Nokes was his aunt or his uncle. The witness appeared uncertain."

The trial transcript contradicts this account of Rastus Nokes's response to Houston and indicates that Rastus not only answered but did so twice. When Houston asked Rastus, "Is Hammond Noakes your aunt or your uncle?," Rastus stated, "Aunt." Houston replied, "Your aunt?" and Rastus said, "Yes."[31] Under oath, Rastus had identified Hannah Nokes as his aunt when questioned by the most prominent African American attorney in the country.

The Black press, including the *Chicago Defender, Pittsburgh Courier,* and *Afro-American,* had extensively covered the double murder case from the time that Crawford was named as the assailant, but few carried in-depth coverage of the trial itself. Two Virginia papers, the *Norfolk Journal and Guide* and the *Richmond Planet,* along with the *Afro-American,* covered the trial and, to varying degrees, also covered Hannah Nokes's court appearance. Coverage by the Black press is especially significant not only because of the case's legal importance but because, as historians have noted, Black newspapers "covered sex and gender nonnormativity with regularity" in the early and mid-1930s, with the *Afro-American* in particular running "sensational stories about 'twilight men' and 'she wolves.'"[32]

Full editions of the *Richmond Planet* for that time have not been located, but at least one article, published as the trial was beginning, still exists. Under the headline "'Girl-Friend' And A 'Fairy' Damage The Crawford Defense," the *Planet*'s article offered a broad overview of the prosecution's case. While never actually identifying Hannah Nokes by name, the article, in addition to the headline, referenced her twice and provided a negative portrayal without any supporting evidence. The *Planet* reported, "It is evident that Commonwealth's Attorney Galleher will attempt to prove: First—That Crawford spent the night before the crime at the home of a colored man, who showed certain sadistic tendencies" and also that the "note found in the abandoned Ilsley car, near Alexandria, was Crawford's notation of the address of the lady-man he was allegedly with the night before the crime."[33] Although "lady-man" and "fairy" are not particularly harsh terms, the reference to Nokes as a person with "sadistic tendencies" is offered without any explanation or supporting documentation. Of the dozens of articles reviewed for this study, the *Planet*'s account is the only one to criticize Nokes in this manner.

Virginia's other major Black weekly, the *Norfolk Journal and Guide*, sent reporter Thomas W. Young to cover the trial. Young, son of *Journal and Guide* publisher P. B. Young Sr., reported on Hannah Nokes's presence in court, and his article included two secondary headlines highlighting her appearance. "Male Witness Comes Into Court In Female Dress" ran on the front page and then again on the inside page, ensuring that readers would be alerted to this aspect of the trial.[34]

Young wrote that in his opening statement, the Commonwealth's attorney said that "Hammond Noake would testify that Crawford spent the night before the murder with him at Herndon, Va., writing Noake's address on notepaper on leaving in the morning." Young added, "When Noake came into court he was wearing female clothes and was frisking and waving to people he apparently knew."[35] Although Young did not include Nokes's actual testimony, the paper did include, under the subheading "Man In Female Attire," the following as a standalone paragraph in bold: "Forty-one witnesses were summoned by the Commonwealth to testify again Crawford, among them a man who came to court dressed in women's clothes, frisking and smiling at everyone. His name is Hammond Noake."

Still, the *Journal and Guide*'s coverage of Hannah Nokes's appearance was limited and restrained compared to the *Afro-American*, which published multiple articles on the trial itself and dedicated a full article to her life. This attention from the *Afro-American* is not surprising, as Kim Gallon observed: "Coverage of female impersonators and black gay men in the *Tribune, Courier,* and *Defender,* and even the *Amsterdam News* to some degree, paled in comparison to the coverage that the *Afro-American* devoted to the subject."[36] Further, the only reporter receiving a byline in *Afro-American*'s trial coverage was its well-known correspondent Ralph Matthews, who had regularly covered gender nonconforming individuals, including female impersonators performing in clubs in Washington, DC.[37]

During the week of the trial, the *Afro-American* ran four articles about the case, three brief items on page two that covered the history of the case, the jurors, and the initial proceedings, and the major story on the front page under the headline "Queer Witness Testifies for Crawford." None of the articles had a byline, but the front-page story indicated that it was an exclusive to the *Afro-American*. The primary headline was somewhat misleading as Hannah Nokes was actually a witness for the prosecution, but it certainly made the *Afro-American*'s focus clear to its readers—Nokes's gender identity received more attention than Houston's challenge of an all-white jury in a death penalty case. The secondary and also inaccurate headline "Red Wigged Boy-Girl Witness for Crawford" was followed by "The Court Speculates Whether Witness Is Miss, Mrs., or Mr.," "Court Approves Lily-White Jury," and "Sensational Trial Gets Under Way."[38] As though the trial would not have been "sensational" enough with a Black man accused of killing two white women in Virginia, the *Afro-American* chose to elevate it by focusing on Hannah's gender nonconformity.

The article, which mistakenly identifies Hannah Nokes as "Annie Dokes" and "Henry Dokes," led with the following account of her appearance and then dedicated the bulk of the article to other aspects of the case:

A mysterious witness who calls herself Annie Dokes is one of the state's star witnesses as George Crawford went on trial for his life again at 10 a.m Wednesday.

Motion to quash the indictment on grounds that Negroes were also excluded from the present trial was overruled by Judge McLemore Tuesday and 20 veniremen were selected from which the final 12 were picked Wednesday.

RED WIG

The mystery witness wears red Clara Bow wig over a dark brown face from which protrudes a closely-cropped beard. 'She' talks in a husky masculine voice, wearing a green gown, beads, silk hose and women's galoshes, smiles coyly at the men in the courtroom. Her bosom and hips are padded a la Mae West. Sometimes the breast pads fall down to her stomach. Court authorities compel her to use the male restroom in spite of feminine attire. She works in a laundry, drives a big auto and lives at

Herndon, Va. Crawford spent the night at her house before his disappear-
ance, the state charges.

Old residents say Henry Dokes has masqueraded as a woman 15 years.

As Dokes took the stand Wednesday Dr. Houston asked is this Miss,
Mrs. or Mr. Dokes?[39]

The remaining twelve paragraphs of the article then explored other parts
of the trial and did not mention Hannah Nokes's testimony or physical appearance again.

This article offered a detailed description of Nokes's clothing, provided
some limited biographical details, and at times referred to her with feminine pronouns, but overall the article appeared to mock Hannah Nokes,
first by portraying her as a "mystery" and "star" witness and then by using
her gender identity as a joke. If she were indeed a star witness offering critical information under oath, then why did the *Afro-American* fail to include
any details from her actual testimony? Instead of focusing on her testimony, the newspaper concentrated on her physical appearance—her wig,
clothing, jewelry, and padded hips and chest—and how it conflicted with
her facial hair and masculine voice. But it also made fun of her by joking
about her "breast pads" falling out of position, and about officials forcing
her to use the men's restroom at the courthouse. This seems especially
insensitive, considering their own readers' experiences in accessing public
facilities in the segregated South, but also suspect as no other newspapers
reported this detail.

When comparing this published account to the court records, it calls the
Afro-American's accuracy and perhaps truthfulness into question. The article
stated that Houston asked if Hannah Nokes was "Miss, Mrs. or Mr." Nokes,
but this question does not appear in the trial transcript and the transcript
shows that Houston never even questioned her.[40] Instead, by publishing this
dubious account, the *Afro-American* chose to make Nokes a punchline before
moving on to the more serious trial coverage in the same article.

A week later, Crawford had been convicted of killing Ilsley, but the jury
spared his life, and the *Afro-American*'s front-page story by Ralph Matthews
focused on Houston's defense, considered by the NAACP to be a success as
Crawford avoided the death penalty. In addition to the front-page story, the
Afro-American also devoted a full page to the trial with twelve different articles, including one by Matthews entirely about Hannah Nokes.

In the profile piece, "Mother Always Wore Pants, Hammond Nokes Wears Dresses," Matthews offered a biographical overview that attempted to explain Nokes's gender nonconformity. Many of the details Matthews provided cannot be verified now and others are not supported by documentary evidence. Matthews called Nokes the "queerest witness ever introduced in a nationally-known murder case since the appearance of the pig-woman in the famous Hall-Mills case of New Jersey," and then explained that "Hammond Nokes is a man of 30-odd years of age who dresses in women's clothes and works as a domestic servant throughout Loudoun County" before providing a detailed description of her attire on the witness stand.

Matthews then explained that the back story of this "queer individual is an interesting and equally queer story" and this "unusual abnormality was created, it is said by older residents here, by an unexplainable and insatiable desire on the part of his mother to have a girl."[41]

Matthews wrote that "Hammond's mother, quite contrary to his effeminate self was a masculine woman" who, according to unidentified neighbors, "always wore pants and could handle a six-horse team with the dexterity of any man in the community." Matthews further described "Mrs. Nokes" as "an expert hunter and angler" who "refused to do the petty household chores of womenfolk but made her living plowing in the fields."[42] However, Hannah Nokes's mother was not actually "Mrs. Nokes" but a woman named Jennie Johnson, and Hannah's father, Albert Carl Nokes, was married to another woman when Hannah was born.

Matthews explained that the mother's desire for a girl was so great that after "the unfortunate child was born" and "turned out to be a boy," the mother "set out to rear her son as a girl." Matthews describes how this "queer child," known as "Annie," wore girl's clothing, played with girls, and "grew into adolescence as a girl," until around the age of eighteen when she "began to grow a beard" and her mother attempted to "put to rest these rumors that Annie was a boy." Matthews then provided this account of Hannah Nokes's employer making a "Great Discovery."

> Sometime later a white resident employed Annie as a house servant and
> it was her duty to attend her mistress even to the point of spending the
> night in her bedroom during the absence of the husband. During a serious
> illness of the wife Annie bathed her and attended to her intimately.

One day the husband inadvertently entered the bathroom without knocking, not knowing that Annie had preceded him. There the husband made a horrible discovery which resulted in poor Annie being driven from the house in deep humiliation. For a while this matter was Loudoun County's most whispered scandal.[43]

While Hannah Nokes did work as a domestic servant in several homes, that specific account cannot be substantiated today, and neither can the events that Matthews shared next. He described how Nokes continued to live as a woman "until the long arm of Uncle Sam reached down into remote little Herndon, Va., and called for Hammond Nokes" during the wartime draft. According to Matthews, the birth certificate for "Annie Nokes" and "Hammond Nokes" were "one and the same" and "so Annie went to war." Matthews explained that her record "could not be ascertained" but implied that Nokes served in the war and even saw combat. Matthews added that after mustering out, "Hammond Nokes disappeared and Annie again became a living personality so far as exterior appearances were concerned."[44]

Matthews did not provide a source for Hannah Nokes's supposed military service, and there are several problems with this account. Like other Virginians born in 1898, Nokes did not have a birth certificate issued at the time she was born. Although she had the option to obtain a delayed one in later years after the Commonwealth began issuing birth certificates in 1912, no birth record for her, under the name of either Johnson or Nokes, has been found, creating doubt as to Matthews's description of the birth certificates for Annie and Hammond being "one and the same."

Further, Hannah Nokes had indeed registered for the draft under the name Hammond Johnson, so it would not have been difficult for her to be called up for military service, even without a birth certificate.[45] But her name, as Johnson or as Nokes, does not appear on the manifests of ships with soldiers sailing to Europe or returning home after the war, adding more doubt to Matthews's suggestion that Hannah Nokes had served on a battlefield. It is highly doubtful that she served in the military at all. Virginia required counties to create muster rolls of residents who were drafted to serve in the military during World War I, and Hannah Nokes does not appear in those records in either Fairfax or Loudoun County under the name of Johnson or Nokes.[46]

Matthews, who had been writing extensively about female impersonators and drag shows during the "pansy craze" at this time, also offered a quasi-psychological opinion to explain that Nokes's "queer desire to wear clothes of the opposite sex need not be a sexual abnormality" but "may be explained as Fetishism which takes many varying forms." Matthews acknowledged that along with "his feminine attire, Hammond has also adopted all the mannerisms of women," ultimately indicating that it was not simply a case of cross-dressing. As further evidence, he offered Nokes's response to the question of her age, writing "Hammond blushed coyly and replied in a peculiar falsetto, 'Well, you can say that I am less than 75.'"[47]

But after speculating about Hannah's childhood and sharing accounts of her domestic work in a private home and supposed military experience, Matthews concluded: "There is no evidence throughout the county to reflect on Hammond's reputation for morality and propriety. He has, so far as is known, been a perfect lady, living above reproach an [as] industrious and energetic laundress and cook."[48] With this assessment, Matthews admitted that, during the Crawford trial, Hannah Nokes's character had not been called into question, regardless of her gender nonconformity.

Despite publishing some fabrications and at times making fun of Hannah Nokes, the Black press is largely responsible for her story being known today, because much of the coverage by wires and daily newspapers did not mention her gender identity. But beyond the sometimes over-the-top press coverage, how did those involved with the case perceive Hannah Nokes?

Walter White, executive director of the NAACP, attended the trial and took notes throughout. In his brief jottings covering Nokes's testimony, he did not comment on her gender identity but did describe her clothing, including a trimmed coat collar and a handkerchief tucked in the left cuff. He wrote that laughter followed when she stood up, put her hands on her hips, and stated, "That favors the man very well," apparently referring to the defendant. White added, "High pitched voice" to his notes about Nokes before moving on to the next witness.[49]

Commonwealth's Attorney John Galleher called Hannah Nokes as a witness to the prosecution, so presumably he did not believe her gender identity would impugn her credibility. He had earlier called her before the grand jury but may not have needed her to testify in a public courtroom. While the note found in Agnes Ilsley's car in the days after the murders referred to the Nokes home in Herndon, Galleher could have established that Crawford had been at the house and written the note with Rastus Nokes's testimony alone. Yet Galleher still chose to call Hannah Nokes as a witness at trial, an indication that he found her to be credible.[50] Galleher's cocounsel, State Senator Cecil Connor, referred to Nokes as "that peculiar host—the he-lady—a male masquerading in the garb of a female" in his closing arguments as he revisited the chain of events before the murders in Middleburg.[51]

In spite of what the *Afro-American* reported, defense counsel Charles Houston did not cross-examine Hammond. However, he and co-counsel James Guy Tyson had interviewed Hannah Nokes at her home near Herndon in advance of the trial, and in their notes they referred to her as "Mr. ? Nokes" and "this Hammond person." Their records also indicate that Nokes was not particularly cooperative and they "thought he was stalling along because someone had posted him not to say anything." They did note that Nokes regularly allowed people such as "weary travellers" to stay at her home, but they found some of her statements to be "tales." Houston and Tyson closed by stating that their visit with Hannah Nokes was "a complete bust so far as an interview was concerned" and that, without explaining why, they considered her home to be a "den for all the thieves, sissies, cutthroats and other depraved and degraded folk of that [sort] surrounding country."[52] Hannah Nokes may not have been forthcoming, and some of her statements may have lacked credibility, but it is unclear why they characterized her home in such a manner, considering it was their client who had stayed there.

Another high-profile advocate for Crawford was also critical of Nokes. Civil rights activist Martha Gruening, a former assistant secretary for the NAACP, described Nokes as a "rather disreputable colored man who had been passing as a woman" and implied that "passing" contributed to a perceived lack of credibility as a witness or at least a negative reputation in the community. Gruening also questioned why Houston had failed to challenge the credibility of the other witnesses, including Rastus Nokes and a Herndon man named Joe Hill, who had stayed at Hannah Nokes's home as well.[53]

While Galleher may have had questions about Hannah Nokes's gender identity, he still called her to the stand to testify, under oath, for the Commonwealth in a high-profile capital murder case. But Houston, Tyson, and Gruening all considered Nokes's gender identity when challenging her credibility. Although Houston's personal view of gender nonconforming individuals is not clearly known, both Howard University, where he served as the law school dean, and the NAACP leadership, which he joined as special counsel, considered them damaging to the respectability that both organizations pursued and promoted. In fact, Kim Gallon notes that in early 1934, just weeks after the Crawford trial, Howard University was engaged in a "public fight to distance itself and respectable black Washingtonians from aspersions about gender-nonconforming expression," a stand that included its president contacting police to shut down a female impersonators' ball at the nearby Prince Hall Masonic Temple.[54]

Five years later, the NAACP refused to take the case of Pauli Murray, a gender-nonconforming civil rights activist, after she was refused admission to graduate school at the University of North Carolina. Roy Wilkins, assistant secretary at the NAACP, believed Murray presented a significant risk to the organization, and Houston, according to Wilkins, "agreed most emphatically . . . that the Association should not be connected in any way with Miss Murray's application."[55] Glenda Elizabeth Gilmore acknowledges that Murray's earlier communist connections and the NAACP's reluctance to accept female plaintiffs may have influenced its decision, but argues that the "NAACP could not represent her because she did not conform to feminine standards." Gilmore explains that Murray used male nicknames, frequently dressed as a man, had intimate relationships with women and experienced a "sexual identity crisis," and concludes that "before the adjective existed, Murray thought that she was a transgendered person."[56]

These events provide some context for how the two organizations most strongly associated with Houston sought to avoid any perception of acceptance or tolerance of gender nonconformity. Further, the trial transcript, in addition to correcting some of the spurious accounts published in the newspaper coverage, confirms that Houston readily challenged Hannah Nokes's nephew about Hannah's gender identity and her relationship to him. As mentioned earlier, Houston began his cross-examination of Rastus Nokes by asking, "Is Hammond Noakes your aunt or your uncle?" Rastus stated, "Aunt." Houston replied, "Your aunt?" and Rastus stated, "Yes." Houston responded, "I see," and then moved to a different topic.[57]

Galleher used the opportunity on redirect to show the jury that Hannah's gender identity was not relevant to the case, and his line of questioning helped to reinforce Rastus's credibility.

JOHN GALLEHER: Do you know whether Hammond Noakes is a man or a woman? Do you know of your own knowledge?

RASTUS NOKES: I don't know.

JG: You don't know.

RN: No.

JG: Has he ever been regarded down there as a man wearing women's clothing?

RN: What is that?

JG: Have you heard persons speaking of him as a man in women's clothing?

RN: Yes, I heard people speak of it.

JG: You heard that spoken about it?

RN: Yes, sir.

JG: Was that discussed when George Crawford stayed there?

RN: No, sir.

JG: Was that talked about?

RN: No.

JG: That is all.[58]

The court then excused Rastus Nokes from the witness stand and the Commonwealth called Joe Hill. When asked where he was living in January 1932, Hill answered, "I was staying at Mrs. Noakes', boarding there." Hill used a woman's title to refer to Hannah Nokes, indicating that he regarded her, in some manner, as female and one deserving of the respectful title of "Mrs." Neither Galleher nor Houston challenged Hill on that point.[59] During his testimony, young Robert Hughes, who knew enough about Hannah Nokes to direct Crawford to her home, referred to her as "he," "the fellow," and "this Hammond" but did not offer any additional description or observations.[60]

The defendant did not take the stand in his own defense; however, an earlier statement is part of the trial transcript. While he was being held in Boston, Crawford gave a statement to Galleher when interviewed at the Suffolk County jail. In recalling the events before the crimes in Middleburg, Crawford stated that he had stayed in a place in Herndon. Galleher asked him if he knew the names of the people at that house and although Crawford said he did not, he did describe his host as the "man that dressed in women's clothes."[61]

No other witnesses provided accounts or shared their perceptions of Hannah Nokes, and no one challenged her credibility on the stand. While some news reports mocked her and some people in the courtroom may have snickered at her appearance, the fact that a gender nonconforming African American testified in a Virginia court for the Commonwealth during Jim Crow is remarkable.

Also remarkable is that just three years after Hannah Nokes's court appearance, a government publication promoting a New Deal program featured her as a working-class success story. The article in the monthly magazine *Rural Electrification News* presented Nokes as an example of a hardworking but "poor laundress" whose life and livelihood would be greatly improved because of electricity.[62]

The Rural Electrification Administration (REA) sought to bring electric power to farms across the country, and in 1936 it used nearby Northern Virginia as an example of how electricity could transform rural life. The REA electrified a farm in Sterling along Leesburg Pike, just a mile or so from Dranesville Road where Hannah lived and worked, to be used as a model.[63] Coincidentally this demonstration farm belonged to the Hughes family, where Robert Hughes, the young man on horseback who had directed George Crawford to Hannah Nokes's home, lived with his parents and siblings.

During this time several families along Dranesville Road electrified their homes and farms and, according to the article, one of Nokes's employers, Mrs. McMillen, signed a loan for her so that her home could be wired. Hannah Nokes also purchased an electric washing machine and ironer "on easy terms," and with electricity and these appliances, Nokes's business of taking in laundry would be more efficient and profitable.[64]

In profiling Hannah Nokes, the *Rural Electrification News* praised her work ethic and community ties, writing:

> Hammond is noted throughout the countryside for her industry, honesty, and good nature. Each morning she rises with the sun to wash and iron the clothes of her employers who live in and about Herndon. Never having been known to disappoint a customer, she has built up a laundry clientele of a scope that only a sight of the stacks of clothes can convey.
>
> Born in the community where she lives, as were generations of her ancestors, she is regarded with affection and respect by her neighbors.[65]

This portrayal of Hannah Nokes gave increased credibility to Ralph Matthews's description of her as someone "living above reproach" who was "an industrious and energetic laundress and cook."[66]

The article featured a photo of Nokes, wearing an apron and mobcap and hand washing laundry in a tub, and described her as "probably the happiest laundress in the Commonwealth of Virginia." The article mentioned Nokes's "inimitable drawl" and that she "sings and laughs about her work even more now" that she would soon be getting electricity. As a Black woman, Hannah Nokes is referred to by her first name while her employer, a white woman, is identified as Mrs. McMillen. Although the article identified her by the name Hammond and mentioned that "she is strong," there is nothing that cast any doubts upon her gender. So despite making racial and class distinctions, the *Rural Electrification News* clearly presented Hannah Nokes as a woman.[67]

The article and the willingness of the McMillens to sign a note for Nokes also help to establish that Nokes was hard-working and trusted by those who employed her. At that point in 1936, Hannah Nokes had already worked for

In 1936, this photo of Hannah Nokes appeared in *Rural Electrification News* in an article that described her as "probably the happiest laundress in the Commonwealth of Virginia." (Wirtz Labor Library, U.S. Department of Labor)

several years for members of the McMillen family, including brothers Zenus F. and J. Richard McMillen, who both had farms along Dranesville Road. By the age of twenty, she was doing housework for the family of Zenus McMillen, and at the time of the *Rural Electrification News* article she was working at least one day a week for the family of Richard McMillen, doing their laundry at their home where she had the convenience of electric appliances.[68]

More than twenty years later, a member of the McMillen family, who Hannah Nokes was still working for, assisted her in registering for a social security account and number. Nokes's ability to read and write was limited, so Selma McMillen Mott, the daughter of J. Richard and Mary McMillen, completed the application for her. Mott's granddaughter recalled that her grandmother assisted other workers at Willow Springs, the family's dairy farm, with similar matters. On Hannah Nokes's social security form, which Nokes signed with an "X," Mott had checked the box for "female," indicating that on some level Mott accepted Nokes's gender identity.[69]

The 1920 census listed Nokes as Hammond Jones, a twenty-three-year-old Black male who lived in a rented home, could read and write, and was employed doing "labor" on a farm.[70] But later census records identified her as female, even if her name varies. The 1930 census recorded her as Hannah Nokes, a thirty-two-year-old Negro female who could neither read nor write, lived in a rented home, and worked in the "Wash and Iron" industry.[71] Ten years later, the 1940 census listed her as Hammond Nokes, a forty-three-year-old Negro female who had a second grade education, lived in a rented home, and worked twelve hours a day as a "laundress," and the 1950 census documented her as Hammond Nokes, as a Negro female, fifty years old, and working sixty hours a week at home in her own laundry business.[72] Throughout this time, Hannah Nokes remained in the rural Dranesville community along the Fairfax-Loudoun border.[73]

This contrasts with the movement of many other transgender people at that time from their home communities to cities. In *Transgender History: The Roots of Today's Revolution*, Susan Stryker notes that when the urban population surpassed rural population in the 1920s, it gave people assigned male at birth who identified as women "greater opportunities to live as women in cities far from the communities where they had grown up."[74] But even with Washington, DC, just twenty-five miles away, Hannah Nokes continued to live in the same area outside of Herndon and near Sterling. She would remain there her entire life.

Hannah Nokes's apparent acceptance in her community and her ability to support herself may be among the reasons that she remained. But her close family ties, especially to her Nokes kin, may be another. The Nokes name was well known in the Sterling area, with the Nokes family of farmers stretching back at least to the mid-nineteenth century and the Nokes School educating African American children during segregation.[75] Although Hannah Nokes was born outside of her father's marriage, she had good relationships with her Nokes half-siblings, cousins, and nieces and nephews.

Hannah Nokes was entrusted by her family to care for their children. Her great nieces and nephews remembered visiting her home when they were young and enjoying caramel cakes that she baked.[76] Her great nephew Calvin Nokes fondly remembered Hannah as his babysitter when he was growing up in the 1960s. When Calvin was a boy he did not "know what transsexual was" but he knew he "loved this woman" who cared for him. As someone who struggled with his own sexual orientation, Calvin also remembered hearing "people joke about me growing up to be just like her."[77] But he said that she was always "very kind" to him and that he was "blessed to have known her."[78]

When Hannah Nokes later became sick and was hospitalized, Calvin remembered being concerned for her. "I had no idea about trans or anything until later when I heard things like being in hospital and nurses discovering she was a man."[79] Selma McMillen Mott's grandson, who believed Hannah Nokes was intersex and preferred to be identified as female, similarly recalled her being upset when she had her wig removed during a hospitalization.[80]

Hannah Nokes died at 74 at Fairfax Hospital in 1972 after suffering a heart attack. Her death certificate identified her as male, but her family had long accepted her as a woman, something that was evident in how they honored her in death.[81] Calvin Nokes, not quite thirteen himself, was concerned about her funeral arrangements and wondered whether she would be dressed in men's or women's clothing. Her funeral was held at Salem Baptist Church on Leesburg Pike, and although the funeral announcement made it clear that the "casket will not be opened at church," the funeral home in Herndon held visiting hours.[82] Calvin wrote, "I am pleased to say she was dressed in a beautiful blue dress."[83]

Obituaries in local papers reflected Hannah Nokes's identity as a woman with both the *Loudoun Times-Mirror* and *Northern Virginia Sun* referring to her as "Miss Nokes." The *Sun* further described her as a "retired domestic worker" and a longtime member of Salem Baptist Church where she had been active in the "missionary circle, dining club, kitchen club, and flower club." In the same obituary, a niece shared that Nokes "loved flowers . . . and people . . . and stray dogs and cats." Hannah was buried among other members of the Nokes family at a Sterling cemetery, beneath a headstone with the engraved name "Hannah Nokes."[84]

Today Hannah Nokes is remembered by her family members and descendants of the families for whom she worked. Her name and gender identity made national headlines during the George Crawford trial, and she was featured in a government magazine as a model of New Deal hope and advancement. Yet the larger community has been slow to incorporate her story into its public history efforts. In 2019, the Loudoun County Heritage Commission completed an eighty-page report looking at the critical role of the courthouse in Loudoun's African American history.[85] Although it discussed the importance of the Crawford case, it never mentioned Hannah Nokes or her significance in testifying in court as a visible transgender woman. But five years later, as Loudoun County pursued National Historic Landmark designation for the historic courthouse, the nomination did mention Nokes's presence as "one of the earliest known instances of an openly transgender person testifying in Virginia court."[86]

Hannah Nokes's remarkable visibility in court and in her own community decades before queer liberation serves as an example of those who risked their family relationships, livelihood, and even personal safety to simply live as their true gender identity. This examination of just one individual, a transgender Black woman in the Jim Crow South, helps in some small part to answer the call by Snorton, Beemyn, and Skidmore to recover the stories of trans people of color. However, to successfully do this, those working in local history, African American history, legal history, and other fields outside of queer and gender history must recognize, document, and attempt to amplify these overlooked stories. Like Hannah Nokes, the names, stories, and struggles of others who transed gender deserve to be acknowledged and remembered, for their sake and for the sake of transgender people today facing increasing oppression from those who fail to understand that gender nonconformity is not new.

NOTES

Amy Bertsch wishes to thank the Nokes family and especially Calvin Nokes for sharing their memories. She would also like to thank the staffs of the Thomas Balch Library, Wirtz Labor Library, Historic Records and Deed Research Division of the Loudoun County Circuit Court Clerk's Office, and Howard University's Moorland-Spingarn Research Center, particularly now retired Chief Curator of Manuscripts Joellen Elbashir, for their expert assistance.

1. For a thorough study of the George Crawford trial, see David Bradley, *The Historic Murder Trial of George Crawford: Charles H. Houston, the NAACP and the Case That Put All-White Southern Juries on Trial* (Jefferson, N.C.: McFarland & Company, Inc., 2014).

2. "Queer Witness Testifies for Crawford," *Afro-American*, December 16, 1933.

3. "Queer Witness Testifies."

4. Ralph Matthews, "Mother Always Wore Pants, Hammond Nokes Wears Dresses," *Afro-American*, December 23, 1933.

5. For clarity, because other members of the Nokes family are referenced and quoted in this study, first names are frequently used to refer to the subject and others with the same last name.

6. Susan Stryker, *Transgender History: The Roots of Today's Revolution*, rev. ed. (New York: Seal Press, 2017), 1.

7. Kritika Agarwal, "What Is Trans History? From Activist and Academic Roots, a Field Takes Shape," *Perspectives on History,* 2018, https://www.historians .org/publications-and-directories/perspectives-on-history/may-2018/what-is -trans-history-from-activist-and-academic-roots-a-field-takes-shape (accessed June 19, 2023).

8. Agarwal, "What Is Trans History?"

9. Clare Sears, *Arresting Dress: Cross-Dressing, Law, and Fascination in Nineteenth-Century San Francisco* (Durham, NC: Duke University Press, 2014). For more on Sears's transing analysis, see her interview on the blog *Notches*, "'Arresting Dress': A Student Interview with Clare Sears," Rachel Hope Cleves, January 12, 2016, https://notchesblog.com/2016/01/12/arresting-dress-a-student-interview -with-clare-sears/ (accessed June 19, 2023).

10. Jen Manion, *Female Husbands: A Trans History* (Cambridge: Cambridge University Press), 11.

11. C. Riley Snorton, *Black on Both Sides: A Racial History of Trans Identity* (Minneapolis: University of Minnesota Press, 2017), 2.

12. Kim Gallon, "'No Tears for Alden': Black Female Impersonators at 'Outsiders Within' in the *Baltimore Afro-American*," *Journal of the History of Sexuality* 27, no. 3 (2018): 370–71.

13. Genny Beemyn, "A Presence in the Past: A Transgender Historiography," *Journal of Women's History* 25, no. 4 (2013): 113–21.

14. Beemyn, "A Presence in the Past," 117; Snorton, *Black on Both Sides,* 145; Skidmore quoted in Agarwal, "What Is Trans History?"

15. Snorton, 139–75.

16. Gallon, "No Tears for Alden," 394.

17. Gallon, "No Tears for Alden," 368.

18. Hammond Nokes, death certificate, June 26, 1972, file no. 72019308, Commonwealth of Virginia Department of Health.

19. Hammond Johnson, registration card serial no. 1624, Local Board for Loudoun County, Va., United States, Selective Service System. World War I Selective Service System Draft Registration Cards, 1917–1918. Washington, DC: National Archives and Records Administration. M1509, 4,582 rolls. Imaged from Family History Library microfilm; Nokes death certificate.

20. Fourteenth Census of the United States, 1920, Census Place: Dranesville, Fairfax, Virginia; Roll: T625_1886; Page: 12A; Enumeration District: 29, accessed through ancestry.com January 9, 2019; Fifteenth Census of the United States, 1930, Census Place: Dranesville, Fairfax, Virginia; Page: 5B; Enumeration District: 0007, accessed through ancestry.com January 9, 2019; Sixteenth Census of the United States, 1940. Census Place: Dranesville, Fairfax, Virginia; Roll: m-t0627–04261; Page: 61A; Enumeration District: 30–7, FHL microfilm: 2342176, accessed through ancestry.com January 9, 2019.

21. *Commonwealth of Virginia, Plaintiff vs. George Crawford, Defendant,* "Transcript of the Shorthand Report of the Proceedings, etc., December 12 to 16, 1933," prepared for Charles H. Houston, NAACP Papers, Group I, Box D-54, Library of Congress, Washington, DC.

22. This piece of evidence remains with the original court record at Loudoun County Courthouse, Clerk of Circuit Court, Historic Records Division, Criminal Cases 1757–1955, *Commonwealth vs. George Crawford,* 1932–090.

23. Rawn James Jr., *Root and Branch: Charles Hamilton Houston, Thurgood Marshall, and the Struggle to End Segregation* (New York: Bloomsbury Press, 2010), 1–15; "Court to Rule on Crawford Defense Today," *Washington Post,* November 7, 1933.

24. "Crawford Case Is Being Crippled by Lack of Funds," *Detroit Tribune*, December 9, 1933; "Brilliant Array of Legal Talent in Famous Case," *Norfolk Journal and Guide*, November 11, 1933; "Geo. Crawford Defense Staff to Be All Negro," *Norfolk Journal and Guide*, November 18, 1933.

25. Associated Press, "Testifies Crawford Abandoned Machine," Baltimore *Evening Sun*, December 14, 1933; and Associated Press, "Crawford Identified," *Boston Globe*, December 14, 1933.

26. "Crawford's Notes Linked in Slaying," Washington *Evening Star*, December 14, 1933; "State Rests Case Against Crawford," Washington *Evening Star*, December 15, 1933.

27. International News Service, "Saw Crawford Near Ilsley Residence, Witnesses Testify," *Alexandria Gazette*, December 14, 1933.

28. Frank Getty, "Hope of Alibi For Crawford Is Abandoned," *Washington Post*, December 15, 1933.

29. Martha Strayer, "Murder Chain Drawn Closer on Crawford," *Washington Daily News*, date unavailable, from James Guy Tyson Papers, Box 108–2, Folder Commonwealth of Virginia vs. George Crawford Clippings, Moorland-Spingarn Research Center, Howard University.

30. "State Tightens Its Case Against George Crawford," *Northern Virginia Daily*, December 15, 1933.

31. *Commonwealth vs. Crawford*, transcript, 284.

32. Simon D. Elin Fisher, "Challenging Dissemblance in Pauli Murray Historiography, Sketching a History of the Trans New Negro," *Journal of African American History* 104, no. 2 (2019): 199; Genny Beemyn, *A Queer Capital: A History of Gay Life in Washington, D.C.* (New York: Routledge, 2015), 31.

33. "'Girl-Friend' And A 'Fairy' Damage The Crawford Defense," *Richmond Planet*, date unavailable, from James Guy Tyson Papers, Box 108–2, Folder Commonwealth of Virginia vs. George Crawford Clippings, Moorland-Spingarn Research Center, Howard University.

34. Thomas W. Young, "Crawford Case Nears End; Jury Plea Overruled," *Norfolk Journal and Guide*, December 16, 1933.

35. Ibid.

36. Kim Gallon, *Pleasure in the News: African American Readership and Sexuality in the Black Press* (Urbana, Ill.: University of Illinois Press, 2020), 141.

37. Gallon, "'No Tears for Alden'," 368.

38. "Queer Witness Testifies."

39. "Queer Witness Testifies."

40. "Queer Witness Testifies."

41. Matthews, "Mother Always Wore Pants."

42. Ibid.

43. Ibid.

44. Ibid.

45. Johnson registration card.

46. "Military Indexes," Loudoun County Clerk of the Circuit Court, https://www
.loudoun.gov/3422/Military-Indexes (accessed January 18, 2020).

47. Matthews, "Mother Always Wore Pants"; Gallon notes, "Reporters' use of modern scientific language and concepts allowed them to operate under the guise
of objectivity in their discussions of homosexuality and gender nonconforma-
tivity even as they sometimes poked fun at female impersonators." *Pleasure in
the News,* 157.

48. Matthews, "Mother Always Wore Pants."

49. Walter White, notes on Crawford trial, December 14, 1933, NAACP Papers,
Group I, Series D, Legal File: Cases Supported George Crawford, Library of
Congress, Washington, DC, ProQuest History Vault.

50. *Commonwealth vs. Crawford,* transcript, 275–79.

51. *Commonwealth vs. Crawford,* transcript, 618.

52. Interview with Hammond Nokes, November 26, 1933, James Guy Tyson Papers,
Box 108–2, Folder Commonwealth of Virginia vs. George Crawford Interviews, Moorland-Spingarn Research Center, Howard University.

53. Martha Gruening, "The Truth about the Crawford Case," *New Masses,* January 8, 1935.

54. Gallon, "No Tears for Alden."

55. Roy Wilkins to Walter White, memorandum, February 2, 1939, NAACP Papers,
Group I, Box C-271, Campaign for Educational Equality, Series A: Legal
Department and Central Office Records, 1913–1940, Library of Congress,
Washington, DC.

56. Glenda Elizabeth Gilmore, *Defying Dixie: The Radical Roots of Civil Rights
1919–1950* (New York: W. W. Norton & Company, Inc., 2008), 288.

57. *Commonwealth vs. Crawford,* transcript, 284.

58. Ibid., 285–286.

59. Ibid., 287.

60. Ibid., 273–274.

61. Ibid., 490.

62. Dorothy Moore, "Happiness—A Rural Electrification By-Product," *Rural Electrification News,* July 1936.

63. "REA Electrified Farm Points Way to New Standard of Rural Life," *Rural
Electrification News,* August 1936.

64. Moore, "Happiness."

65. Ibid.

66. Matthews, "Mother Always Wore Pants."

67. Moore, "Happiness."

68. Johnson registration card; Moore, "Happiness."

69. Hammond Nokes, Application for Social Security Account Number, October 7, 1959, U.S. Social Security Administration; Mary Mott, telephone conversation with author, October 19, 2019.

70. Fourteenth Census of the United States, 1920, Census Place: Dranesville, Fairfax, Virginia; Roll: T625_1886; Page: 12A; Enumeration District: 29, accessed through ancestry.com January 9, 2019.

71. Fifteenth Census of the United States, 1930, Census Place: Dranesville, Fairfax, Virginia; Page: 5B; Enumeration District: 0007, accessed through ancestry.com January 9, 2019.

72. Sixteenth Census of the United States, 1940. Census Place: Dranesville, Fairfax, Virginia; Roll: m-t0627–04261; Page: 61A; Enumeration District: 30–7, FHL microfilm: 2342176, accessed through ancestry.com January 9, 2019; Seventeenth Census of the United States, 1950. Census Place: Dranesville, Fairfax, Virginia; Roll: 3017; Sheet Number: 20; Enumeration District: 30–8, accessed through ancestry.com June 19, 2023.

73. Despite thorough reviews, the author has been unable to find documentation of Hannah Nokes as a child in the 1910 or 1900 census.

74. Stryker, 48–50.

75. For more on the Nokes family, see Nathaniel Cline, "Sold, Demolished: Community Remembers Sterling Home of Historic Black Family," *Loudoun Times*, June 15, 2021, updated July 2, 2021, https://www.loudountimes.com/news/sold -demolished-community-remembers-sterling-home-of-historic-black-family /article_c7b86f56-cd22-11eb-8dc8-f36e575f253b.html (accessed September 21, 2021), and "Loudoun's Disappearing Villages: What has Become of Eastern Loudoun's African-American Villages and Communities?," *Connection Newspapers*, February 11, 2003, http://www.connectionnewspapers.com/news/2003 /feb/11/loudouns-disappearing-villages/ (accessed September 21, 2021).

76. Author's notes from meeting with Nokes family members, Loudoun County, Va., May 29, 2019.

77. Calvin Nokes, "Advocating for Change," in *Cancer Up the Wazoo*, edited by Angela G. Gentile (Care to Age Press, 2018), 222.

78. Calvin Nokes, email message to author, May 29, 2019.

79. Nokes, email message.

80. Mott, conversation with author.

81. Hammond Nokes death certificate.

82. Hammond (Hanna) Nokes death notice, *Washington Post,* June 25, 1972.

83. Nokes, email message.

84. "Miss Nokes Dies in Home June 22," *Loudoun Times-Mirror,* June 29, 1972; "Hanna Nokes Services Held," *Northern Virginia Sun,* June 26, 1972.

85. Robert A. Pollard, ed., and Loudoun County Heritage Commission, *History of the Loudoun County Courthouse and Its Role in the Path to Freedom, Justice and Racial Equality in Loudoun County* (Leesburg, Va.: Loudoun County Government, 2019), https://www.loudoun.gov/DocumentCenter/View/151802/Heritage -Commission-Report-Final?bidId=, accessed October 20, 2019.

86. Nancy A. Holst, "Loudoun County Courthouse," National Historic Landmark Nomination, 2024, 58, https://irma.nps.gov/DataStore/DownloadFile/700837, accessed September 2, 2024.

EXIT 5,
MUSEUM OF TRANS
—

Sex Work and the Making of Roanoke, Virginia

G. SAMANTHA ROSENTHAL

ave you seen my body reflected in the sky-high windows outside of Billy's? Sometimes I walk beside the panes, so close I can reach out and leave a streak of finger grease on the glass. I tread slowly, catching the eyes of well-dressed gentlemen and ladies on a summer evening sitting inside grasping tightly to their silverware. I watch their eyes journey from my legs to the mop of curls atop my head and back down to my hips and beyond like an X-ray machine piercing my skin. I am out here conjuring ghosts.

People who looked sort of like me—trans women and transfeminine folks, self-described transvestites and drag queens—once walked this same sidewalk, beside the same windowpanes, looking in while fancy people looked out. Walt Whitman once intoned, "Just as you feel when you look on the river and sky, so I felt," and as I walk these streets I, too, feel across a generation—across the time and space of transgender history.[1] The corner of Salem Avenue and Market Street in downtown Roanoke was once a whole world condensed into a small spot. Here was a flashpoint over the ability of trans people to survive and belong, what Henri Lefebvre has called the "right to the city."[2] What happened on this side of the windowpanes over forty years ago—on the streets outside of Billy's in the 1970s and 1980s—was a fight over public space that reshaped the history of Roanoke, Virginia. That fight also thrust trans sex workers into the spotlight of the story that Roanokers tell about who we are, a story of postindustrial rebirth and downtown revival.

Several years ago, *Politico* published a long-form essay about Roanoke's twenty-first-century renaissance. It was titled "Trains Built Roanoke. Science Saved It."[3] City boosters pointed to the *Politico* article as evidence that Roanoke had turned the corner on its dirty past. The city's railroad-powered industrialization, an economic force that once made Roanoke the "magic city of the New South" in the late nineteenth century, was now only apparent in urban heritage tourism and the crisscross of squeaky railroad lines that divide downtown into disjointed quarters.[4] The city's reputation as a sexual marketplace, also dating back to the late nineteenth century when brothels ringed the blocks on either side of these tracks, also appears now in the rearview mirror. This sentiment was summarized in a quote from a local newspaper editor who, in the *Politico* article, points to the 1970s, 1980s, and even 1990s as a low point when downtown Roanoke was corrupted by the presence of "hookers, transvestites, dealers, all manner of shady characters." "Decent people didn't go there," he leveled.[5] Transvestites and sex workers were not only indecent in his estimation, but they were also the very agents holding Roanoke back from its destiny as a postindustrial twenty-first-century city.[6]

At a community book club meeting in 2017 held at Roanoke's Center in the Square—a six-story downtown structure full of museums and cultural institutions, itself a product of the city's turn toward an arts-and-culture-based economy—the CEO of that center, in talking about the building's history, claimed that downtown used to be so awful because it was overrun by "prostitutes."[7] A local city council member, sitting next to him, agreed. And then I spoke up. "Actually, those prostitutes were real people, people we have interviewed, people with amazing stories. They are local heroes of LGBTQ history." The room grew silent. I am not sure that the previous speakers even realized that someone sympathetic to trans sex workers was in attendance. No one responded, but also no one tried to bad-mouth sex workers again that night.

Even a colleague of mine at Roanoke College once said to me, "You did not want to go downtown in the 1980s. It was full of prostitutes." What is amazing to me about these comments on late-twentieth-century urban life is that in attempting to define the city as corrupted, fallen, disorderly, and undesirable, these narrators all clearly mark prostitutes, particularly trans sex workers, as the boogeymen (or, more accurately, the boogeywomen) of Roanoke's recent past. It is as if, were I to ask some of the leading historians, cultural brokers, and politicians in Roanoke today to define the character of the city's history in the 1970s and 1980s, they would not be able to do so without mentioning "transvestites" and "hookers."[8] Isn't it wild that trans sex workers are such a dominant part of this city's narrative? Trans sex workers are seemingly front and center in the minds of historically minded politicians and business leaders in Roanoke. Somehow, in spite of these very important people's own prejudices and perversions, they have counterintuitively memorialized trans sex work as a key moment in Roanoke's history.

In this essay I argue that sex work was a foundational arena of transgender community formation in Roanoke in the 1970s and 1980s, just as the city's multipronged effort *against* sex work provides a key origin story for the contemporary urban renaissance. In this era two simultaneous and interconnected processes were at work: trans people and sex workers carved out increasingly visible spaces in the city just as the city cracked down on these newly visible communities in the name of urban redevelopment. Trans people and sex workers are not just central actors in the city's history, but the erasure of them from history was part and parcel of the city's path towards rebirth.[9] I am actually tempted to reach out to *Politico* and suggest a typo in their headline. Rather than "trains built Roanoke," perhaps it should read "trans built Roanoke."

Opened in a former hotel on the cusp of the 1980s, Billy's Ritz was a fixture of the city's revanchist dreams. To understand just how the city's twenty-first-century story has come to focus on a history of reclaiming downtown from "hookers" and "transvestites," we must first understand how sex work became central to downtown's informal economy. In 1979, just as the owners of Billy's Ritz were readying to open, a report from the urban design firm Moore Grover Harper stated that "nighttime in the Market District brings fear of crime to many Roanokers."[10] But to those on the outside of Billy's windowpanes, the area was simply a coordinate on an already-extensive map of queer and trans spaces. Christy, one of many Black trans sex workers who used to work that block, remembers, "The transvestites used to hang out in front of Billy's Ritz." She continues, "That's what made Billy's Ritz so much money. People watching them get in cars and this, that, and the other." Grace, a legendary Black drag queen and part-time sex worker, had similar recollections. "They had a restaurant called Billy's Ritz and we used to stand right across the street from there." Like Christy, she states that "people would come there for dinner and it stayed packed and we wondered why and they was coming down to see us stand there and carry on."[11]

Even cisgender gay men, who at that time had as many as five or six hangouts in downtown Roanoke—including gay bars that were explicitly hostile to folks "in drag"—knew about Billy's and the reputation of the "girls" working the street.[12] Sam, a white gay man, remembers shortly after moving to Roanoke in 1981 heeding the warnings he heard about the crowd outside of Billy's Ritz. "I can remember being at work and one of the girls at the office," assuming that Sam was straight, warned, "Be careful if you go downtown to pick up a female." Sam asked why. She responded, "Because it might not be a female." Sam replied, "Okay, I understand!" But he did not fully understand the sex workers' world. "I had not ever lived anywhere where you had female impersonators on the street corners soliciting business," he recalls.[13] Another white gay man, Rodger, recalls actually making it inside Billy's in the late 1980s. Sitting at "the bar with my brand new significant other," he says they "held hands hiding under the bar and it wasn't winter time so we had no coats to cover our hands up. . . . So we sat there at a straight bar holding hands, and that was kinda neat but you're always looking over your shoulder to see if anyone was gonna see."[14] For Black trans sex workers like Christy and Grace, there was no hope of sneaking into Billy's and holding hands underneath the countertop. There were other places that they could go with straight johns and find some modicum of acceptance, but this was not it. Trans life at that time was largely confined to the street beyond the windowpanes.

The transgender sex workers' world was forged in Roanoke's gritty 1970s. Whereas men seeking sex with other men had flocked since the 1960s to a block of Bullitt Avenue abutting Elmwood Park on the edge of downtown, "the Block," as it was called, was primarily for cruising and not often a space for paid sex work—although Leonard, a Black gay man, remembers that by the 1980s it was a place to go see "male hustlers" and "where guys got picked up."[15] But for straight men seeking sex with women, it was rather those blocks surrounding the City Market building downtown, right outside of Billy's Ritz and around Market Square, where for over a century Roanokers located their red-light district.

A sexual marketplace first emerged downtown in the 1880s and 1890s as thousands of people flocked to Roanoke, a new city at the intersection of crisscrossing railroad lines. Dozens of "male-only" saloons sprouted up in those early decades, clustered around Railroad Avenue (now Norfolk Avenue) alongside the railroad tracks. Middle-class white women in Roanoke helped push for legislation, enacted in 1903, that restricted the presence of women in those very spaces. But respectability politics never protected the young working-class women who continued to work in these male-only spaces as prostitutes. An early twentieth-century photograph of the Capital Saloon, an establishment on Salem Avenue, depicted a sign behind the bar advertising "Oysters Upstairs." Male patrons of the bar knew that the word "oysters" was a euphemism for prostitution.[16]

Sex workers were everywhere in early Roanoke, but the geography of their labor was starkly divided by race. According to historian Rand Dotson, Railroad Avenue's scores of saloons included whites-only saloons and Blacks-only saloons. Race mixing was forbidden. Meanwhile, by 1890, brothels existed away from Railroad Avenue, clustered in the all-white Southeast neighborhood and in the overwhelmingly Black Gainsboro neighborhood north of the railroad tracks.[17] While vice was seemingly strictly segregated, the reality is that white men could traverse the sexual marketplaces of both white and Black spaces, while Black men and white women's movements were, conversely, strictly policed. The tension in the city around race mixing was so intense that a major riot exploded downtown in 1893 after a Black man was accused of assaulting a white woman. An angry white mob engaged in a firefight with city leaders in an effort to extract the accused man from the city's jail. Gunshots rang out on the street outside the Municipal Building, leaving eight Roanokers dead and thirty-one wounded. In the middle of the night a mob was successful in kidnapping the alleged assailant and lynching him. These acts of violence were born of downtown Roanoke's unique spaces of racial and gender mixing, and pronouncedly of white men's violently paranoid concerns about the sexual activity of Black men and white women.[18]

The sexual geography of downtown did not change that much during the Jim Crow era. Across the tracks, Gainsboro developed into a thriving area of Black cultural achievement and entrepreneurship. Downtown yet remained the only place where race mixing was largely possible, and then only at certain times and in certain spaces.[19] Records of the Roanoke City Police Department in the 1920s indicate that sex work continued to thrive in the city throughout the early twentieth century, as evidenced by arrests for keeping a "Disorderly House" (a brothel), for "Solicitation on street," and for "Operating house of ill fame," among other charges.[20]

As in other cities across the United States, it was ultimately a caustic mix of deindustrialization, suburbanization, and the momentum of the Civil Rights Movement that brought about changes to downtown Roanoke that would lead to the emergence of a visible transgender population in the 1970s. Black activists worked behind the scenes in Roanoke to bring about the integration of downtown lunch counters in 1960. That was just the opening salvo in Roanoke's civil rights movement, although activists had begun to resist the city's urban renewal program even earlier in the 1950s. School integration occurred more slowly, and mostly peacefully, beginning in 1960. Yet the desegregation of all public and private institutions, including the city's school district, would drag on in the face of white segregationists' massive resistance into the early 1970s. All throughout this process anxious white families packed their bags and moved out of the city to Roanoke's suburbs—predominantly into the rapidly growing Roanoke County—in search of an American dream predicated on segregation and white supremacy.[21]

The city of Roanoke had long stemmed population decline—ever since the Great Depression when the city began losing population—through the strategic annexation of suburban neighborhoods. By the 1970s municipal leaders were fighting harder than ever to annex more land—especially the nearby suburbs now populated by white-flighters. Ultimately, in 1979 the state of Virginia passed a law banning Virginia municipalities from engaging in any more annexations. It meant that Roanoke would henceforth have to focus on luring residents and consumers back to within the city limits. It is also notable that if not for these late twentieth-century annexations, Roanoke's population today would probably be majority Black instead of, as it currently stands, approximately 30 percent Black.[22]

Middle-class white people did not just flee for the suburbs; they also began to engage in new geographies of consumption. Whereas they used to go downtown to purchase clothing, fine foods, and other consumables, by the 1960s they were now drawn to the area's first shopping malls, located far outside the downtown core. By 1965 the abandonment of downtown by middle-class white folks was so pronounced that the city released a new study recommending ways to revitalize the area around the Market build-ing. "Downtown is bereft of what is commonly called 'night life,'" the report claimed. The city's Department of Planning recommended that a "Restaurant-Entertainment Complex" might attract middle-class white consumers down-town again. This would balance out the "skid row" businesses that, according to the report, included "pawn shops, tiny cafes, low cost hotels, and various second-hand stores." They also recommended that the city explore creation of a "gas light" district with a "gay nineties" feel, following in the foot-steps of one of the country's first experiments in downtown revitalization in St. Louis's gaslight district in the 1950s.[23] The St. Louis project had sought to use a "glory days" facade of history as a means of reclaiming real estate from certain undesirable populations, including "transvestites," and replac-ing them with a returning white middle-class clientele. This was the gene-sis of the "festival marketplace" concept in urban planning, one that would return to Roanoke in the late 1970s just as transgender sex workers' grip on downtown was peaking.[24]

For whatever reason, Roanoke city leaders did not take the recommended steps in the late 1960s to revitalize downtown, and by the mid-1970s the city's downtown nightlife was increasingly dominated by sex work, includ-ing the presence of a visible transgender community. Grace spent many an evening outside of the Market building in the late 1970s. She recalls how she first got started in the trade. Hailing from Martinsville, Virginia, fifty miles to the south along the North Carolina border, she decided in 1976 to hop into the car one evening and travel to Roanoke with a friend. Land-ing at the Horoscope, the city's first discotheque, she quickly befriended a drag queen named Carolyn. Grace later packed her bags and moved to Roa-noke for good in 1977, and she, along with Carolyn, started performing on stages for money. "I started doing shows at the Horoscope," she recalls, "and then later on they was talking about the Market. I said, 'The Market?' So I went down to the Market and there were cars that were there and there were drag queens on every corner and I was like 'What kind of madness is this?'" Her friends, other queens, explained that "this is where everybody was pros-tituting." They also told Grace, "We don't call it that. We call it selling after hours produce!"[25]

Another name for the area was even more apt: this was the "meat market." The blocks ringing the City Market building were where straight johns would drive by in the evenings, or in the wee hours of the morning, looking for a sex worker to pick up, either a cis woman or a trans woman. That was "the only thing going on downtown, nothing else," recalls Leonard, a Black gay man who was friendly with many of the queens. "There was no restaurants, there was no walk-in, at five o'clock it became that . . . the dark light, the red light district."[26] There were more to these streets than just sex work, however. Carolyn remembers the Market as a site of community formation and socializing for the girls. "The City Market downtown, that's where we used to hang out . . . , and then they ran us from down there."[27] Grace remembers a string of dive bars and restaurants that would allow trans sex workers in from off the street with their johns. "They had a lot of redneck bars and things downtown," she recalls, and "a lot of people didn't like us because of the way we were. [But] some people accepted us for what we were." She and other sex workers found a tenuous acceptance in places like the New Market, the Manhattan ("redneck," but "we knew the woman who owned it"), the Capitol, and Miss Tony's. Don, a Black gay man who was friendly with the street queens, remembered hanging out inside the same spaces. "These places are all gone," he says. "But they were full of gay people."[28]

One notable feature of this downtown social world, as remembered by Carolyn, Grace, Don, and Leonard, is that it was a space of special significance for Black queer and trans people. The dive bars and street corners that they recall barely register at all in the memories of white LGBTQ people. Across dozens of oral history interviews conducted in and around Roanoke from 2016 to the present, only Black gay men and Black queens remember this patchwork of hole-in-the-wall restaurants and "redneck" bars and the intricacies of late-night survival in and among these spaces. Leonard remembers the distinctive racial geography of sex work downtown. In the city's bars and nightclubs "you had the black drag queens and the white drag queens," he says, but there were "two different poverty levels, too. If that's what you want to call it." Most of the white queens had daytime jobs, but "you know most of the black drag queens were the ones who worked the street and prostituted themselves to make a living off of." The trans sex workers' downtown Roanoke was a distinctly Black queer world.[29]

On a wintry walk around downtown in 2019 with Don and Peter, another Black gay man, the two of them talked for over an hour about vibrant

The City Market area south of Campbell Avenue in 1975. (Historical Society of Western Virginia, 1976.38.7)

memories of decades past that came flooding back to them as we walked from block to block through the remains of this once-queer world.[30] Don stood in front of what was once decades ago the Manhattan and talked of Black queens hanging on the arms of white johns seated inside at the long bar still visible through the foggy window. Peter and Don recalled the Pagoda, a Chinese restaurant that once stood where now a skyscraper looms over downtown, and the owner who would periodically come out of the store and tell the transvestites to go somewhere else. (Other downtown business owners apparently appreciated the sex workers. One shop owner in the early 1990s told the *Roanoke Times* that the nighttime activity of trans sex workers "keeps people away" from his store. "Kind of like a burglar alarm.")[31]

There was a whole world here in the late 1970s—a remarkably visible world of trans people, Black queer men and women, sex workers, and all the ways that those identities overlapped. Roanoke city leaders despised this world. In 1977, the city began to crackdown on sex work around the Market building. This was a major policing campaign—one of the largest crackdowns on sex work in the city's history, and the first known police operation in Roanoke to explicitly target transgender people.

The Roanoke City Police Department vice squad was at the forefront of this operation. The "vice," as it was known by sex workers, was then led by Sergeant John Barrett, who by 1977 was already well known among the broader gay community. Gay men in Roanoke, especially those who cruised on Bullitt Avenue, had faced off with the police over public sex since at least 1971 when a local newsletter, the *Big Lick Gayzette*, announced the presence of an undercover cop in Elmwood Park posing as a gay man.[32] Entrapment was a common policing technique. Gay men interviewed by the *Roanoker* magazine in 1977 recalled stories of undercover cops getting into cars with them, then putting them into handcuffs instead of kissing them, or, in one case, picking up a guy at the discotheque, getting a hotel room together, and then only finally pulling out the police badge and making an arrest.[33] By 1977, Sergeant Barrett was overseeing a major campaign against "homosexuality" in the city, timed perfectly alongside the country's first major backlash against gay rights led by singer Anita Bryant (and with substantial support from televangelist Jerry Falwell in nearby Lynchburg). In September 1977, the *Roanoke Times* reported that the city's vice squad had already arrested at least 77 men that year on charges of "Soliciting for Immoral Purposes."[34] By February 1978, the number of arrests for "homosexual" activity had jumped to over 140 according to the police.

A local gay rights group, the Free Association for Individual Rights (FAIR), formed in response to the city's crackdown on public sex. They claimed that the true number of gay men arrested as of that February was more like 250.[35] FAIR used their own newsletter, the *Virginia Gayzette*, to poke fun at Sergeant Barrett. When Barrett was quoted in the *Roanoke Times* self-flagellating because he worried that he had given the gay rights group too much publicity with all the arrests, FAIR responded "To Sgt. Barrett[,] You did not unite us. We have done that on our own!"[36] But FAIR's activism was primarily focused on the concerns of gay men—especially the safety of cruising spaces. Gay women complained that FAIR did not represent them, and trans women and sex workers were unrepresented in this battle against the police department.[37]

Meanwhile, by the fall of 1977, the vice squad campaign against sex in the city had moved downtown to the area around the City Market building. An article in the *Roanoke Times* referred to the "market queens" who worked as sex workers after nightfall. The city council was then considering legislation

The intersection of Wall Street and Salem Avenue in the early 1980s. The City Market building is on the right. (Historical Society of Western Virginia, 1998.24.255)

that would have made "men posing as women to sell sexual favors" an illegal act, thereby targeting trans people in particular while leaving cisgender sex workers off the hook.[38] While the city considered legislative responses, the vice squad did not hold back. Carolyn remembers the police crackdown began around the Market building. "We was working. We were doing tricks back then," she recalls. "They wouldn't let us come down there! They wouldn't let us come down and standing and stuff. Which we weren't down there doing anything mean. We just go down there and stand and whatever . . . whatever happens, it happens. But, they ran us," she continues, and "they told us we couldn't stand around down there."[39] Don also remembers the police crackdown on the sex workers. "Through the seventies," he says, "downtown Roanoke was the red-light district. We're talking hoes." Back then, he continues, "The police would arrest you if you were in women's clothing. You never seen so many drag queens jump over a car like Elly May Clampett from the Beverly Hillbillies trying to run from the police. Because they would arrest you even if you weren't soliciting sexual favors or whatever."[40]

By April 1978 the *Roanoke Times* was running near-weekly stories on the vice squad's successes. Every week, two to three more prostitutes were arrested "in the market area," Sergeant Barrett proudly informed the newspaper. The vice squad also now had a female officer on the force who posed as a cisgender sex worker in an effort to entrap johns. An op-ed in the *Roanoke Times* argued, "Roanoke is mounting an all out war on prostitution. The war is being staged on the City Market." The headline suggested that "A Far Better World Awaits Streetwalkers" once they were removed from the downtown core and resettled into less desirable areas of the city.[41]

And it worked. By the 1980s Roanoke's red-light district had been pushed westward up Salem Avenue towards more industrial parts of the city. Sex work also reemerged in the late 1980s east of downtown, along Campbell Avenue outside the railroad shops and the hulking ruins of the city's postindustrial landscape. These new spaces of sex work were more dangerous for transgender workers. There was less lighting and less legal nighttime activity in more marginal zones, leaving sex workers to face extreme violence at the hands of johns, police officers, and parading homophobes, transphobes, and nighttime thrill-seekers.[42] "I was real tiny," Carolyn recalls of that era. "They used to call me 'mop legs,' and stuff like that. But I was real tiny." Her stature made her more attractive to some johns, she suggests, but also more susceptible to violence. "You know, it got so bad where they were killing you and shooting you. I had a friend that has been stabbed, shot, and everything, from there. And I got out of the business. And I said, 'I have to find a better business to go into.'" She continues, "They start trying to rob you and killing you and stuff and stabbing you and cutting you, shoot you, whatever. And I said 'not today.' It's not for me no more. But we had fun doing it. It was exciting. It was interesting."[43]

Grace continued to work along Salem Avenue throughout the 1980s. She, too, faced the increasing violence of this newly marginalized sex work scene. One night, she recalls, "a bunch of redneck boys rolled by and you know how you can have a can of beer with it not being open, they threw it and they hit me in the back with it and they called me a faggot." As the car of boys circled the block with an intention to come around a second time, Grace "got a big huge cinder block" from behind a nearby building. "Honey," she says, "I came around that corner and stepped out with that cinder block, threw it over my head. I had threw it so hard that the windshield fell in their lap." She was arrested and became entangled in the local criminal justice system. Indeed, the city's jail cells and court rooms became ever-more frequent spaces in sex workers' lives in the 1980s as Roanoke, like the rest of the country, stepped up its commitment to policing and incarceration. Christy was of a younger generation than Grace and Carolyn; she came of age working on Salem Avenue in the 1980s under Grace's wing. Christy carried a hammer with her at times, and she recounts several violent encounters with clients as well as the police. She was in and out of the city's criminal justice system dozens of times within the span of just a few years.[44]

Trans sex workers also faced another threat at this time. The first recorded case of HIV/AIDS in Roanoke was documented in 1983, and by the late 1980s HIV was coursing through the city's public sex and sex worker communities.[45] Grace recalls in 1985 stepping inside the Health Department building in Roanoke with her friend to get tested for the virus. Her friend "went in one room, I went in the other one. When they told her I heard her hit the floor, I heard her scream and holler." Grace, too, received a positive diagnosis. "It didn't phase me," though, she says. "I knew what I had to do." And she survived. But not every queen was so lucky. Leonard recalls, "I knew a lot of drag queens" back then, but "it's only two that I know left," one of those being Grace. "A lot of 'em died, a lot of them started dying in the eighties, '83, '88," he says. "But the ones that I really knew, that you know we went together, partied together, rode around together and all of that—a lot of them are gone. A lot of them are gone."[46]

The AIDS crisis also transformed public perceptions of sex work. Whereas in the late 1970s sex workers were seen as nuisances to the revival of a downtown economy, by the late 1980s they were seen as vectors of a deadly disease. Indeed, the late 1980s witnessed explicit calls on the local level to quarantine people living with HIV. Some city leaders even questioned whether to round up the city's prostitutes and put them in jail or test them against their will for HIV.[47] A renewed crackdown ensued, with the Roanoke Police Department stepping up its arrests of sex workers—particularly trans sex workers—across the city. In 1989 the *Roanoke Times* reported that the police had arrested thirty sex workers in just the past week—most of them trans. "Roanoke is a prostitution hub for Western Virginia," the *Times* noted, with clients driving into the city sometimes from hours away.[48] Christy, who at the time worked most often on Campbell Avenue east of downtown, was quoted in the paper that year stating that "Roanoke City ought to put up a banner and fly it around on an airplane that says 'We have prostitution at Eighth and Campbell' because nobody knew about it before" the city began its crackdown. Christy used to take the condoms she received from the city's health department and blow them up into balloons which she released into the sky. These condom balloons floated high above the inner-city neighborhood—a visual reminder that trans sex workers were still here, some ten years after their initial expulsion from the city center.[49]

The expulsion of trans sex workers from downtown Roanoke was part of an urban redevelopment strategy that unfolded throughout the early 1980s. Policing and violence on the streets was one arm of urban planning; the other unfolded within stuffy board rooms and via telethons. In 1979, the city hired the firm Moore Grover Harper to lead an urban redevelopment plan called Design '79. It was a revolutionary process, utilizing a televised call-in show to solicit the public's aspirations for what downtown could become. Residents called in to express their dreams of a utopian arena, a space that was clean and safe for middle-class white people—those same folks who decades earlier had abandoned downtown for the sanctuary of the suburbs. The Design '79 plan ultimately centered on transforming two areas of downtown: the vicinity around Elmwood Park that, since the 1960s, was the city's main gay cruising block, and Market Square, which by evening was the sex workers' world.[50]

As dreams became realities in the 1980s, Bullitt Avenue—the Block—was closed to vehicular traffic and ultimately turned into a pedestrian mall so that gay men could no longer drive through and literally "cruise" in automobiles to meet other men. Meanwhile, outside the Market Building a new six-floor cultural institution, Center in the Square, full of museums and theaters, was established as an anchor for the new downtown. Alongside these municipal projects, private enterprise began to swoop in: Billy's Ritz opened at the northeast corner of the Market; other upscale eateries followed. Moore Grover Harper called for the area around the Market building to become a "Downtown Celebration Zone," a manifestation of the festival marketplace concept in which white middle-class consumers remain after dark. They would open their wallets on imagined outings to dinner and to the theater.

They would not feel threatened by trans sex workers and their johns and the community that had formed in these streets.[51]

One by one the places that Grace and Don remembered, those dive bars where a transvestite on the arm of her john might sit for a drink, shuttered their doors. By 1981 the New Market and the Belmont were closed; the Manhattan followed suit in the late 1980s. The Capitol and Miss Tony's turned off the lights in the late 1990s.[52] Today one of these former hangouts is a Thai restaurant, and another is a Louisiana-style creole restaurant (with a conspicuous "Oysters Upstairs" sign hanging behind the bar, a veiled reference to early twentieth-century sex work). Two of them have been absorbed into a major downtown brewery, and one more, part of an entire demolished block, is now on the site of the city's contemporary art museum. Standing in front of Billy's on our memory walk in 2019, Don pointed east along Salem Avenue to an inconspicuous side entrance to the art museum. "That was Miss Tony's," he said. "Right there." Later we walked past the former site of the Manhattan. Don peered inside the front windows amid the daytime glare, remembering the wild scenes of his youth. Further down the road we stopped outside the site of the Last Straw, one of Roanoke's earliest gay bars, opened in 1973 but closed in the early 1990s. Don pointed yet further down the block to a parking garage and remembered it as a site of anonymous sexual trysts. It was wintry and cold with tiny snow particles circulating in the air. I offered to give Don a ride home. Walking back to my car he stopped several more times to point out the sites of former adult bookstores from the 1980s—one here, one there. A whole world is now gone. Downtown has changed. It is all but a memory palace to the Black queer and trans people who once knew it so well. It is a place of erasure and forgetting.[53]

Processes of remembrance and forgetting are foundational to the stories that Roanokers tell about our city today. Black activists in Gainsboro and throughout Roanoke have continually used what Erica Meiners and Therese Quinn call "defiant memory work" as a way to bring to light histories of redlining, urban renewal, destruction of Black wealth, and displacement of Black families as central narratives in Roanoke's story.[54] They have raised issues such as reparations and the question of community control over spaces including the Dumas Hotel on Henry Street, Roanoke's former Black Wall Street.[55]

In the summer of 2020, an elderly white man toppled Roanoke's downtown Robert E. Lee monument. The city ultimately voted to get rid of the monument (now broken in two), handing it off to a local cemetery rather than restoring it downtown.[56] The successes and failures of these movements ebb and flow, yet they reveal the dynamic relationship between history and memory and the grassroots activism that uses remembrance as a strategy for reimagining the city that we call home.

Queer and trans memory work in Roanoke has unfolded in chaotic ways, often without much consensus about what actually happened in the good old days. Since the late 2000s, a transgender support and advocacy nonprofit, led primarily by white trans women, has been at the forefront of transgender memory work in Roanoke. There have been fights, however, both within and beyond this organization over the true origins of the city's trans community. Two older white trans women—identifying more in the tradition of so-called heterosexual cross-dressers—have argued that they were, in fact, part of an earlier transgender advocacy group in Roanoke started in the mid-1990s.[57] Yet the view of all these white women discounts the community formation and movement work of Black queens such as Carolyn, Grace, Christy, and others, all of whom were, at times, part of an even earlier visible trans community in Roanoke in the 1970s and 1980s.

Notably, Miss Grace and Miss Carolyn, as they were so often called, are akin to Black queer royalty in Roanoke—at least among the Black queer people who knew them. They are women of legendary status in Roanoke's worlds of drag performance, pageantry, and nightlife. Interviews with Grace, Carolyn, and Christy reveal trans sex worker networks that emerged in the late 1970s around the City Market building and continued through the 1980s and early 1990s along Salem Avenue and elsewhere on the edges of downtown. Investigative reporting by the *Roanoke Times* in the late 1980s and early 1990s, in which journalists actually interviewed trans sex workers about their lives, fill out a portrait of community life among trans women and transfeminine people, transvestites and street queens, teaching each other the tricks of the trade, forming chosen families and new forms of kinship, and looking out for one another in their interactions with the police.[58] It is not so much that LGBTQ people today have forgotten about the world that trans sex workers made, but somehow the lineage between yesterday's queens and today's transgender community has been ruptured, and I am curious as to why and how that happened.[59]

The truth is that even during the 1970s and 1980s when trans sex workers formed a world of their own in downtown Roanoke, there were many
other transgender people in the city who did not relate to the queens and
perhaps even sought to distance themselves from them. Through archival
research, I discovered a white trans woman named Rona who had, since the
early 1970s, been an active member of Virginia Prince's Foundation for Personality Expression (later Tri-Ess). Rona endeavored to create a space for
trans women in Roanoke. For example, in 1974 she worked to convince the
Roanoke City Public Library, as well as the Roanoke County Public Library,
to acquire copies of Prince's book, *The Transvestite and His Wife*. She also
discussed sharing a pamphlet, *Introduction to Transvestism*, with the local
police department.[60] By 1980, Rona had connected with a few other white
trans women in the Roanoke area and was in the process of attempting to
formalize a Tri-Ess chapter in Southwest Virginia.[61] It is important to note
that, as far as I can tell, Rona and her comrades were all white trans women
who did not engage in sex work. At the very same time as Grace, Carolyn,
and other Black queens were manifesting spaces of belonging and survival
in the city's nightclubs and on the streets of downtown, Rona and her comrades were envisioning other new, yet exclusive, white trans worlds within
the sanctity of their homes and in printed newsletters. For many Black
transfeminine people, sex work was crucial to livelihood. One can only
hope that Rona understood this when she sent that information to the city's
police department.[62]

Rona's world of domestic transness in the 1970s and 1980s was, in fact,
fiercely oppositional to the rival world of downtown sex work and drag performance. Articles in transgender magazines and newsletters from that era
celebrated the white middle-class trans women who were able to dress as
women yet sustain their "heterosexual" marriages. They dreamed of becoming women within the confines of white middle-class norms including marriage, heterosexuality (even though they really were becoming lesbians), and
suburban domesticity.[63] Trans women who had sex with men, on the other
hand, especially for money, were potentially reinforcing stereotypes that
associated all trans women with criminality and perversion.

Yet there was hope that some domestic, heterosexual white trans women
might find common cause with the mostly Black trans sex workers. Lucy J, a
transgender reader of the *Journal of Male Feminism* and a resident of nearby
Blacksburg, Virginia, wrote about this issue in a letter to the editor she

penned in 1977. She spoke up in defense of the so-called market queens: "It does seem very unjust," she argued, "for the city to permit discreet female prostitutes to flourish while trying to subvert their male counterparts." This crackdown on trans sex work was potentially an attack on all transvestites, she wrote. An editor's note added that more "heterosexual" transvestites such as Lucy J should speak up against the "denial of basic human rights to our sisters."[64] But this imagined "sisterhood" between white middle-class transvestites and Black trans sex workers never really materialized in the 1970s and 1980s in Roanoke.

It seems over time that white trans women aspiring to lead middle-class heteronormative lives rallied around a collective memory of transness that did not for the most part include the city's trans sex workers—Lucy J's efforts notwithstanding. Indeed, many transgender women to this day remain hostile to historical narratives of sex work because the stereotype of trans women as sex workers is one that perhaps brings them shame or, at least, a real feeling of misrecognition.[65] It is true that stories of trans sex work have the potential to sideline and marginalize the important work of people such as Rona and her crew who fought for trans rights in Roanoke in a separate yet important way. It is also true that stories of sex work serve to make invisible histories of transgender men and transmasculine people in our community. The contemporary transgender support group in Roanoke has worked hard to move beyond a women-only space and facilitate a community of support and uplift for trans men and transmasculine people. It is also true that trans men's histories are much harder to resurrect because they did not have a voice in the dominant transgender magazines and newsletters of the 1970s and 1980s, were not profiled in exposes by local newspapers such as the *Roanoke Times*, and were simply not as visible as the conspicuous downtown sex workers. For all these reasons, focusing on trans sex worker histories can sometimes manifest negative consequences.[66]

And yet, despite the memory battles of our own transgender community, Black trans sex workers remain central to the stories that straight cisgender people tell about the history of this place. Newspaper writers speak of "hookers" and "transvestites" in the same breath as they praise the city's efforts to turn around downtown. CEOs and city council members talk of downtown as once "full of prostitutes" but now a safer place reclaimed for all Roanokers. When the *Roanoke Times* first published a story in 2016 about our efforts to interpret the history of trans sex work downtown, a white, presumably straight older gentleman asked me, "Are you sure those folks were transgender?" The question strikes me as a query about bodies. There is an intimacy—a kind of bodily intimacy—that hundreds if not thousands of people in Roanoke have with this history. This includes a local congressman who at least one former trans sex worker mentions as a past client. Perhaps the reason trans sex workers live so large in straight memories of Roanoke is because so many straight men lived that history, too—whether picking up a woman on Salem Avenue at night or connecting with one at the Thrifty Inn near the airport. For every straight man who remembers trans sex work as a crucial chapter in downtown's history, I wonder, much as they might wonder about me and the queer histories I am intimate with, "So did y'all fuck?"

In 2020, most visitors to Roanoke enter the valley through a tiny gap cut through the Blue Ridge mountains. Trucks and cars speed down Interstate 81 beneath towering cliffs and emerge into this Appalachian oasis that I call home. A city of a hundred-thousand residents, Roanoke sprawls across the valley floor. A small mountain rears its head just above downtown. Interstate 581 breaks off from the main highway north of the city. Vehicles barrel down 581 at warp speeds heading toward the city center. One of my favorite highway signs is on this stretch of asphalt. It reads "Exit 5, Virginia Museum of Trans."

Besides the Museum of Transgender History and Art (MOTHA), which has no permanent home but rather roves throughout the country's museums, this is the only other "Museum of Trans" that I know of in the United States. So let's say you take exit 5. It will deposit you on Williamson Road in Gainsboro, just north of the city center.

Back in the 1970s and 1980s there was a different off-ramp for downtown. If you took the former Hunter Viaduct, your car would descend a highway spur coursing above the railroad tracks, flying right behind Billy's Ritz, and deposit you onto Salem Avenue. If you got off the Hunter Viaduct at night, you would have entered immediately into the sex workers' world. On our wintry walk in 2019, Don remembered a public sex space right underneath the viaduct behind Billy's, although if you stand there today you only see a small patch of grass behind the art museum. Yet you can perhaps imagine, in your mind's eye, the concrete ceiling above you, and the many activities available to those seeking pleasure underneath its protective cover.

Today if you follow the sign to the "Museum of Trans," you will turn right onto Salem Avenue off of Williamson Road. You drive past the Taubman Museum and Billy's, past the Market building, past a skyscraper, past the lingering hulk of a former gay bar, past the parking garage where men once met up for a quick fuck. When you get to the 300-block of Salem Avenue—home to another famous former gay bar—you have arrived. But the "Museum of Trans" turns out to be Virginia's official Museum of Transportation. They just couldn't figure out how to spell out the whole word "Transportation" on the deceitful highway sign.

Yet this street *is* a Museum of Trans. Grace and Christy used to walk these blocks. Cars came off the viaduct and cruised down Salem Avenue—looking for pleasure, looking for trouble. The police headquarters is just one block away. Christy was arrested on this street for blocking the path of a police cruiser. Grace threw a cinder block into the windshield of a car full of violent harassers here. Carolyn had "five boyfriends" back in the day, she says, some of whom she met on or around this street. Today, Salem Avenue is festooned with flags announcing new downtown housing projects—former industrial warehouses converted into lofts and condominiums with exclusive keypad entrances. Young professionals look out their windows upon this Museum of Trans. At night the avenue is haunted by the ghosts of trans people nearly yet not completely forgotten. For those of us who remember, we stomp our feet and chant their names in celebration of their lives. Sometimes I see their painted faces and long legs in the glimmer of the glass outside of Billy's. I can't tell if the reflection is theirs, or my own.

NOTES

1. Walt Whitman, "Crossing Brooklyn Ferry," in *The Portable Walt Whitman*, ed. Mark Van Doren (New York: Viking, 1973), 149–56.
2. Henri Lefebvre, "Right to the City," in *Writings on Cities*, translated and edited by Eleonore Kofman and Elizabeth Lebas (Malden, Mass.: Blackwell, 1996), 63–181.

3. Colin Woodard, "Trains Built Roanoke. Science Saved It," *Politico Magazine,* September 15, 2016.

4. Rand Dotson, *Roanoke, Virginia, 1882–1912: Magic City of the New South* (Knoxville: University of Tennessee Press, 2007).

5. Woodard, "Trains Built Roanoke."

6. Sex work continues to be framed as an obstacle to ongoing gentrification in Roanoke; see Matt Chittum, "Corbin Prydwen Invests in Roanoke's West End for Diversity and Profit," *Roanoke Times,* August 16, 2014; RM Barton, "How Communities Pathologized Sex Workers," *WUSSY,* April 19, 2018.

7. This section includes reprinted material from Gregory Samantha Rosenthal, *Living Queer History: Remembrance and Belonging in a Southern City* (Chapel Hill: University of North Carolina Press, 2021), 144–45.

8. On the way that defining a "bad" period in a city's history helps rehabilitate an earlier "golden age" as well as lay the groundwork for contemporary renaissance, see Andrew Hurley, *Beyond Preservation: Using Public History to Revitalize Inner Cities* (Philadelphia: Temple University Press, 2010), 22–30.

9. On the ways that urban redevelopment relies on the policing of undesirable populations, see Neil Smith, *The New Urban Frontier: Gentrification and the Revanchist City* (New York: Routledge, 1996). On how this intersects with queer communities, see Christina B. Hanhardt, "Broken Windows at Blue's: A Queer History of Gentrification and Policing," in *Policing the Planet: Why the Policing Crisis Led to Black Lives Matter,* edited by Jordan T. Camp and Christina Heatherton (New York: Verso, 2016), 41–61. On the complicity of queer communities in this policing, see Hanhardt, *Safe Space: Gay Neighborhood History and the Politics of Violence* (Durham, N.C.: Duke University Press, 2013); Zachary Blair, "Boystown: Gay Neighborhoods, Social Media, and the (Re)production of Racism," in *No Tea, No Shade: New Writings in Black Queer Studies,* edited by E. Patrick Johnson (Durham, N.C.: Duke University Press, 2016), 287–303. On transgender sex work histories, see Susan Stryker, *Transgender History: The Roots of Today's Revolution,* 2nd ed. (New York: Seal Press, 2017); C. Riley Snorton, *Black on Both Sides: A Racial History of Trans Identity* (Minneapolis: University of Minnesota Press, 2017).

10. Moore Grover Harper, *Roanoke Design 79 Catalog* (Essex, CT: n.p., 1979), n.p. ["Market District"].

11. Southwest Virginia LGBTQ+ History Project, "Oral History Interview with Christy," 2017, Virginia Room, Roanoke Public Libraries (hereafter VR-RPL); Southwest Virginia LGBTQ+ History Project, "Oral History Interview with Grace," 2018, VR-RPL. I conducted member checks in 2020, and again in 2023,

with all the oral history narrators featured in this essay. Some narrators asked to go by their real names; others preferred that I use a pseudonym. In order to protect everyone's privacy, I have identified everyone by first names only. There is no need for the reader to be able to trace any given person to a file in the LGBTQ History Collection, but readers are welcome to explore the entire oral history collection at http://www.virginiaroom.org/digital/collections/show/19.

12. "A Bar Critique," *Virginia Gayzette* 3, no. 2 (February 1978).

13. Southwest Virginia LGBTQ+ History Project, "Oral History Interview with Daddy Sam," 2016, VR-RPL.

14. Southwest Virginia LGBTQ+ History Project, "Oral History Interview with Rodger," 2016, VR-RPL.

15. Southwest Virginia LGBTQ+ History Project, "Oral History Interview with Daniel," 2016, VR-RPL; Southwest Virginia LGBTQ+ History Project, "Oral History Interview with Leonard," 2018, VR-RPL.

16. Dotson, *Roanoke*, 21–22, 47, 86–87, 212. This section includes reprinted material from Rosenthal, *Living Queer History*, 22–28.

17. Dotson, *Roanoke*, 50, 108.

18. Dotson, *Roanoke*, 132–41; Ida B. Wells, "Southern Horrors," *On Lynchings* (Amherst, NY: Humanity Books, 2002), 25–54.

19. Reginald Shareef, *The Roanoke Valley's African American Heritage: A Pictorial History* (Virginia Beach, VA: Donning Co., 1996).

20. City of Roanoke, Virginia, *1928 Review of the Department of Police, City of Roanoke, Virginia with Report of the Superintendent of Police 1922 to 1928* (Roanoke: n.p., 1928), 55–57.

21. "Roanoke, Va., City Council Holds Urban Renewal Hearing," January 8, 1958, WSLS-TV (Roanoke, VA) News Film Collection, 1951–1971, University of Virginia Library; Henry Chenault, "Roanoke Lunch Counter Desegregated Quietly," *Roanoke Times*, August 28, 1960; Robert B. Sears, "Racial Bars Dropped at Roanoke Memorial," *Roanoke Times*, March 18, 1964; Marietta E. Poff, "School Desegregation in Roanoke, Virginia: The Black Student Perspective," *Journal of Negro Education* 85, no. 4 (2016): 433–43. On these processes throughout Virginia and across the nation, see Kristen Green, *Something Must Be Done about Prince Edward County: A Family, a Virginia Town, a Civil Rights Battle* (New York: Harper Perennial, 2016); Richard Rothstein, *The Color of Law: A Forgotten History of How Our Government Segregated America* (New York: Liveright, 2017).

22. U.S. Department of Commerce, Bureau of the Census, *Population of Urbanized Areas Established since the 1970 Census, for the United States: 1970* (Washington, DC: US Government Printing Office, 1976), 22; Patrick J. Weschler,

"Annexation and Other Municipal Boundary Changes," *Virginia Law Review* 66, no. 2 (1980): 329–39; Clare White, *Roanoke, 1740–1982* (Roanoke: Roanoke Valley Historical Society, 1982), 108.

23. John T. Morse, *The City Market: A Redevelopment Study of the Roanoke City Market Area* (Roanoke: Department of City Planning, 1965), 37, 88, 93.

24. Alison Isenberg, *Downtown America: A History of the Place and the People Who Made It* (Chicago: University of Chicago Press, 2004), 273–83, 408. On the Festival Marketplace concept, see M. Christine Boyer, "Cities for Sale: Merchandising History at South Street Seaport," in *Variations on a Theme Park: The New American City and the End of Public Space*, ed. Michael Sorkin (New York: Hill and Wang, 1992), 181–204; M. Christine Boyer, *The City of Collective Memory: Its Historical Imagery and Architectural Entertainments* (Cambridge, MA: MIT Press, 1994), 6; Hurley, *Beyond Preservation*, 14–15.

25. "Oral History Interview with Grace"; Stefan Bechtel, "The Long Road from Man to Woman," *Roanoker* 4, no. 6 (November/December 1977), 25.

26. "Oral History Interview with Leonard."

27. Southwest Virginia LGBTQ+ History Project, "Oral History Interview with Carolyn," 2018, VR-RPL.

28. "Oral History Interview with Grace"; Southwest Virginia LGBTQ+ History Project, "Oral History Interview with Don," 2017, VR-RPL.

29. "Oral History Interview with Leonard."

30. Cassius Adair, "The Lost Queer World of Roanoke, Virginia," in "How to Go Clubbing," *With Good Reason*, Virginia Humanities, February 8, 2019, https://www.withgoodreasonradio.org/episode/how-to-go-clubbing/.

31. Laurence Hammack, "Sex, Drug Indictments Returned," *Roanoke Times & World News*, September 9, 1992.

32. "Oral History Interview with Daniel"; "Special Edition: Something New Has Been Added," *Big Lick Gayzette* 1, no. 7 (December 3, 1971).

33. Stefan Bechtel, "What It's Like to Be Gay in Roanoke," *Roanoker* 4, no. 6 (November/December 1977), 25–26, 73, 76.

34. Bechtel, "What It's Like to Be Gay in Roanoke," 28.

35. Douglas Pardue, "Homosexuals Organize, Publish Own Newspaper," *Roanoke Times & World News*, March 2, 1978; "Out of the Closet Onto the Newstand," *Virginia Gayzette* 3, no. 3 (March 5, 1978); "The Heat Is Never Off," *Virginia Gayzette* 3, no. 3 (March 5, 1978).

36. "To Sgt. Barrett," *Virginia Gayzette* 3, no. 3 (March 5, 1978).

37. Bechtel, "What It's Like to Be Gay in Roanoke," 77; "Womensline," *Virginia Gayzette*, 3, no. 4 (April 1978).

38. John Witt, "City May Outlaw Market 'Queens,'" *Roanoke Times & World News,* September 18, 1977.

39. "Oral History Interview with Carolyn."

40. "Oral History Interview with Don."

41. Douglas Pardue, "Punish Vice Patrons, Prosecutor Says," *Roanoke Times & World News,* April 21, 1978; Mike Ives, "A Far Better World Awaits Streetwalkers," *Roanoke Times & World News,* April 24, 1978.

42. "Oral History Interview with Christy"; Laurence Hammack, "Complaints Bring Prostitution Busts," *Roanoke Times & World News,* September 2, 1989; "7 More Face Prostitution Charges," *Roanoke Times & World News,* September 7, 1989; Mary Bishop, "Roanoke's Lurid Street Circus a Hard Show to Close," *Roanoke Times & World News,* September 10, 1989; Hammack, "Sex, Drug Indictments Returned."

43. "Oral History Interview with Carolyn."

44. "Oral History Interview with Grace"; "Oral History Interview with Christy."

45. Roland Lazenby, "AIDS Causes Second Death in Western Va." *Roanoke Times & World News,* November 6, 1983; "Southwest Virginia Sees Eight AIDS Deaths," *Blue Ridge Lambda Press,* 3, no. 7 (December 1985–January 1986).

46. "Oral History interview with Grace"; "Oral History Interview with Leonard."

47. "Southwest Virginia Sees Eight AIDS Deaths"; Victoria Ratcliff, "Street Life's a Drag, Transvestite Says," *Roanoke Times & World News,* June 28, 1992; Laurence Hammack, "Prostitutes to Be Tested for AIDS," *Roanoke Times & World News,* September 21, 1992.

48. "7 More Face Prostitution Charges"; Bishop, "Roanoke's Lurid Street Circus a Hard Show to Close."

49. "Oral History interview with Christy"; Bishop, "Roanoke's Lurid Street Circus a Hard Show to Close."

50. Moore Grover Harper, *Roanoke Design 79 Catalog*; Adair, "The Lost Queer World of Roanoke, Virginia." This section includes reprinted material from Rosenthal, *Living Queer History,* 40–42.

51. Moore Grover Harper, *Roanoke Design 79 Catalog,* n.p. ["Elmwood Park Extension" and "Development Concept"]; Mag Poff, "Facelifting Begins for Elmwood Park," *Roanoke Times & World News,* June 23, 1982.

52. Roanoke city directories were utilized to provide estimated opening and closing dates for these establishments. See *Roanoke, Salem and Vinton (Roanoke County, Va.) City Directory* (Richmond, VA: Hill Directory Company Publishers, 1950–81); *Roanoke, Salem and Vinton (Roanoke County, Va.) City Directory* (Richmond, VA [later Livonia, MI]: R. L. Polk & Co., 1982–2000).

53. On downtown Roanoke's gentrification, see also "Oral History Interview with Don"; Nate Berg, "Are These the Fastest-Gentrifying Neighborhoods in the

U.S.?," *CityLab*, June 11, 2012; Lyman Stone, "Is Roanoke Really an Appalachian Comeback Story?," *Medium*, November 8, 2016.

54. Erica R. Meiners and Therese Quinn, "Introduction: Defiant Memory Work," *American Quarterly* 71, no. 2 (2019): 353–61.

55. Martin Jeffrey, "Dumas Sale is Watershed Moment," *Roanoke Times,* May 18, 2017; Martha Park, "When a 'Green Book' Site Goes Up for Sale," *CityLab,* July 11, 2017; Shayne Dwyer, "Walking Tour of Roanoke's 'Black Wall Street' Capitalizes on Growing Juneteenth Energy," *WSLS 10* (news), June 19, 2020.

56. Shayne Dwyer, Lindsey Kennett, and Jeff Williamson, "Roanoke's Lee Monument Will Be Moved to Evergreen Burial Park," *WSLS 10* (news), September 21, 2020.

57. Southwest Virginia LGBTQ+ History Project, "Oral History Interview with Valerie," 2016, VR-RPL; Southwest Virginia LGBTQ+ History Project, "Oral History Interview with Terri," 2016, VR-RPL.

58. Bechtel, "The Long Road from Man to Woman"; Ratcliff, "Street Life's a Drag, Transvestite Says." See also Gregory Samantha Rosenthal, "How to Become a Woman," *Southern Cultures* 26, no. 3 (2020): 122–37.

59. On generational divides within transgender communities, see Jack Halberstam, *Trans*: A Quick and Quirky Account of Gender Variability* (Oakland: University of California Press, 2018), 63–83.

60. Rona, letter to the editor, *Transvestia* 14, no. 80 (1974): 69.

61. "New Chapter Organizes: Roanoke, Va. New Site," *Femme Mirror* 5, nos. 2–3 (1980), 24.

62. On the racialized experiences of trans women, see Snorton, *Black on Both Sides,* 139–75.

63. Stryker, *Transgender History,* 57–77.

64. Lucy J, "Roanoke May 'Outlaw' Transvestites," *Journal of Male Feminism* 77, nos. 4–5 (1977), 9–10.

65. Julia Serano, *Whipping Girl: A Transsexual Woman on Sexism and the Scapegoating of Femininity,* 2nd ed. (Berkeley, CA: Seal Press, 2016), 16. See also Nihils Rev and Fiona Maeve Geist, "Staging the Trans Sex Worker," *TSQ: Transgender Studies Quarterly* 4, no. 1 (2017): 112–27.

66. For trans men's perspectives on Roanoke's history, see Southwest Virginia LGBTQ+ History Project, "Oral History Interview with Anton," 2018, VR-RPL; Southwest Virginia LGBTQ+ History Project, "Oral History Interview with Theodore," 2019, VR-RPL; Southwest Virginia LGBTQ+ History Project, "Oral History Interview with Nathaniel," 2020, VR-RPL.

MAPPING
QUEER RICHMOND

———

Space, Place, and Community Building
Around Diversity Richmond

JAY WATKINS

n 1979 Cal Yeomans' play *Richmond Jim* took the stage at San Francisco's
Theatre Rhinoceros. Yeomans was a southerner who was as unhappy in
Atlanta, New York, and San Francisco as he was in his native rural central
Florida.[1] In the play, Jim comes to New York with friends on vacation from
the Department of Education in Richmond. He has abandoned them and
improbably ended up at the Spike, a leather bar. He goes home with Mike,
and during an evening of sex, poppers, and pot punctuated by moments of
deep intimacy, Jim is awakened to his kinky desires. The curtain falls with
Mike on his knees in submission to Jim. Over the next several years, the show
played in New York, San Francisco, Los Angeles, and Portland to generally
good reviews. The show is not really about Richmond at all. Instead, Richmond is shorthand for the simple, backward, repressed, uneducated "country bumpkin" who was insufficiently liberated until he arrived in New York.
Audiences were supposed to understand that Richmond represented the
opposite of a city with a progressive gay community.[2] Though Yeomans's use
of Richmond telegraphed a particular message to audiences in America's
queer capitals, the reality of Richmond in 1979 was far queerer than many
realized. Richmond was not hiding. There was, in fact, a vibrant queer world.

There was even a Richmonder on the executive board of the National Gay and Lesbian Task Force.

This chapter aims to counter the narrative of Richmond's lack of queer cultures and builds on previous works by Bob Swisher, Beth Marschak, Alex Lorch, Cindy Bray, Leisa Meyer, and myself.[3] It makes extensive use of five oral histories collected during the partnership between the William & Mary LGBTQ Research Project and Diversity Richmond, which is detailed in the next section.[4] I have used long quotes so that the chapter tells a story of Richmond through the voices of some people who lived it. Rather than a linear progress narrative that culminates in Diversity Richmond as *the* community center, the narrators in this chapter illuminate some of the distinct—though not wholly unique—struggles and movements that morphed, melded, and divided over the period as queer people in Richmond made their way in the shadow of their city's confederate history. The chapter ends with Diversity Richmond because it is a useful counter-monument in a city that was, until recently, home to some of the largest Confederate monuments in the country.

A NOTE ON SOURCES

Since 1961, the Mattachine Society of Washington, DC, has worked for visibility and legal equality. In recent years, they have been engaged in "archive activism" and supplied seed money to various research projects around the country to educate about the LGBTQ past.[5] In 2015, Leisa Meyer, professor of history and American studies at the College of William & Mary, received some of Mattachine's funding for research into Virginia LGBTQ history.[6] Through meetings with other college stakeholders, Professor Meyer secured additional funding, and the call went out for William & Mary students interested in documenting the queer past. "The William & Mary LGBTIQ Research Project: Documenting the LGBTIQ Past in Virginia" officially launched in the spring semester of 2016. Those first student researchers came from undergrad and graduate levels in majors as diverse as gender, sexuality, and women's studies; history; sociology; anthropology; and American studies. The project's first graduate research fellow, Jan Hübenthal, established and ran the social media presence. Swem Library Special Collections led the initial training for the student researchers in archival and digital records research. The undergraduate student researchers then spent many Saturdays in special collections at William & Mary, Virginia Commonwealth University, and the Library of Virginia. The research from that first semester culminated in an exhibit at William & Mary's Swem Library. The well-attended opening event and roundtable session provoked thoughtful discussion.[7] One of the primary critiques to come from the early research and exhibition was the over-representation of white gay men compared to other groups. Much of that was a function of the available source material in the archive, a more extensive problem of which projects such as this should always be cognizant. Oral history helps to remedy these silences and gaps.[8]

The fall semester of 2016 brought a new group of students, increased faculty involvement, and a partnership with Diversity Richmond. I was hired as a visiting assistant professor in the Department of History. When I arrived on campus, I was most looking forward to working on the research project because of my previous work with southern queer history.[9] Partnering with Diversity Richmond expanded the research opportunities available to students. In addition to traditional archival research, student researchers and fellows assisted with digitizing the pictures and other ephemera donated or loaned to the project by community members. Oral history necessitated a different approach to research than many students had encountered before. Professor Meyer and I conducted a series of training sessions to prepare the students for the particularities of conducting interviews with older LGBTQ+ individuals. We found it helpful to develop core areas of inquiry: biography, identity, community, and activism.

Before COVID-19, I would wake up early a few Saturdays every semester to pick up a van to meet Professor Meyer and the students at Wawa for breakfast and coffee before hitting the road. The drive over was generally quiet since most of us were not quite awake yet. The days tended to progress in a similar fashion. We arrived at Diversity Richmond to meet Rodney Lofton and set up our recorders. We often had a few minutes to collect our thoughts and assign appropriate students to the interviewee, often balancing gender presentations and ethnicities as best we could.

The benefits of oral history have been theorized and explored by several scholars, and bearing in mind that this produces a base of evidence grounded in the late-twentieth century, the practice has become essential for modern

LGBTQ+ scholarship.[10] Indeed, the strides we have made as a field would not be possible without oral history, since the politics of archives have erased, excluded, and occluded queerness in traditional archives. This work has not been without problems. Issues of inclusion, identity, and respectability continue to plague LGBTQ+ politics. These issues play out on the ground in sometimes surprising ways. When the Gay Community Center of Richmond became Diversity Richmond, some resisted involvement and did not welcome the change. Some have questioned why certain letters appear in the title of our research project. The word "queer" continues to be troubling for some. Though one sometimes meets resistance to speaking, participants are generally happy (some might even be grateful and enthusiastic) to have the opportunity to tell their stories. Zakia McKensey, in her 2017 interview, said: "I thought it was awesome that you all are taking time out to capture that part of history because I think it's important, and they're going to be important for those who come after me to know our struggles and what we did in Richmond as a community."[11] Others have resisted student involvement. At least one interviewee expressed the opinion that undergraduate students could not possibly conduct sufficiently rigorous interviews or relate to their subjects, whilst others were overjoyed at being interviewed by students who represent future generations. This variation necessitated flexibility with students and community members as we collected dozens of hours of oral histories.

QUEER RICHMOND

Like many American cities, Richmond was segregated in law and practice. Though never a singular community, white queer Richmonders coalesced around cruising, bars, and select private homes.[12] Men cruised for sex in downtown Richmond at least from the 1940s. Bob Swisher wrote, "Broad Street (railroad) Station, the Greyhound bus station, and the USO were full of servicemen on leave or en route to or from military assignments."[13] Small spaces away from prying eyes all over downtown could be requisitioned for sex, with the most popular being the alley behind the Colonial Theatre or the hotel basement across Broad Street.[14] The area became known as "the block," a name that signified a cruising space rather than a firm attachment to a particular block. Initially downtown around the downtown hotels and the other train station, the block moved around in response to police crackdowns. The cruising space was active well into the 1980s. Bill Harrison recalled, "After the bars closed, guys would go down. There was a lot of hustlers down there, and you would ride around and ride around and ride around and maybe pick up somebody, and it's interesting because everybody knew that place existed, and I don't remember a lot of police being down there, at the time."[15] While walking this area today, one is confronted with uneven gentrification. The Science Museum now occupies the former Broad Street train station in a neighborhood called the Fan District. The architecture of the downtown station on Main Street remains, and it is still a functioning train station. Further into downtown, unhoused people are sleeping in the doorways of fancy brunch restaurants and coffee shops.

Separate from the world of street cruising, though sometimes overlapping with it, a few bars and private homes offered community to Richmond's queers.[16] Smitty's opened in 1954 and was initially popular among women's softball teams. Carol S. recalled, "I thought for a long time that all the lesbians in the world played softball except for those few of us who sat in the stands."[17] Because of the association of lesbians and softball and the restrictive Virginia Alcoholic Beverage Control laws, this was an unofficial lesbian bar. Later, Richmond's softball lesbians would take over Tanglewood, a "beer joint in Goochland County" whose popularity stretched back to World War II.[18] By the 1960s, new owners converted Smitty's to Leo's and began catering almost exclusively to gay men. In 1976, new owners renamed it the Male Box before a firearm incident and a patron's death forced it to close.[19] After Marroni's closed in 1962 another queer spot, Eton's, opened on West Grace Street, between downtown and the museum district.[20] Because of its location just two blocks from the Richmond Professional Institute (RPI, now part of Virginia Commonwealth University), it frequently ran afoul of the law. The bar was closed in 1967 due to Virginia's ABC law (overturned in 1991) that outlawed selling alcohol to or allowing the congregation of notorious homosexuals.[21] This was after several years of the RPI banning students from going to the bar because of its reputation as a queer space.[22]

Richmond's gay activism got off to a rocky start. Tony Segura, a gay Cuban immigrant, moved to Richmond in 1959 after living in New York and helping to found the city's Mattachine Society.[23] His partner Marsh Harris made a name for himself writing gay fiction, some of the first with happy endings. Segura was already imbued with an activist spirit and attempted to start a Richmond chapter of Mattachine.[24] This never really got off the ground. Still, in 1977 Segura and his partner would go on to be at the forefront of queer organizing in Richmond as founding members of the Virginia Gay Rights Association, where many of our narrators honed their activist skills.

GUY KINMAN

Guy Kinman was born in 1917 in Heavener, Oklahoma, a town at the far eastern edge of the state, to a family that frequently moved because of his father's military service. He finished college in 1940 and entered the seminary, which spared him from the draft during World War II. He served as a minister and then a chaplain in the Korean War. In 1957 he abruptly quit the ministry after an experience with another man. Kinman says:

> When I woke up the next morning, I was a different person. I said, 'Oh, there's been something missing in my life.' And I immediately, and I do mean immediately, probably that day, because there was no one to talk with about it—I knew what I was going to do. So, I resigned the chaplaincy, notified my church that I would be demitting the ministry, coming back [to America], and that I would be starting a new career. I had no idea what I had wanted to be. I had been a good minister. I had been honored with the commendation ribbon as chaplain. There are people that said I was fine, but my life was not being daily or did not have any potential for being fulfilled in the personal way.[25]

He arrived in a still deeply segregated Richmond in 1960 as a photocopier salesperson after choosing Virginia over Pennsylvania as his preferred territory.

Kinman's experience of his identity echoes that of many other men at midcentury who did not have words for what they were or what they were feeling at the time. At least in the popular imagination, homosexuals were still "dirty psychopaths," and many did not feel well-served by the label.[26] By the time

Kinman recognized his desires, the fledgling homophile movement, exemplified by the Mattachine Society, was only a few years old.[27] He recalled "experiences of closeness, [but] there was no thought that I would find a great person for life."[28] So he did what many men in his position did: married a woman. "I was very, very physically and otherwise attracted to her. And I married her in 1962, and the day I married her was the unhappiest day of my life because I realized that, getting dressed, I didn't want to marry her."[29] It would be ten years before the couple separated and divorced.

Kinman's "liberation" from his marriage coincided with the gay liberation that was happening nationally. Philadelphia's "annual reminder march" started in 1965; the Compton's Cafeteria riot occurred in San Francisco in 1966, then Stonewall in New York in 1969, and in 1970 the first Christopher Street Liberation Day (now Pride) happened in New York. Coupled with events such as the Emma Jones Society conventions (more beach parties than conventions) in Pensacola, Florida, every Fourth of July weekend, many queer people across the country embraced a politics of visibility.[30] Those publicly declaring their sexualities and those more reticent to do so cautiously intermingled in Richmond. Some, like Kinman, were "free all along. For instance, when I would go to the symphony between '72 and '85. . . . Uh, I was there, just the same, mingling during the intermission. If I would see a lesbian or gay, I would have seen them at the gay bar or the lesbian bar, they would blanch. They would be frightened seeing me. They would be so afraid that this awful truth might be out."[31]

BOBBIE WEINSTOCK

Barbara "Bobbie" Weinstock is a Virginia native. She was born in Newport News in 1946 to a military family. Like Kinman, she spent her formative years moving around before landing in Georgia in the 1960s. She attended a segregated high school in Warner Robbins before beginning classes at the University of Georgia in 1964, just three years after the university desegregated.[32] She recalled just a few Black students, but there were "many, many, many armed guards."[33] Though unaware she was a lesbian—"the gay part came after"—Weinstock spent her college years working in the Civil Rights and anti-war movements. This informed her activism in the War on Poverty after her return to Richmond after college, where she took up a social service position. She "met some men who were bisexual and started dating them, and came out, in that environment." She joked that, for a long time, she did not know anyone else who was white and gay.[34]

Her entry into lesbian politics came in 1974 when she reached out to the Atlanta Lesbian Feminist Alliance (ALFA) upon returning to Georgia for graduate school. ALFA was a lesbian separatist group founded in 1972 when a group of radical (many socialist) lesbians broke away from the Atlanta Women's Liberation Center and the Gay Liberation Front because of insufficient intersectionality.[35] Her involvement with lesbian separatists and the larger lesbian and gay movement led to her work within and then election to the National Lesbian and Gay Task Force board during grad school.

When Weinstock returned to Richmond in the late 1970s, she found a city already creating activist spaces and visible gay and lesbian community organizations. Gay Awareness in Perspective (GAP) was founded in 1974 and held weekly meetings at the Pace Memorial United Methodist Church.[36] The Richmond Lesbian Feminists followed in 1975. Weinstock began organizing a state chapter called the Virginia Coalition for Lesbian and Gay Rights to supplement and coordinate the smaller organizations on campuses such as Virginia Commonwealth University in Richmond and Old Dominion University in Norfolk. About this time she says: "The early lesbian feminist movement was so incorporated in environments and everything! And not separate. Anything that affected your life was involved. And how you looked at the whole political perspective on looking at something." The organization's newsletter went out "twice a month, and we were getting together. We'd bring food. Like a potluck get-together, and talk and get real involved in everybody's full life. Very much of a support group, very much of a family."[37]

BILL HARRISON

William "Bill" Atkinson Harrison Jr. was born near Richmond in 1953 and grew up in a Southern Baptist household on a peanut farm in Southampton County. His gay awakening came early in life. "I was in the 8th grade, and I was walking in the hallway and Jerry Flowers was in front of me, and I thought, hmm [*laughs*], and that's when I realized."[38] He first heard the word "homosexual" soon after when a fellow student intervened in an instance of bullying. Though these realizations came early for Bill, it would be several tumultuous years before he grew to accept himself.

On that journey to self-acceptance, Harrison found community in the bars of the early 1970s. After rejecting and reconnecting with a client he met while studying to be a mortician, Bill went to his first gay bar:

> It's down in Carytown, and it was a restaurant during the day and a bar at night, and it was called the Dial Tone because the telephone company was located right in that neighborhood, and a lot of people from the telephone company would come over and eat lunch. That's how it got called the Dial Tone. There was this old story that the tables had phones on [them] where you could call to another table. That never happened. That was just an old story somebody made up. It was all men. I don't think there were any women who went there. There was no dancing. It was just a bar, probably about seventy-five men there every night that you went, and it was about the only game in town, at the time, of the bars opened up. . . . It was a part of Ukrops grocery store. They renovated it. It was the health food section, and I told this story. We had a history thing that we did here at Diversity a couple of years ago. In the middle of the bar, there was this pole that went from the floor to the ceiling, and there was a light up at the top that shined down. All the hot guys would stand there and lean up against the pole like being on display, and I never did that because I wasn't a hot guy, but whenever I would go into Ukrops, in their food section, I would always go over to that pole. It was still there, and I would lean up against it. Here I am. And now they're going to tear that building down. I would love to get that pole and put it in our archives.[39]

Spending time at the bars caused Harrison's work and grades to suffer. When his boss learned of his homosexuality, he fired him. Harrison entered a period of despondence that included psychotherapy and a search to be "normal." Like Kinman and many others, Harrison married, but the marriage did not last long.

Though Harrison was rejected by his hometown Baptist church, his parents never left his side, and he later found a way to marry his activism with his faith.

I went to St. Paul's, and the rector, the priest, there was a man by the
name of Craig Biddle, and he was very pro-gay, and he preached a sermon
entitled "Different, But No Less Decent," and he talked about gay and
lesbian people, and I sat there, and I thought, these people are going to start
turning pews over at any given moment, and they didn't, and so that's why I
thought, again, there is a God, because I don't think it was an accident that
I went there and I heard that, and I couldn't believe that this was happening, and I got involved with the church, and there's a lot of homophobia in
the church, and so I started writing letters to the editor of their diocesan
newsletter, which I look back at that, and I think, I can't believe I did that,
you know, but I did, and it's just a part of my journey. . . . Several years later,
the bishop formed a Human Sexuality Commission, and we met on a regular basis up in Northern Virginia; and I was on the commission, and it
was our task to go around the diocese and talk to different churches
and get their impressions about how do you think the church should move
with this? . . . I got involved in this group called Dignity Integrity, which
was a Catholic and Episcopal support group for gay and lesbian people,
and I became an Episcopalian and just became involved in the community.
I started writing letters to the editor, you know, about their homophobic
editorials, and I got involved and became an activist back in the '70s,
and forty years later, I'm the executive director of the LGBT Community
Foundation.[40]

Local Quakers, Methodists, Episcopalians, and Roman Catholics were surprisingly progressive at various points—though, as in most places across the
South, this tolerance was tenuous and fraught at the best of times. At the national level, mainline denominations such as the Methodists were beginning
to unravel over questions on the status of homosexuals. The Methodist's 1972
General Conference declared homosexuality incompatible with scripture,
but in 1976 some clergy and laity introduced language welcoming all sexual
orientations, a proposal that was soundly defeated.[41] Growing up in tight-knit
communities, often centered on church life, queer southerners frequently
kept their strong connections to faith, which worked to the detriment of political organizing that too narrowly defined appropriate queerness and failed
to account for the importance of southerners' faith. Historian John Howard
found that "these queer Christians, black and white, rarely responded to a

narrow gay movement driven by identity politics. Instead, they joined only when a more expansive definition of gayness was fashioned."[42] Sometimes southerners founded their own churches, such as the Metropolitan Community Church founded in Los Angeles in 1968 by Troy Perry. Harrison's experience was echoed by other narrators who left their childhood faith to seek one that worked holistically for them as God's children.

Whilst Harrison was grappling with his place in gay life, the 1970s were a pivotal time for Richmond's queer folks generally. In 1970 a group of committed activists, using the free university and free clinic model of other cities, opened the Fan Free Clinic (now Health Brigade), which would go on to be one of the earliest health organizations to respond to and care for those impacted by AIDS in Richmond.[43] The Richmond Gay Liberation Front was formed in late 1970 and held its final meeting in 1971. In the meantime, they hosted two dances near the campus of VCU, and after the group folded, Kenneth Pederson continued to distribute literature on the block. Pace Memorial United Methodist Church became the heart of queer Richmond activism, with GAP and the Richmond Lesbian Feminists meeting in the space. Guy Kinman was living as a free man, Bobbie Weinstock returned to Richmond and set up the Virginia Coalition for Lesbian and Gay Rights, and the city celebrated its first Pride in 1979. Weinstock recalls:

> In '79, Bill Harrison and I—we were both working at Social Service at
> the time—[during] lunch hour went over to the police department and
> got the permits for the first gay pride festival in Richmond. And he was
> working part-time at a funeral home and had access to different stuff. So,
> we made the theme "Death of Denial, Birth of Pride," and we made it like
> a funeral procession. We got a hearse t' to lead the way. And, we figured
> people wouldn't walk in the streets in '79, but maybe they would ride in
> their car. As it turned out, there were maybe ten cars 'cause people were so
> afraid, and they covered their license plates, they wore sunglasses, they did
> everything, and so afraid of being identified. And the media was there in
> full force. But we had lots of good police protection. And we weren't sure if
> it was going to be good police protection or attacks. But we did the-the pro-
> cession, and then we went down to Byrd Park, and there were more people

there who joined in, and it was like a picnic in the park—music, entertainment, that kind of thing, and speakers. So that was in '79. And I used to have fun because I started chairing the committee, so I could get friends of mine from New York, especially coming down for Pride Festival in Richmond as a keynote speaker. Got to—got to see my friends easy that way. So we did the festivals in the park, and then it kept on raining, so we moved it inside to the convention center. And people were still scared to show up. And then there was kind of this made awareness, at some point, where people wanted to march in the streets and wanted to . . . felt safe— some people felt safe doing it. And Pride Festival now is pretty much taken over by the bars and liquor distributors. So it's lost some of that same community sense of organizing. But there's thousands of people who show up. And in the first ones, ten in the parade and a couple of hundred at the park.

Cal Yeomans's *Richmond Jim* might have painted Richmond as desolate and backward for queers, but as Guy Kinman, Bill Harrison, and Bobbie Weinstock have shown, this was far from the truth. Whilst they were "coming out" and building queer Richmond's infrastructure, two more influential queer Richmonders were born.

CHEVELLE MOSS-SAVAGE

Chevelle Moss-Savage is a native southerner. She was born in Richmond in 1969 with an extended family stretching to Blackstone, Virginia, and down into North Carolina and Georgia. She self-identifies as a southern belle and did not "come out" until after her mother's passing. "I always knew, but I tried to fit into the scope of what society expects of women such as myself and also what my parents expected of me. Like I'm truly a southern belle, and my mom, there were certain things that women did in the household and certain things that men did in the household, and so just trying to redefine those gender and social constructs, I recognized that that is not really how I am, but when I came out to my friends, it was a shock."[44] By that point, Moss-Savage and the woman she would later marry had been together for several months. Her family's reaction was mixed, with a brother who was not accepting but a son who was excited by the news.

Her activism started young. During Apartheid, she had to educate a boyfriend who bought her BK brand shoes, and she stopped drinking Coke because they supported South Africa's regime. After training as a therapist, she worked at Virginia State University where she was one of the only out faculty, "which is like a two-edged sword, so it puts a target on your back, but also it provided a resource for students to know that they could come to me, that I was open, and that it did not matter what your sexual identity or your gender identity was." Being an out lesbian at an HBCU came with its own set of difficulties.

> I remember when I was pushing something forward or trying to get VSU
> to adopt a sexual orientation antidiscrimination statement, and I had to
> go and meet with the president or vice president. At one point in time, my
> hair was very long. It was down to my back, and it's always been natural,
> but I was straightening it, so depending on who I needed to go talk to would
> depend on how I would present myself, and so I felt that every time I had to
> do that, I had to mortgage myself a little bit. Like I had to mortgage my little
> soul just a little bit, straighten my hair, wear a skirt so that I'm easier to look
> at so that when you sit across from me, and I'm pitching something that
> you don't want to talk about, mental health and queer stuff, those are two
> subjects that black folks don't want to have a conversation about. So, I'm
> pitching both of those, and I needed to go forward, so I'm going to do what
> I need to do to make sure that goes forward. In the same instance, it got
> to a point where like, it kills you a little bit, so right when I decided I was
> going to leave, I cut all my hair off, and it was liberating. . . . It went
> from it being totally non—it was not even tolerated. It wasn't a place of
> tolerance. . . . I think I moved them to a place from not being tolerant to
> some are tolerant, and then some are accepting.[45]

At VSU she also worked with student groups to start the first pride balls and lavender graduation. She left VSU in 2016 to pursue her therapeutic practice and has since continued to work with Richmond's diverse populations. Her legacy of activism with queer students established an infrastructure that continues to provide a space for queerness at VSU.

Like Bill Harrison, Moss-Savage struggled to find a spiritual home.

It got to a point where we were giving an offering one day, and somebody was doing an offertory prayer. You just ran over the money that we were about to give, and then it says, you know, and people who are dealing with lesbianism. I was like, what the hell does that have to do with me giving you my goddamn money? So, guess what? I don't have to go there. I don't have to go there but miss the black church experience. Other churches that are affirming and welcoming don't have that black church experience that I enjoy.[46]

There continues to be a racial divide between the worship experiences of Black and white mainline protestant denominations. However, the rise of multicultural and nondenominational evangelical churches in the twenty-first century has changed that for many. Sadly, many queer people are subjected to increasingly virulent homophobia from the evangelical movement, which is at the forefront of efforts to block civil rights and liberation for LGBTQ+ people.

ZAKIA MCKENSEY

Zakia McKensey was born in Richmond in 1972. Growing up in Richmond during the 1970s "was pretty different. It's a very conservative state and the capital city. I guess it was like, normal like anywhere else, just people weren't as friendly."[47] McKensey does not recall other queer people in her life growing up. "No, there wasn't any. Well, I mean as in like the clubs, but if you weren't old enough to go to the clubs, you kind of like, ran across people that you knew was they were . . . it was kind of an unspoken sort of thing"[48] Cruising for sex or simply noticing other queer people in public and striking up a friendship is a practice that cuts across generations of queer people, and it is often the first way into larger queer worlds for people unwilling or unable to partake in the liberation economy of visible gay bars, coffee shops, and other places that are traditionally found in larger cities.[49] After she came out in the late 1980s, McKensey built a network of queer kin through a variety of interactions.[50]

McKensey came out to her mother at a young age, and the process was "hellacious." Her mother threw her out of the house, and she spent her teen years living with relatives or couch surfing. Once she turned sixteen, she expanded her chosen family through the club scene. "We would all go, and then we met other people and became part of like a family or group, and then we started hanging out with them more and get invited to a bunch of different parties and so stuff like that." Drag houses became her family, and she went on to compete in national competitions. This time in her life was integral to her later activism with trans youth of color through T-Gurlz Rock and Nationz Foundation.

> I work for the Virginia antiviolence project and, and I'm also the founder and executive director at the Nationz Foundation, which is a nonprofit organization which focuses on LGBTIQ-identifying people and we provide testing services, care services, trans advocacy and support, emergency housing and stuff like that. . . . We provide syphilis testing, HIV testing. It's completely a volunteer-based organization. We've done a lot this year or the last couple of years, and I'm really proud of the two years of work that we have done and how many people we've tested and made them aware of their status, how many we've found that are positive and connected those to care, the amount of people we have through our food pantry program. And when I sit back and think about [it], it's like awesome, the work that we've done. . . . I worked for Richmond City Health District for ten years, and I worked, no six years, and I worked for Fan Free [clinic] for ten years and in working in the two, just having a relationship with the clients that come in because us talking and I know them from the community, they felt more comfortable talking to me. . . . They didn't like coming into the health department or to the clinic. People weren't respectful to them, weren't using proper pronouns, they had some type of negative experience, some type of misgendering sometimes, so it just turned them off from going because, you know, they felt like they were being disrespected while trying to get a service. The service that we provide is a very personal experience. It's like if people come for testing, it's like a separate area that we go to test them, and a lot of the times, because it's just really me, and I only really like pull in like volunteers for special events and stuff but they have a one on one, you come into my office for your testing, and it's just you and I. And instead of just sitting in a room waiting, you can go back to a conference room and play the Wii, or you can watch TV, or watch ball tapes

or drag pageants to take your mind off of that, so that's not the longest twenty minutes of your life and chill out. So, we try to do a lot of fun stuff to get people engaged and educate them in different ways. We have game nights and stuff like that, and we do education. We just make all of these services available, so we're not ramming it down their throat, but that they see it as regularly there, and if they need it, they can access it.[51]

McKensey has fundamentally transformed the lives of countless queer people of color. She has created a safe space for people to just be themselves. In addition, the STI testing services at Nationz are open to all and provide a space for people to take charge of their sexual health. This is especially important for queer people because many medical offices are not equipped (or accommodating) for people who have sex in ways other than a penis in a vagina.

LIKE A PHOENIX

As the 1990s opened with Jesse Helms' vitriolic Senate campaign, southern queer organizations shifted to grapple with broader issues such as identity, race, region, religion, longterm AIDS, and the future of queer politics in the South. They imagined new ways of being and thriving in the 1990s as many southerners claimed a distinctive—though not wholly unique—experience of American queerness. Comedian Robyn Tyler proposed the phoenix as the symbol for the coming decade. The previous decade had been devastating, but Tyler proclaimed in a speech that a change in attitude will prompt a tremendous shift in the coming years.[52] This shift held true for Richmond's queer communities. Richmond Triangle Players formed the city's first LGBTQ+ theatre company. The Richmond Metropolitan Community Church added AIDS ministries and purchased their permanent home. Queer softball, volleyball, and bowling leagues, as well as a running club, were active in Richmond. Richmond Lesbian Feminists continued to sponsor their potlucks, Christmas events, and Women's Festival.

Richmond Lesbian Feminists dates back to the 1970s, but women of color through the 1980s were frustrated with the whiteness of queer spaces. In 1987, the same year Guy Kinman and the Richmond Virginia Gay and Lesbian Alliance sponsored a billboard,[53] Terri Pendleton started a bachelor's degree in social work at VCU. Soon she found herself in need of community. She founded the Richmond Lesbian Women of Color in 1990 because she did not see the needs of lesbians of color being met in predominantly white organizations.

> We weren't at the friggin' table, and if we don't bring our voice, we cannot expect others to take up our cause. . . . What was most important was African American lesbian women, and I started an organization called Lesbian Women of Color due to the fact that I was in Richmond and I couldn't find any of them. I was like, where are they, you know? Are they hiding or what? And they were. They were hiding, I mean, or they were just not—maybe I shouldn't say they were hiding. Maybe I should just say they were just not out. They were just not involved. They were just not a part of the groups that were up and coming in the Richmond area. . . . I was involved with Richmond Lesbian Feminists. I was involved with Fan Free Clinic. I was involved with all these other community agencies, and there were very few African American people in these organizations. So I thought that my job was to find a way to reach out to African American lesbians and pull them out, educate, and build something with them, and so this agency, not agency, this group. . . . And the ad [in *Style* magazine] said something like, I think, where are all the lesbians of color? Here's my phone number. Call me. You cannot believe the calls on that phone. Oh my God, it was unbelievable. It's like lesbians of color saw that ad, and they were like, oh my God, you know, so here we were, so we had our first meeting at my small apartment in the Fan; couldn't even fit everybody in, and out of that came an organization that sought to be social, political, educational, as you can see, and to bring about awareness to lesbians of color about their worth and about our need to engage in this political process of LGBT stuff. So I think most of the lesbians of color that came were living their lives but did not see that there was more to just their small community. So LWOC was seeking to engage the larger mainstream community that lesbian women of color matter, and why don't you have any of them in your organizations? And then, lesbian women of color, why aren't you in any of these organizations? So that organization went as it was, Lesbian Women of Color, for about three years with me predominately at the head.[54]

Pendleton worked closely with Richmond Lesbian Feminists, but her experience illuminates some struggles to build communities that meet a broader range of needs.

> I raise them up, because I don't know how they've been able to keep it, you know. LWOC didn't make it, and I still in my mind kind of wonder about why we didn't, but Richmond Lesbian Feminists is an organization here in Richmond that was organized by lesbians to meet the needs of lesbians . . . I don't know if I can ever be considered a member of Richmond Lesbian Feminists. I sent money to them, and I got their newsletter, and I went to some of their events. Yes, I guess I could be considered a member. I knew and was involved with Richmond Lesbian Feminists before starting LWOC, but I never voted or anything like that. I think I was just a member-at-large, not a core member. When I started LWOC, Richmond Lesbian Feminists were very supportive. I worked with Beth Marschak quite a lot. Beth Marschak is an icon in the LGBTQ community of Richmond. I worked with Beth Marschak quite a lot in getting Richmond Lesbian Feminists and LWOC to do things together. For a long time, they contributed material from their newsletter to our newsletter, *Lesbian Women of Color Information You Can Use* newsletter, and Robin Troublefield managed our newsletter. Many women of color did not get the Richmond Lesbian Feminists newsletter. They didn't even know who they were. So anyway, that was about RLF. RLF is still going on. They have grown in their thinking, in their ways of inclusion, so many more lesbians of color have joined and are involved, but they were, at one time, very exclusive.[55]

Pendleton highlights the struggles over how people prioritize their identities in justice work. Prioritizing one particular identity can lead to marginalization from those who prioritize another. As people form communities of support and work for justice, their identities clash against others for whom whiteness is the default position. The racial politics of a city with Richmond's history meant that an acrimonious split was more likely. Across the United States, LGBTQ organizations have split over questions of gender and racial inclusion, such as when the Human Rights Campaign was rightfully castigated for excluding trans people from their platforms. Diversity is an easy concept to speak about but a more challenging concept to live. It involves continually asking how one might do better and then actually doing that.

DIVERSITY RICHMOND

The Gay Community Center of Richmond was founded in 1999 as a place "to provide support for the agencies and groups that serve Central Virginia's sexual and gender minority people, and to educate the public about the many issues facing our community."[56] In 2004, they purchased a 47,000-square-foot building that now houses Diversity Thrift, event spaces, an art gallery, and meeting rooms. In 2008, they completed renovations and dedicated the first queer-focused community center in Virginia.[57] As the organization worked in the community, their thinking and activism became more diverse in name

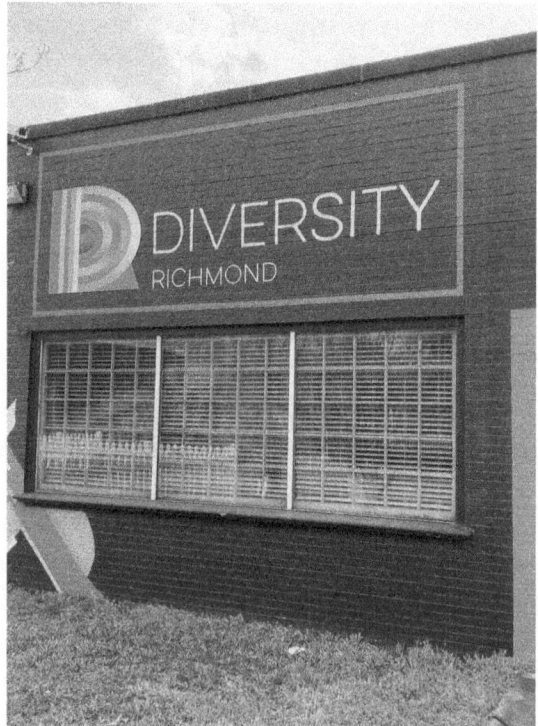

Diversity Richmond's logo (as of 2023) as seen on the building facing Sherwood Avenue. (Photo by author)

and action. In 2012, they were dealing with declining revenue and mounting debts. They put the building up for sale. The organization was saved when they brought in Bill Harrison and restructured. From re-evaluating their programming to making structural improvements to increase efficiency, they made sweeping changes. Within a few short years, they were able to give community grants again and were running a surplus. The Gay Community Center of Richmond rebranded as Diversity Richmond in 2015 to better include trans people, women, and the larger community and to better show a "commitment to inclusion, fairness, and equality."[58] The long wall that faced Interstate 64 was changed from a rainbow that ran its length to a mural of brightly colored flowers and geometric shapes on a black background, along with the new Diversity Richmond logo below.

If a counter monument forces the viewer to face a subject head on without easy answers and asks viewers to think differently about the landscape, then these murals serve as counter monuments.[59] From 1890 to 1929, the city of Richmond erected five statues to Confederates along Monument Avenue. Robert E. Lee (1890), Jeb Stuart and Jefferson Davis (1907), Stonewall Jackson (1919), and Matthew Fontaine Maury (1929) were all honored with enormous statues in the middle of roundabouts. By the middle of the twentieth century, Richmond was also home to the national headquarters of the United Daughters of the Confederacy, with their mausoleum-like building on Arthur Ashe Boulevard. Richmond also has the White House of the Confederacy and countless other smaller sites, statues, and named structures or roads dedicated to the Confederacy or white supremacy. The Gay Community Center's rainbow wall, unmissable when driving along Interstate 64, was placed there specifically to force viewers to confront the presence of queer people in Richmond. When the organization shifted to Diversity Richmond, the wall was also changed. Though more subdued, it still clearly announces the purpose of the building. The discourse around diversifying the monumental landscape was crucial to removing Confederate statues around the city. The name change and the repainting of the building should be seen as part of this discourse and an essential addition to the visual and monumental landscape of the city.

Some parts of Diversity Richmond's operation are well known, but others are not. Diversity Thrift remains one of the most prominent parts of the organization. Even longtime LGBTQ residents were unaware of how extensively

This mural is located on the Diversity Richmond building's longest wall, which faces Interstate 64. Painted in 2015, it is the result of a partnership between Diversity Richmond, Mickael Broth of Welcoming Walls, and artist Hamilton "Ham" Glass. It was painted in 2015. (Photo by author)

Diversity Richmond supports the community. As Bill Harrison told the *Richmond Times-Dispatch* in 2015: "Everybody knew that it was a 'gay' thrift store, but they did not know what we did with the proceeds from the thrift store. Most people know that we do diversity bingo here, but they didn't know what we did with the proceeds."[60] In his interview with the LGBTIQ Research Project he added:

> One of the things I'm very proud of here is that we have connected with a lot of organizations that are not LGBT. For example, with the Diversity Thrift, which is our main source of revenue, we have partnerships with public school systems in the area where if their families are on public assistance, they can come shop for clothing for free here, and I got a letter several years ago, about three years ago, from a mother who told the story that her daughter, who was in the third grade, had been crying for months every morning and did not want to go to school, and a teacher finally notified the

mom that her daughter was being ridiculed and bullied, because she wore the same clothes all the time, and so they came and went shopping here, and in her letter, she said, 'Now for the first time in months my daughter wants to get on the school bus.' And when I think about this little innocent baby, and in the letter, the woman said, 'I want you to know that I grew up in a household that gays were bad because God said so,' and she said, 'I wrote my mother this morning, and I told her that God is alive and well at Diversity Richmond.'[61]

The thrift store and event spaces continue to help the community beyond direct aid. The building has classrooms and other areas that provide free meeting space to community groups. The building also houses the Iridian Gallery, one of only a handful of specifically LGBTQ+-focused art galleries in the country and the only one in the South. The gallery has showcased dozens of queer artists over the years and remains a vibrant part of Richmond's arts scene.

Part of Diversity Richmond's focus on diversity in action is an effort to center and celebrate Black Richmonders. Rodney Lofton, one of Diversity Richmond's first Black executives, organized a variety of Black and PoC programming at Diversity Richmond. "We celebrated LGBT Black History Month, and we had a big response. We gave out recognitions to Black people who had done extraordinary work, and we had a partnership that we're extending with the Black History Museum here in Richmond. It's the first time in the United States a Black history museum has ever partnered with the LGBT community in the country, so we made history again."[62] Before COVID-19, one of the most important events in this series was the Black and Bold awards.[63] Chevelle Moss-Savage recalled:

I think it was very important because a lot of times, I don't believe that we're asked to have a seat at the table, especially when it comes to decisions within the community. . . . I was excited that I was honored and to be able to see all of the other work that everybody else is doing. Like when I see queer folk who are my son's age who are organizing and involved in social justice work, it just warms my little social justice mind and heart to see that at such a young age, that you could be so committed and so dedicated, and I thought back to myself like, what was I doing at that age? . . . That's why the Diversity Richmond Black and Bold gala was so important.[64]

In subsequent years, the work begun by Lofton to celebrate the achievements and contributions of Black LGBTQ+ leaders in Richmond and the Commonwealth has expanded to a collection of events under the umbrella of Black and Bold 2.0.

The bifurcated racial system of the South means that when organizations focus on diversity and multiculturalism, they often default to Black and white. The increasing demographic changes happening in the South mean organizations have had to confront this unconscious bias in sometimes powerful ways. Bill Harrison faced this after the massacre at the Pulse nightclub in Orlando.

> I started getting all these emails from different organizations around the city. We want to have a vigil. You've got this big event hall. We need to do something. What can we do? So in forty-eight hours, we organized this service. I cannot remember when I realized that the vast majority of people who were murdered were people of color, Hispanic folks, like people from Puerto Rico, and we were going a hundred miles an hour, and so one of the people on the committee got two VCU students, two young women, who were Puerto Rican, and they read the names and lit candles, and they also took that as an opportunity to express their outrage on how, once again, white people had claimed their pain and tried to tell their story. The governor was here. We had two thousand people. We had as many people in the park. We had speakers in the parking lot, and I was pretty paralyzed listening to that, so I struggle with it a lot because there was a lot of conversation going on about that afterward and one of the realizations I had the following week was, had I been working on this service and I found out that forty-nine out of the fifty people killed were African American. I'd have stopped in my tracks, and I would have reached out to the black community and say, "How can we make this a meaningful service?" and I didn't do it, and we have so little connection with the Hispanic community here.[65]

It is easy to lose sight of other communities in the former capital of the Confederacy that only in 2021 removed the last white supremacist statues on Monument Avenue. Harrison and many others at Diversity Richmond have taken the criticism to heart and have used this as a time to grow.

On February 23, 2021, Diversity Richmond and Virginia Pride announced a merger. Since the first Pride festival organized by Bobbie Weinstock and Bill

Harrison, the organization has been run entirely by volunteers. James Mill-ner, interim executive director of Virginia Pride, told the *Richmond Times-Dispatch* that "over the last five years with the growth of Virginia Pride, it became really strained. Diversity Richmond gives us the organizational infra-structure and additional staff resources. I think it will be a really wonderful partnership."[66] With this merger, the umbrella that is Diversity Richmond grew a bit bigger. Though the giant warehouse space has only existed for twenty years, Diversity Richmond has become the anchor for much of queer Richmond. Diversity Richmond has been built carefully by activists over the years and now provides an infrastructure to support LGBTQ and community work throughout Richmond.

The recent past has not been without problems for the organization. In the last half of 2021, employees of the thrift store staged a protest about low pay and overwork. There were also allegations of sexual misconduct and harassment. Their official statements charged Bill Harrison and other board members with gross mismanagement. The fight resulted in Bill Harrison's retirement, along with several others who left the board and leadership posi-tions in the thrift store operations. It also resulted in the hiring of a human resources officer to oversee working conditions and a pay raise for employees. As of this writing, the organization seems in better shape than ever.

In this tiny sampling of queer Richmonders, we have taken a whirlwind tour of the city's past. The oral histories have allowed us to glimpse the Richmond that they experienced. The place of Diversity Richmond has allowed a coales-cence of LGBTQ history. Within the walls of the massive former-warehouse, activists and regular folks have worked to build a community. Its highway-facing wall a counter monument against the city's confederate and racist past. Diversity Richmond shows us the possibilities for great things when people come together to hold space and make a place for the whole rainbow. Despite conservative talking points about "divisive concepts" or the novelty of LGBTQ+ history, the oral histories in this chapter and in archives around Richmond show that queer people have been integral to the city and to Amer-ica. They show us some of the ways that regular queer people have inhabited the city and worked to make the world better. They show us the struggles and the triumphs. It has never been easy for queer people here, but the activ-ists in Richmond give me hope.

NOTES

Jay Watkins would like to acknowledge and thank the students involved with the William & Mary LGBTIQ Research Project, and Professor Leisa Meyer for organizing the project. Watkins would also like to thank the Harrison Ruffin Tyler Department of History for their generous support of his research throughout this project.

1. Robert Schanke, *Queer Theatre and the Legacy of Cal Yeomans* (New York: Palgrave McMillan, 2011).
2. Newspaper clipping of Trebor D., "Discovering Leathersex," Box 3, Folder 7, "Richmond Jim, 1979–1981," Southeastern Arts, Media and Education (SAME) Project records, 1985–96, Coll2008–020, ONE National Gay and Lesbian Archives, Los Angeles, CA.
3. Cindy Bray, "Rainbow Richmond: LGBTQ History of Richmond, VA," *OutHistory,* accessed September 7, 2021, https://outhistory.org/exhibits/show/rainbow-richmond; Beth Marschak and Alex Lorch, *Lesbian and Gay Richmond* (Charleston SC: Arcadia Publishing, 2008); Bob Swisher, "A Small, but Hidden, Community Thrived in the 50s," *Our Own Community Press,* May 1990; Jay Watkins and Leisa Meyer, "William & Mary LGBTIQ Project Update," *Public Historian,* 42, no. 3, ePublication, June 2019.
4. I have edited the interviews for clarity and length. Whilst removing vocal fillers such as "um" I have tried to maintain each narrator's unique cadence and voice.
5. "Mission," Mattachine Society of Washington DC, accessed September 7, 2021, https://mattachinesocietywashingtondc.org/mission/.
6. Cortney Langley, "Mattachine Project Unearths W&M's Lost LGBTIQ History," April 1, 2016, William & Mary News, accessed September 7, 2021, http://www.wm.edu/news/stories/2016/lgbtiq-research-project-helps-unearth-lost-history-of-william--mary123.php.
7. Langley, "Mattachine Project."
8. Nan Alamilla Boyd and Horacio N. Roque Ramirez, eds., *Bodies of Evidence: The Practice of Queer Oral History* (Oxford: Oxford University Press, 2012).
9. Jerry T. Watkins III, *Queering the Redneck Riviera: Sexuality and the Rise of Florida Tourism* (Gainesville: University Press of Florida, 2018).
10. Nan Alamilla Boyd, "Who Is the Subject? Queer Theory Meets Oral History," *Journal of the History of Sexuality,* 17, no. 2 (May 2008), 177–89. See also John Howard, *Men Like That: A Southern Queer History* (Chicago: University of Chicago Press, 1999).

11. Zakia McKensey, interview by Maya and Erin, February 25, 2017, transcript, William & Mary LGBTQ Research Project, Williamsburg, VA.

12. Cindy Bray, "Developing Identity: A Prelude to Activism," OutHistory, accessed September 7, 2021, http://outhistory.org/exhibits/show/rainbow-richmond/developing-identity.

13. Bob Swisher, "While Straights Slept, Gays Played, Part 1, 1944–1952" *Our Own Community Press,* April 1988.

14. Swisher, "While Straights Slept, Gays Played."

15. Bill Harrison, interview by Maya Farr-Henderson, November 18, 2017, transcript, William & Mary LGBTQ Research Project, Williamsburg, VA.

16. Bray, "Developing Identity."

17. Carol S., quoted in Bob Swisher, "City Lesbians 'Took Over,' Danced at Beer Joint," *Our Own Community Press,* June 1989.

18. Bray, "Developing Identity."

19. Yelyzaveta Shevchenko, "Reconnaissance Survey of LGBTQ Architectural Resources in the City of Richmond," Virginia Department of Historic Resources LGBTQ Heritage Working Group, accessed September 7, 2021, https://www.dhr.virginia.gov/wp-content/uploads/2018/09/LGBTQRichmondSurveyReport.pdf.

20. Bray, "Developing Identity."

21. Cindy Bray, "ABC Regulations Challenged in Court," OutHistory, accessed September 7, 2021, https://outhistory.org/exhibits/show/rainbow-richmond/the-fight-continues/abc-regulations.

22. Bray, "Developing Identity."

23. Brandon Carwile, "Queer Revolutionaries Tony Segura and Marsh Haris Helped Build Richmond's LGBT Community," *Dogwood,* December 2, 2020, https://vadogwood.com/2020/12/02/queer-revolutionaries-tony-segura-and-marsh-haris-helped-build-richmonds-lgbt-community/.

24. Bray, "Developing Identity."

25. Guy Kinman, interview by Maya Farr-Henderson, Alyssa Luz-Ricca, and Kate Avery, December 3, 2016, transcript, William & Mary LGBTQ Research Project, Williamsburg, VA.

26. David K. Johnson, *Lavender Scare: The Cold War Persecution of Gays and Lesbians in the Federal Government* (Chicago: University of Chicago Press, 2004).

27. Jonathan Ned Katz, "Harry Hay: Founding the Mattachine Society, 1948–1953," OutHistory, accessed September 7, 2021, https://outhistory.org/exhibits/show/hay-mattachine/hhfm.

28. Kinman, interview.

29. Kinman, interview.

30. Watkins, *Queering the Redneck Riviera.*

31. Kinman, interview.

32. "Black History Month: UGA's Desegregation," accessed September 7, 2021, https://online.uga.edu/node/5341; Bobbie Weinstock, interview by Sarah Rodriguez, Bre Adey, Parker Ronquest, December 3, 2016, transcript, William & Mary LGBTQ Research Project, Williamsburg, VA.

33. Weinstock, interview.

34. Weinstock, interview.

35. "Biographical/Historical," catalog description, Atlanta Lesbian Feminist Alliance (ALFA) Archives, circa 1972–1994, https://archives.lib.duke.edu/catalog/alfa.

36. Marschak Lorch, *Lesbian and Gay Richmond,* 40.

37. Weinstock, interview.

38. Harrison, interview.

39. Ibid.

40. Ibid.

41. Howard, *Men Like That,* 230

42. Howard, *Men Like That,* 231.

43. Marschak and Lorch, *Lesbian and Gay Richmond,* 72.

44. Chevelle Moss-Savage, interview by Maya Farr-Henderson, Alyssa Luz-Ricca, February 11, 2017, transcript, William & Mary LGBTQ Research Project, Williamsburg, VA.

45. Moss-Savage, interview.

46. Ibid.

47. Ibid.

48. Ibid.

49. John Howard, "Southern Sodomy; or What the Coppers Saw," in *Southern Masculinity: Perspectives on Manhood in the South Since Reconstruction,* edited by Craig Thompson Friend (Athens, GA: University of Georgia Press, 2009), 196–218;. Jerry T Watkins III, *Queering the Redneck Riviera: Sexuality and the Rise of Florida Tourism* (Gainesville, FL: University Press of Florida, 2018).

50. "Personality: Zakia Mckensey," *Richmond Free Press,* November 6, 2015. http://richmondfreepress.com/news/2015/nov/06/personality-zakia-k-mckensey/.

51. McKensey, interview.

52. Robin Tyler, "A Love Letter to the Movement," *Alabama Forum,* October 1989, 3.

53. Bray, "The Billboard Project and Guy Kinman," *Rainbow Richmond,* outhistory.org.

54. Terri Pendleton, interview, transcript, William & Mary LGBTQ Research Project, Williamsburg, VA.

55. Pendleton, interview.

56. Bray, "The Gay Community Center of Richmond," *Rainbow Richmond,* outhistory.org

57. "About Us," http://diversityrichmond.org/27-about-us/64-about-us.html.

58. "Diversity Richmond Announces $33,000 in Community Contributions and Unveils New Name and Look," press release, April 15, 2015, https://diversityrichmond.org/media-resources.html.

59. Thomas Cauvin, "Counter Monuments, Interpretation, and Interactive Memory," *Monuments in History,* 2019, https://monumentsinhistory.wordpress.com/2017/09/25/counter-monuments-interpretation-and-interactive-memory/.

60. Bill Harrison, quoted in Tammie Smith, "Gay Community Center of Richmond Changes Name," *Richmond Times-Dispatch,* April 15, 2015, https://richmond.com/news/local/gay-community-center-of-richmond-changes-name/article_75da8417-773b-5b9a-99d3-873463b4f450.html.

61. Harrison, interview.

62. Harrison, interview.

63. Bill Harrison, "Why We Host the Black and Bold Awards," https://diversityrichmond.org/commentary/569-why-we-host-the-black-and-bold-awards.html.

64. Moss-Savage, interview.

65. Harrison, interview.

66. Colleen Curran, "'Stronger Together': Diversity Richmond and Virginia Pride Are Merging," *Richmond Times-Dispatch,* February 23, 2021, https://richmond.com/news/local/stronger-together-diversity-richmond-and-virginia-pride-are-merging/article_4b00e39b-c676-55ee-82cd-62b9d304e30a.html?fbclid=IwAR1sBWB37_1e5KnR0NXNdeX0j99X4wvFI21l27d6MT-uJFMmgq6BqQLBwOc.

CHARLOTTESVILLE'S QUEER HISTORY ACROSS THIRTY YEARS

———

SENLIN MEANS

n early 1986, Hospice of the Piedmont needed help with a patient who had less than a month to live. The organization's purpose, then and now, is to care for terminal patients, but this patient had AIDS, and AIDS patients were different.

By the end of 1984, there were 10 reported AIDS cases in Charlottesville, 42 in Virginia. A year later, the total number in the state had jumped to 102, and Hospice board member Jim Heilman began pondering the idea of a group devoted solely to their treatment. Given the hysteria and fear surrounding the disease, as well as how quickly and miserably the patients died, AIDS cases required a special kind of care. When a particularly horrific case came to the door in 1986, Heilman called Blaise Spinelli, a thirty-six-year-old med tech at UVA, and asked him if he wanted to help.

The patient was a young man in his mid- to late-twenties, living outside of town with his sister and her husband in a rundown house with holes in the walls. The sister and the husband both worked, leaving no one to look after him during the day. When Spinelli walked into the room, he saw a head, a skull really, lying on a pillow, and below that nothing. His body was so thin the sheets were barely wrinkled.

"I remember you," the young man said. "I used to see you at the bars."

The development of an effective treatment for AIDS was still far in the future, and people were trying anything: prayer, acupuncture, bone marrow transfusions, even drinking urine. The man wasting away on the bed was being given chemotherapy, which did nothing except leave him vomiting into a trash can. Spinelli sat next to him and gave what comfort he could, which wasn't much.

That night, when he got back to the farm he shared with his partner, Spinelli wanted to wash his hands forever, to scrub his skin until it was raw. The window opposite the patient's bed looked out over a graveyard. In two weeks the young man would be dead; for now, all he could do was gaze out at the rows of tombstones.

"I'm not sure I'm up to this," Spinelli thought.

THE BAR

Word on the street in the 1970s was that the Virginian, a popular restaurant that's been on the Corner since 1923, was gay-friendly. (The Corner is a strip of restaurants and bars that caters to students from the University of Virginia) When twenty-four-year-old Joan Schatzman and her girlfriend moved to town in June of 1976, they headed straight there, spotted three lesbians sitting at a table, bought some beers, and sat down.

Despite the promising introduction, Charlottesville was very different from Boston, where Schatzman lived before moving down south. Boston had overt gay bars, gay neighborhoods, even an openly gay state senator in Elaine Noble; Charlottesville had none of those things.

There were places in Charlottesville back then that were gay-friendly, or at least places where gays and lesbians could go and dance and not worry about being bothered. In addition to the Virginian, there was Brianna's, a jazz club down Route 29 South; Oasis nightclub on 250 East; and the occasional dance at Newcomb Hall put on by UVA's Gay Student Union. There were other places you could go and dance, but you wouldn't want to be seen holding hands with your same-sex partner.

Schatzman was out and proud when she arrived in Charlottesville, but the same wasn't true for most of the people she met. Compared to other liberal college towns, Charlottesville was fairly conservative, with a largely covert gay community hidden amongst the professorial ranks at the University, encountered at upper-middle-class dinner parties or private gatherings in the county. "You had to get lucky," Schatzman said. "And meet somebody who could give you entrée into the fragmented circles."

The idea of opening a gay bar in Charlottesville seemed crazy to pretty much everyone. It was one thing to hang out together at certain places, to wink and nudge and let whispers carry the word to those who needed to hear it, but opening a place that was just plain gay, no bones about it, was a different story. Everyone in the scene shared the general belief that the redneck hordes gathered just outside the town walls would attack, break the windows, paint the walls with slurs. Everyone except Schatzman.

She quit her job counting bottles at the Pepsi Cola plant, used her severance pay to rent a house just off the Downtown Mall on Water Street, and opened a gay bar called Muldowney's Pub.

Except it wasn't a gay bar. It couldn't be, not in Virginia in 1980. For one thing, the state's Alcoholic Beverage Control Authority had, and still has, a problem with bars; if you want to serve alcohol, you must counteract its sinfulness by serving food, so Schatzman found herself becoming an accidental restaurateur.

But the ABC also had a problem with gays. At the time, Section 4–37 of the ABC rules and regulations read "a bar's license may be suspended or revoked if the bar has become a meeting place and rendezvous for users of narcotics, drunks, homosexuals, prostitutes, pimps, panderers, gamblers or habitual law violaters."

And Section 4–98 forbade "a licensee from employing any person who has the general reputation as a prostitute, homosexual, panderer, gambler, habitual law violater, person of ill repute, user of or peddler of narcotics, or person who drinks to excess or a 'B-girl.'"

Although rarely enforced, the rules not only made gay bars illegal in Virginia, they effectively made it illegal for gay people to drink in any bars at all. It wasn't until a 1991 lawsuit against the ABC forced the matter into a U.S. District Court that the antigay regulations were deemed unconstitutional and struck down.

Schatzman knew the rules, and while she didn't advertise Muldowney's as being gay, every gay person in town knew what it was. She didn't worry about the possibility that she might be breaking the law. How could anyone prove she was "knowingly" serving homosexuals? Opening the bar, she felt, was a form of civil disobedience.

Muldowney's was, Schatzman said, "straight 'til eight," serving turkey sandwiches and Chicago-style chili to anyone who came in, with free delivery on the Downtown Mall. But after 8 p.m., the kitchen closed and the music started, and Muldowney's became, for all intents and purposes, Charlottesville's first gay bar. The place was tiny, a dive really, and fifty people were enough to fill it. The restaurant hosted live bands and gay comedians, and there was always a DJ and dancing.

Originally, Schatzman wanted to open a lesbian bar, but Charlottesville didn't have enough lesbians to make that financially feasible, so Muldowney's became a place where everyone was equally welcome, gay men and women more equally than others. Charlottesville also had a surprisingly large, but hidden, drag scene, and so Saturday night became drag night. Later, near the end of its run, Muldowney's began to host punk shows, because like drag queens and gays, Charlottesville's punks often found themselves without a place to call their own.

There were fights at Muldowney's, but no gay bashing. The feared redneck hordes never arrived, although some of their members did, surreptitiously, not to gay bash . . . but to be gay themselves.

THE PATIENT

America celebrated its bicentennial in the summer of 1976 with huge parties in every major city. New York's harbor filled with ships and sailors from all over the world, a moment captured in Randy Shilts's book *And the Band Played On*. Shilts theorized that this was when AIDS first arrived on our shores, spreading from the sailors to the men they had sex with on shore, as New York's thriving gay community threw a giant party, unwittingly toasting the last heady days of innocence.

Blaise Spinelli had been kicked out of his parents' house at nineteen, after a shrink failed to cure his homosexuality with pictures of naked men and a cattle prod, and ended up in Washington, DC, living in the gay village of Dupont Circle, in a commune with members of the Gay Liberation Front.

For seven years, his life had been a mix of glittering fun and radical politics, but by 1976 most of his friends were heading for San Francisco, and Spinelli was tired of being defined by his sexuality. He was ready for a change, and in the midst of the bicentennial craziness, he found it in a beautiful young man who was in town to celebrate the end of his undergraduate degree at UVA.

"It was one of those magical relationships," Spinelli said about his time with Michael. "I was twenty-six years old. I guess it's always magical when you meet someone when you're twenty-six."

Spinelli moved to Michael's hometown, Charlottesville, a place that seemed to him like it had no gay life at all. But that was okay. He'd had enough of all that; he had Michael, and they were happy.

When, in 1981, the first reports began to filter in about a new disease that seemed to be targeting gay men, Spinelli took notice. Social activism was part of his fabric, part of life as he knew it growing up in the 1960s and 1970s. He started posting news reports and fliers at Muldowney's, warning people that there was something going on, something that seemed to be coming after them.

The disease was called GRID at first, Gay Related Immune Deficiency, and although Spinelli and a few of his friends watched with growing interest, most people paid it no attention. There was no test yet, and there wouldn't be until 1985. The only sign was the appearance of rare illnesses in otherwise healthy young men, illnesses that a normal immune system would have easily destroyed but that had begun to mean certain death.

The first cases of AIDS in Charlottesville almost certainly went unrecorded, slipping by as anomalies before anyone knew what to look for. The first known AIDS case at UVA hospital was in May of 1982, making it one of the first in the state. By then, Spinelli was working in the lab at the pathology department, analyzing blood and bodily fluids. When he heard about a formal presentation, or grand rounds, on the first local case of the new disease, he made sure to attend. Here it was, this thing he'd been posting warnings about at Muldowney's. It had finally come to town.

The grand rounds was held in one of the hospital theaters, a circle of chairs arranged around a stage where the white-robed chorus of doctors performed their clinical drama. In the old days, the patient might have been on stage with them, but by now the cases were kept anonymous. Even so, Spinelli knew who the patient was. It was a small town, with an even smaller gay scene.

Sitting in the room, he felt afraid.

"This is a time bomb going off here," he thought. "This is going to be an epidemic."

There were six known cases of AIDS in Virginia in 1982, four of which were at UVA. Over the next two years, sixty-three more cases would be reported in Virginia, eleven in Charlottesville.

Afraid to enter patients' rooms, hospital workers would leave food trays on the floor outside the door, careful to avoid touching the used forks when they picked them up afterwards. Spinelli didn't like it, but he understood. People were afraid, because they didn't know what was happening. No one did.

Spinelli had friends in DC, California, Texas—friends all over who would call and give reports of the disease in their city, of who was in clinics and who was dying. He called his friend Bob, a lawyer still living in DC, and told him to be careful. It was a strangely quiet phone call, with Spinelli doing most of the talking. A few days later, Spinelli got the call that Bob was dead; he'd been too ashamed to admit he already had it.

Schatzman started seriously hearing about AIDS around 1984. It was still considered a "gay disease," something whispered about in fear and shame. Although the first female cases had been reported the year before, they were all contracted via sex with men. It would be a while before the fear began to spread through the lesbian community. But she realized that the disease was impacting Muldowney's, as more and more of the men who came to dance began coming down with AIDS. By the end of the 1980s, most of them were dead.

In June of 1985 Schatzman sold Muldowney's. It had been a lot of fun, and she was proud of what she'd created. But being a restaurant owner had never been her dream. Several months later, Spinelli got the call from Hospice of the Piedmont about the AIDS patient they didn't think they could handle.

If they couldn't, who could? There was no outside group to act as advocates for the victims, many of whom had been disowned by their families. Others hadn't even told their families they were gay yet, let alone that they were dying. How do you make that phone call? "Mom, dad, I have to tell you something. And then I have to tell you something else . . ."

That winter, when Spinelli went to see the hospice patient—saw his skeletal body under the sheets, saw the tombstones outside the window—he was frightened. But he was also angry. He and Michael got together with Jim Heilman and Wynne Stuart, and the four of them created the AIDS Services Group of Charlottesville.

ASG began with thirteen people meeting at Muldowney's, including members of the Gay Men's Health Clinic in DC who'd agreed to train its nascent staff. Every week the number grew as UVA students, local doctors, and others showed up wanting to volunteer. By July of 1987, ASG was officially recognized by the state of Virginia, with Kathy Drabkin as its first director and seventy-five clients from Charlottesville and the surrounding counties. In the first year, the budget increased from $1,000 to $100,000. By 1989, ASG had seventy-five volunteers and a permanent staff of six. That year, the number of U.S. AIDS cases reached 100,000.

AIDS is a thread that winds back through all of modern gay life. It very nearly destroyed the gay community, but the fight against it made the community stronger than ever before. Before AIDS, gay pride meant sexual freedom and a public identity; afterwards it meant political activism, as the focus shifted away from the fight to define a lifestyle toward a fight for the right to live and, in many cases, to die with dignity.

In a way it was AIDS that made marriage equality the central issue it is today.

Getting married had always been something straight people did, and being queer and proud of it meant rebelling against the straight world as much as possible. But then came this plague, and gays found themselves turned away from their partner's hospital rooms, watching as their loved one's property was taken by the same families that had previously disowned them.

ASG was the model for all other AIDS groups in the state. With a budget over a million dollars by 2012, it covers what's called the Thomas Jefferson Health district: Charlottesville/Albemarle, Fluvanna, Greene, Louisa, and Nelson, but also Staunton, Waynesboro, Harrisonburg, and wherever else it's needed.

"I was talking to a younger gay guy recently," said Peter DeMartino, the current executive director of ASG. "And I started talking about the history of AIDS and the history of ASG, and he was like, 'Wow. Thank you for sharing that.' I was like, 'You're thirty, you really don't know this?' and he was like, 'No.'"

THE CLUB

Clyde Cooper and Mike Fitzgerald met at Muldowney's in 1982 when Cooper was forty-five and newly out of the closet, and Fitzgerald was nineteen and newly out of high school. They began dating and would stop by Muldowney's for a beer most nights after work (eighteen was the legal drinking age at the time), where they were often joined by their friends Charles Ferneyhough, Ned Holt, and Ronnie Roberts.

Cooper would later dub the group "the five dreamers," and their conversations inevitably returned to the particular dream they all shared: how nice it would be if Charlottesville had a real, honest-to-god gay bar. Muldowney's was the unofficial gay bar in town, a great place to socialize and meet people, but it was small and leaned a bit too much toward the lesbian end of things as far as they were concerned. Plus, given the antigay ABC laws, no place could really be out of the closet.

Finally Cooper proposed that they just go for it, the five of them; Clyde could be manager, Mike could handle the door, someone could be bartender, and someone else could DJ. It was 1985; by then Muldowney's had moved across the street to 212 W. Water St., and as luck would have it, Joan was looking to sell. And so, with credit cards and borrowed money, the five dreamers bought the place and reopened it as the Silver Fox.

Cooper was born in 1936, joined the Navy at seventeen and was married by twenty-three. In 1974, he left the Navy and moved with his wife and three daughters to Lake Monticello. He'd known for a long time that he was gay but hoped that "with religion and real effort" he could change. In 1981, at the age of forty-five, he finally quit fighting it. When Clyde Cooper does something, he doesn't fuck around. He came out of the closet, met and began dating Fitzgerald, and a few years later found himself running Charlottesville's one and only gay nightclub.

The Silver Fox was basically the same idea as Muldowney's, a restaurant by day, nightclub after dark. Like Muldowney's, it wasn't advertised as being a gay club, but Cooper never denied the fact when asked or when talking to the police or ABC.

Technically, they were admitting to breaking the law, but Cooper found that the law, in this case, was his best friend. Just before the restaurant opened, he introduced himself to the police chief. "I'm a gay man opening a gay restaurant and nightclub," he said. "Any problems, please come see me. Any issues or questions about the gay community in town, let me know and I will help in any way I can."

People would drive by the club and yell insults and slurs. They would throw bottles and vandalize the building. Cooper always called the police and they always prosecuted, and by supporting the police, he ensured that the police and the ABC board were never anything but supportive of him. They were, he often says, his "best allies."

To Cooper, the Silver Fox was Charlottesville's gay bar, a mantle passed down from Muldowney's, and as such he expected the gay community to support it. The support was limited, however, partly because of competition from Eastern Standard, a new restaurant at the west end of the Mall that was very gay friendly. But the fact that they were open about being gay worked against them as well. The Silver Fox was known as "gay" even in the straight world in a way that Muldowney's hadn't been, and in those more closeted times, many people were afraid to be seen entering a place like that.

By 1990, Cooper and Fitzgerald were tired of struggling to run the restaurant, and it seemed like a good time to pull out. The idea was hatched to turn the Silver Fox into a private club, which would give it the advantage of being able to ignore the city's 2 a.m. curfew for bars and stay open until dawn. Legally, however, private clubs can't be owned by private individuals, so Cooper and his partners started a nonprofit group called the Piedmont Triangle Society and sold the restaurant to the group. The license application stated that it was a gay group intending to establish a gay club; technically, it was against the law, but again, no one said anything.

In September of 1991, the PTS bought the Silver Fox and renamed it Triangles, and Cooper took the opportunity to retire. He was fifty-five, and it seemed like the right moment to fulfill an unrealized dream of his father's: to travel around the country in an RV visiting national parks. He and Fitzgerald traveled thirty thousand miles across thirty-three states and Canada.

Free from the stress of running the restaurant, alone together, it was, Cooper said, absolutely wonderful.

When the couple returned to Charlottesville, Cooper found Triangles in a state of disrepair, having gone through six managers in one year. PTS quickly asked him to come back on as manager and set the house in order. Clyde moved the club to an upstairs location in the building next door, rechristened it Club 216, and oversaw a redesign, adding a dance floor, a glass enclosed chill-out room, dressing rooms, pool tables, and a stage with a runway for drag queens to strut their stuff. With the new space and the freedom to stay open until dawn, Charlottesville's gay club hit its stride. In its heyday, Club 216 had over two thousand members and more money, Cooper said, than they knew what to do with.

"We were so big," Clyde says, "that it was like New York City. At two o'clock people would hit us, and they'd be [lined up] around the building . . . They would stand outside and wait. We closed at five o'clock and sometimes they couldn't even get in until four o'clock."

Clyde Cooper managed Club 216 from 1993 to 1998 and again from 2001 until 2007, and he was PTS treasurer from mid-2010 to mid-2011, but despite his best efforts, the club's days were numbered. In January of 2012, Calvin "Trey" Wilkerson, 216's last manager, was found guilty of a charge of misdemeanor embezzlement. New Year's Eve 2011 was the last night Mike Fitzgerald worked the door. Club 216 closed the first day of the new year.

THE EPIDEMIC

Peter DeMartino moved here from Palm Springs, California, in 2010 to take over as director of AIDS/HIV Services Group. Despite having roughly the same population as Charlottesville, Palm Springs has one of the biggest populations of gay and HIV-positive men in the country. His clinic had 80 residential units on 3.5 acres of land, a pool, a staff of 96 and a $13.5 million budget. It was probably the easiest place in the world to do that kind of work, and DeMartino came to Charlottesville looking for a challenge, which he found. It just wasn't the challenge he expected.

AIDS was no longer just a gay disease, and ASG was no longer a gay organization. In 2011 it served 1,409 people, 83 percent of whom were HIV-negative, and only 36 percent of whom were men having sex with men. Many of its clients were simply people unable to talk to their regular doctor about sex, or who needed an easy place to get tested and get condoms.

Sometimes DeMartino forgot this. On the first Saturday in October 2012, ASG held its annual AIDS walk, and the current director found himself being taken to task by some of his staff and board members for being too gay; they weren't talking about his behavior, but his focus.

"What about hemophiliacs," they asked. "What about pediatric cases? What about women?"

But the way DeMartino saw it, he could only speak his truth, and his truth was that, thirty years into their fight against the disease, gay men were still the population most impacted by AIDS, and still one of the most marginalized communities anywhere, particularly in the South, particularly in Virginia, and, yes, even in Charlottesville. AIDS work, as DeMartino sees it, is social justice work. It's his truth as a gay man living with HIV.

Born in 1972, DeMartino grew up in New York City in the 1980s and by fifteen was hanging out in gay bars looking, as he puts it, for the elders of his tribe. What he found was that those elders were gone. Everyone over thirty-five was dead.

"I use the word 'tribe' a lot," DeMartino said. "Because it's part of why I do the work I do. Being a young adult gay male in the 1990s, you sort of recognize, 'Wow. So much of my life has been defined by what AIDS did to the generation before me . . . that first generation that didn't know better, that just got hit by this disease.'"

DeMartino watched his generation cultivate a sense of inevitability about AIDS, a "not if, but when" attitude. They had sex without condoms, snorted crystal meth, and partied not like AIDS didn't exist but like it didn't matter. It was in 2000, while working on his PhD in Chicago, that he was diagnosed with HIV himself. Looking around at his friends and peers, he realized that, as a community, they'd watched this happen before and were watching it happen again. They knew better, but they kept on dying. Where, he asked himself, did he want to be when history wrote about the Time of the Plague? What did he want to do?

He knew the answer: he wanted to help his tribe, to work with people who had AIDS and HIV, and that work brought him to Charlottesville and ASG. His work there seemed easy at first, so easy he honestly thought he'd be in charge of shutting the clinic down. Charlottesville is rich in available resources, from UVA hospital to many nonprofits and charitable organizations, and like a lot of people, DeMartino assumed that the hardest thing about being an AIDS patient here would be choosing who to get your treatment from.

He was wrong. In 2012, going to the doctor with something like a sinus infection should've been simple; being HIV-positive shouldn't make a difference. It didn't in Palm Springs where, DeMartino said, he wouldn't have even thought to tell most doctors he had HIV. But in Charlottesville, if you went to your neighborhood doc with that sinus infection and you were HIV-positive, you were likely to be sent to UVA or told that the doctor needed more advance notice to prepare. Even at the state level, there was an immediate push to send HIV patients to infectious disease doctors instead of primary care physicians.

"If you have diabetes, not every friggin' appointment you go to is going to be with an endocrinologist," DeMartino said. "If you've had a stroke, not all of your care for the rest of your life is going to be delivered by a cardiologist."

Throw in a lack of education or money, and finding quality care in the area became even harder. Many of those who used ASG lived on the margins of society; IV drug users, people with mental problems, the homeless. Over a third of them had no insurance, with 41 percent on Medicaid or Medicare. Over half lived below the poverty line.

HIV/AIDS was largely ignored or forgotten about. When DeMartino spoke with other health care organizations about the need to connect with HIV-positive people, they said they didn't serve anyone with HIV. But, he learned, the organizations didn't ask their patients' status, and so in reality they didn't know. When he sought donations, people questioned the need for disease-specific organizations. Haven't we, they asked, solved the problem?

Not only did the problem remain, but so did the stigma against people with AIDS, even in a town so full of intelligent, liberal people. When he began his job, DeMartino was shocked at the level of secrecy at ASG; from the confidentiality agreement each HIV patient signed with his individual caseworker, to the back door for patients to come and go unseen.

"Really?" he thought. "The stigma is that bad?"

Even in 2012 patients described situations he thought had died out ten years before, like not wanting to visit their family for the holidays because they're forced to eat off paper plates.

"I wasn't expecting that I would constantly have to remind people of what HIV was," he said. "I wasn't expecting the level of care to be as inadequate as it is."

Nor did he expect to find a town without a built-in gay community to provide support. DeMartino's boyfriend moved here with him but soon found Charlottesville's gay community to be essentially nonexistent and left. There weren't a lot of dateable men in town to begin with, even less if you were HIV-positive. If DeMartino didn't love his work and, he begrudgingly admitted, the town, it's unlikely he would have lasted long either.

The problem was professional as well as personal. ASG was a community-based organization without an organized community. DeMartino got into this work to assume his role in his tribe, and now found himself filling that role in a town where the tribe seemed to be missing.

"I very personally feel like it is my job as a functional gay man living with HIV that when I get to the top of the mountain, it's not just so I can enjoy the view, it's so that I can turn around and pull the next one up. Because the view's only worth it if there's someone to share it with."

PRIDE AND TOLERANCE

The modern gay rights movement was born in a bar, on a hot June night in 1969 when a police raid led to a riot, which led to a civil rights movement, which led to rainbow flags and, eventually, to visibility in the mainstream media. Probably as long as bars have existed, gay bars have existed as well, if for no other reason than this: bars are a unique combination of public and private, both welcoming and walled in.

Bars form their own community, and throughout history gay people have needed community more than most. Shunned by their families, their gods, sometimes even themselves, gays have always needed a place to be safe, to learn the rules of their tribe, and to have fun.

Impulse Gay Social Club, which replaced Club 216 in 2013, closed in 2019, leaving Charlottesville without that particular institution that for decades had been the center of the town's gay world. The question is, does it matter?

On Saturday, September 15, 2012, the entrance to Market Street Park (then Lee Park) was framed by an arch of rainbow balloons, leading to a maze of booths and pamphlet-wielding volunteers, and the air was full of every conceivable anthem to self-discovery and self-acceptance that pop music has produced in the last forty years. It was Charlottesville's Pride Festival. The official slogan was "It's about Time."

When the event's organizer, Amy Sarah Marshall, moved to Charlottesville in 2001, she was married with children. Seven years later, at the age of thirty-three, she came out as a gay woman. It took her eighteen years to get to there, and it wasn't easy.

"When I came out I knew a handful of people who were gay," she said. "And I was like, are there any gay people in Charlottesville? I didn't see them, the visibility is not there, and I really needed a community, I needed to connect with people."

Charlottesville can be a hard place to get your bearings when you're new to the whole gay thing. The community is small, cliquish, and scattered, with no central gathering place, so Marshall decided to try to build one. She started an annual event called Pride in the Park, a potluck for the gay community that ran for three years. At one of the picnics people started giving her money. "What am I supposed to do with this?" she thought. "I'm not a nonprofit organization!"

To her surprise, people began looking to her for some kind of leadership. People who had newly come out or just moved to the area emailed her asking for help in finding their community. So she started Charlottesville Pride Community Network, a nonprofit organization intended to be the thing that brings the whole Charlottesville gay community together, starting with the Pride Festival.

"Part of [Pride Fest] was wanting to see allies show up and show their support, which meant so much to so many people," Marshall said. "You have no idea how many people were just kind of crying because it was like, 'Oh, this is where I live and it's okay for me to be here.'"

Which brings us to the idea of pride versus tolerance, and the idea of Charlottesville as a liberal haven.

"I've never lived somewhere that's so obsessed with being liberal," Peter DeMartino told me. "Like, I've never heard people talk about being liberal as much as people in Charlottesville talk about being liberal. I'm not quite sure they believe it, or they have to keep reminding themselves."

When Marshall came out in 2008, everyone was fine with it. It's not a problem, they said, so you like girls, we're totally cool with that. Only, it wasn't fine, not for her. It was a massive life change, one that her parents didn't accept. Not to mention that, despite the enormous progress that's been made, being gay in this country still carries considerable risks.

"There's still crazy people," Marshall said. "If your student finds out you're gay, if your client, your social worker finds out you're gay, that's still not safe. It's still risky out there . . . When I was getting divorced from my husband my lawyer was like, 'Do not have a relationship with a woman, do not have any woman spend the night, do not tell the judge you're gay.'"

As Marshall sees it, the problem is tolerance.

"I kind of hate that word now," she said. "Because you tolerate somebody that you don't necessarily like. When you tolerate people you put up with them. And I [don't] want to be put up with, I [want] actually to be cared about."

For Marshall, the Pride Fest was an attempt to change the message in Charlottesville from "We will tolerate you and not abuse you" to "We celebrate you and love you."

"This is a liberal city? Show me," she said. "Say it to me so that when I'm walking around Charlottesville I'm not wondering, or guessing, or assuming. Be explicit. Explicitly tell me that it's okay for me to walk down the Downtown Mall holding hands with somebody."

C-VILLE Weekly, a local alternative paper, ran an article right before the Pride Festival called "Queer 101: Everything you need to know about the LGBTQ community." Two comments on the article perfectly illustrate where Charlottesville is socially.

"As a gay man . . . I'm a little taken aback. This is Charlottesville. Do we really need a gay slang dictionary? Is it 1995 in Middle America?" And then: "I feel very strongly that there is NOTHING that I or anyone else needs to know about such a community. The world works better when everyone's intimate life remains intimate."

Having grown up in Charlottesville, I think those attitudes sum up where we are with a lot of our issues: It's hard to tell if we're over them or if we never dealt with them in the first place.

EPILOGUE

Blaise Spinelli and Michael broke up around 1981 but remained very close. Spinelli would often tell Michael, who was single and dating, to be careful.

"Blaise," Michael would say, "It's like .001 percent of people that are getting this."

One winter, Michael went on vacation to Hawaii. The man he was dating at the time stayed behind in his condo in DC, and while Michael was gone, he came down with pneumonia, locked his door, and crawled into bed with a bowl of chicken soup. He was found dead seven days later. A year after that, Michael found out he was HIV-positive.

"When Michael got diagnosed, I wanted to make sure that the AIDS support group would be there for him when he got ill," Spinelli said. "I said that when Michael died, that I would back off. That would be the end of my involvement [with ASG]."

He and Michael would finish each other's sentences. Spinelli always thought that when he was old, when he was the age he is now, they would be sitting on a bench together, enjoying a beautiful day. When his illness got bad, Michael moved to a hospital bed in his parent's den. It wasn't easy for his father to accept, but his mother didn't think twice. She brought her child home and cared for him as he went blind and his mind started to go.

Spinelli visited Michael in the mornings, then went to work the evening shift at the hospital, came home to sleep, got up, and went to see Michael.

"I can't tell you how many nights it would be dark . . . that phone would ring in the middle of the night, and you'd just lay there with your eyes open and say, 'Who's turn is it to get that phone.' Cause you knew what it was," Spinelli said.

I asked him if he's been to a lot of funerals, and after a pause, he said yes.

"Those funerals were just a lot of fun here in Charlottesville, in those Baptist churches, where all the gay people were on one side and the family was on the other."

Michael died in April 1991. Spinelli made appearances at a few fundraisers and private gatherings, but for the most part he slowly withdrew from ASG.

Clyde Cooper lamented the loss of Club 216, the place where everyone was welcome, where everyone was free to be themselves. He knew that a lot has changed in his lifetime, that you could be openly gay in pretty much any restaurant in town. You might not want to dance together, or kiss openly, but still, a lot had changed.

One of the things he treasured most about his time running Club 216 were his memories of the many people who met in the club, of the relationships that started there. Cooper celebrated his seventy-sixth birthday in 2012, thirty years after he met Mike Fitzgerald in Muldowney's.

"Probably the ten fingers I've got would be more than I need to count how many nights we've not been together," Cooper recollected.

When official forms asked your marital status, there was usually no choice that worked for him and Mike, no box to check for "not allowed to marry." Cooper nonetheless checked the box that said married, and then wrote beside it, "gay, lifetime partner." After the 2012 elections, same-sex marriage was legal in nine states, two Native American tribal jurisdictions, and the District of Columbia, but Cooper and Fitzgerald didn't head to Maryland or DC to get married, because that marriage wouldn't be recognized in Virginia, and Virginia was their home. But when same-sex marriage became legal in the Old Dominion after October 6, 2014, following the decision of the U.S. Supreme Court not to hear an appeal of the Fourth Circuit Court of Appeals' ruling in *Bostic v. Schaefer,* they happily took that next step. When Clyde died on May 16, 2019, the news of his passing noted he was survived by his husband of thirty-eight years, Michael Allen Fitzgerald Cooper.

"You know," he said, "I don't think a lot of people realize how much [Club 216] meant, what that club did."

"They thought it was just a beer joint," Fitzgerald said. "It was a lot more than that."

There's still a lot that needs to change, Clyde realized, but young people growing up gay today have no idea what it was like for people his age.

And that made him very happy.

NOTES

To Jasper, and all the other baby queers fighting to be free.

This chapter originally appeared in the November 13, 2012, issue of *CVILLE Weekly* and appears here courtesy of CVILLE.

YOU DON'T HAVE TO GO HOME BUT YOU CAN'T STAY HERE

—

The Struggle to Save Virginia's Oldest Lesbian Bar

CATHLEEN RHODES

t is 2000, and I am a young woman in Norfolk, Virginia, following Loriely and Bonnie to my first lesbian bar. I have my first job out of college and live an hour away with my parents in the rural town where I grew up. I know little of the world, myself, or this city. Loriely, a recently befriended coworker who I am struggling not to lose in traffic, struck up a conversation in the elevator at work one day. "I like your necklace," she said, referring to the cheap pewter goddess figure on an even cheaper chain, with tiny pride rings[1] on either side of her head. That is how we became friends, exchanging, as queers often do, a complex series of hints in the weeks that followed. When she introduced me to Bonnie, another coworker, it felt as if the skies had opened and rained down gays.

That is how I came to be following these two women to Hershee Bar, one of only two (soon to be the only) lesbian bars[2] left in a city that had housed more than a half dozen in the twenty-two years before that day. I was not thinking about the history of women's bars, though. I was only thinking about what it meant to be going to this one bar on this day. I had been to a gay bar before. Having come out a few years earlier in college, I drove with new friends to the one gay bar that any of us knew of in the southwestern corner of the state. It was a forty-five-minute drive down I-81 to a dark, dank bar in Roanoke with way more men than college-aged women. I had been fewer than a handful of times—half of a handful—and I never had anything to show for it but the self-loathing and sadness that a young, newly out lesbian too shy to approach women might have after visiting a gay bar.

None of this bolstered my confidence as I drove toward Hershee wondering what a lesbian bar would be like. Would I be gay enough? Would they laugh at me, parting as I walked in so that everyone could get a good view and point? I worried that I would not know the secret lesbian codes. What do you say? Where do you put your hands? On your hips? In your pockets? Slung across someone's shoulder? What do lesbians drink? What kind of liquor or beer says, "I'm a dyke, and I'm not to be trifled with"? Would dykes say "trifled"?

I had been fully out to family and most friends for three years, but going to a lesbian bar felt very different than going to a gay bar. There was nowhere for a slightly masculine twenty-something with short hair, combat boots, and a flannel shirt to hide in a dyke bar. It was thrilling, and it was terrifying. A lesbian bar was the real deal.

I do not remember actually crossing the threshold at Hershee. The only memory that remains is how scared and unsure I felt on the drive there. It was an important step for me as I grew into my lesbianism, learning what being a lesbian meant outside of my own personal relationships with the two women I had dated by then. Being a lesbian is certainly about one's intimate relationships, but the larger circle of friendships and acquaintances with other queer women are crucial in helping develop an understanding of oneself in a society that has done everything it could to silence and discredit lesbian identity and culture.

No doubt hundreds, maybe thousands, of women have crossed through Hershee's door and stepped into a lesbian bar for the first time, and each of those women has their own story to tell. These personal stories are important because they demonstrate the development of women—young, old, and in between—as lesbians negotiating the homophobia of mainstream culture and the misogyny of gay culture. Many of those women have also been navigating the even more difficult intersections of class, race, gender identity, and disability. The stories of working class and disabled women, of transgender women, and women of color share similarities with those of middle-class, able-bodied, cisgender, white lesbians, but they also diverge in many complicated ways. Despite these differences, many of them share the experience of walking into a dyke bar for the first time. Yet our chances of hearing those stories, of reading about them in books or seeing them reflected on television, at the movies, or in popular music are still relatively rare.[3] The denial of lesbian culture's importance, its necessity, and sometimes even its existence continues.

In the last decade, there has been a flurry of writing, particularly in the mainstream and queer presses, about the decline of the lesbian bar, and more recently there has been much more academic writing on the subject.[4] Despite the dwindling numbers of these bars,[5] the sheer volume of this writing indicates that they must still be important. In 2018, a small group of local activists, myself included, fought to keep Hershee Bar open. We believed the bar meant something—both in its particular time and place and also in a more general sense as a lesbian bar still viable in a country with so few remaining lesbian bars.[6] It is not insignificant that, in 2018, the year of its thirty-fifth anniversary, Hershee was one of only two lesbian bars in Virginia[7] and one of the oldest lesbian bars in the country. Even more significant is that Hershee was not faced with closure due to declining attendance. Contrary to popular narratives about the death of lesbian bars, Hershee's patrons were not all getting married and staying home or finding one another on dating apps. Hershee faced many of the same challenges that queer bars around the country were facing, but the more imminent threat came from a deal between city leadership and the bar's landlord.

Understanding what happened to Hershee is important because the threat of its closure, the fight to keep it open, and its ultimate fate demonstrate a reluctance to acknowledge the importance of lesbian cultures and spaces. The refusal of most city leadership to intervene during months of protestations at city council meetings, an underwhelming response from the gay community at large, and the refusal of politically connected queer community members to intervene on behalf of Hershee suggest that the bar's existence as the only space specifically for queer women[8] mattered little to anyone but those queer women, many of whom lacked political and social connections that could help them in their fight to save the bar. Thus, the fight for Hershee reflects the larger struggles of queer women, particularly of working-class women and women of color who often have fewer financial and social resources to carve out both figurative and literal space.

I present here what I hope can serve as a record of a lesbian bar.[9] Hershee's story is important to those who knew it because of their personal connection to the space, but it also complicates the narrative of lesbian bar closures. The use of dating apps, increasing acceptance in mainstream spaces, reluctance to financially support lesbian businesses,[10] and changes in entertainment habits that come with committed relationships are overly simplistic explanations of the shuttering of so many lesbian bars[11] over the last three decades. These explanations rely heavily on sexism, misogyny, and lesbophobia as they blame lesbians for destroying their own spaces via their intimate personal relationships.[12] What the struggle to save Hershee Bar demonstrates is that queer spaces, particularly those catering to women and femme-identified people, are still devalued and endangered by revital-ization and redevelopment initiatives. After months of interactions between community activists and city leadership, the latter failed to acknowledge the importance of the physical structure of a lesbian bar to its community. Month after month in city council meetings, Hershee was described by many as their "home." Suggestions from Norfolk leadership that the bar simply relocate ignored Hershee's historical significance and the emotional con-nection many felt to the physical space. Physical spaces powerfully connect us to our individual and collective pasts,[13] but queer people have very few such opportunities.[14] Though same-sex desiring and gender nonconforming people have always existed, the identities themselves—lesbian, gay, bisexual, transgender, queer, and the many variations among and between them—are relatively new. Lesbianism as a distinct identity has existed for only about a century and a half. A bar that was open, continuously, for thirty-five years spans more than a third of that time. Hershee, and spaces like it, have made significant contributions to lesbian and queer history, at times ensuring the absolute survival of queer people, and those spaces deserve protection.

THE SIGNIFICANCE OF LESBIAN BARS

In my work as a university professor and director of a community history project,[15] I spend a lot of time talking to people about queer bars. Sometimes they wonder, and occasionally even muster the courage to ask aloud, what is so important about a bar. Bars are associated with loud, sometimes uncontrolled drunkenness and unabashed, libidinous behavior. To some, they seem lurid, dark, and a little shameful. Many do not consider them worthy of academic study or of possessing any historical relevance, but this narrow view obscures the important and varied functions of queer bars over the last century. They were places where queer people could escape at least some of the harassment they encountered in their everyday lives and where they were at least partially protected from the violence, both physical and psychic, of the outside world. Inside the queer bar, queer people could dress, talk, walk, and dance the way they wanted and with whom they wanted while private memberships, obscure locations, and the scrutiny of bouncers working the front door provided at least some protection.

Though mixed gay bars have been important to the development of a lesbian identity and culture, women's bars have played a particularly important role. Writer Judy Grahn's explanation of the importance of Maud's, a San Francisco lesbian bar open from 1966–89, aptly illustrates the importance of lesbian bars more broadly: "It became a primitive social center, an entry point into the Lesbian lifestyle and point of view, a doorway to a different world entered by women from all over the country, and ultimately, the world." Grahn also differentiates between a bar for women owned by a woman and "the male-owned bars, where women were barely or not at all tolerated and, as in most of the culture, by and large invisible as individuals and as a public force."[16] As Grahn illustrates, the bars did not simply provide a place to meet other women; rather, they centered women's interests and desires and provided an opportunity for understanding themselves *as lesbians*. This idea that women could come to some self-understanding of what it meant to be a lesbian is echoed in Marie Cartier's study of mid-century lesbian bars. She describes the women's bar as a place where a lesbian could potentially "find solace, develop meaning, create home, and perhaps find someone to love. In many cases that person they found to love was themselves."[17]

In their groundbreaking work *Boots of Leather, Slippers of Gold*, Elizabeth Kennedy and Madeline Davis argue that early lesbian bars were crucial in shaping lesbian identity: "The culture of resistance that developed in working-class, lesbian bars and house parties contributed to shaping twentieth-century gay and lesbian consciousness and politics."[18] They emphasize the importance of community as "key to the development of twentieth-century lesbian identity and consciousness."[19] Women's bars, in cultivating spaces that brought women together, both created and maintained community and were therefore an essential part of the development of lesbian identities and culture.

Historian Lillian Faderman considers lesbian bars "the single most important public manifestation of the [lesbian] subculture for many decades."[20] She emphasizes the importance of lesbian bars alongside women's colleges, military units, and sports leagues as essential to creating lesbian culture and community: "Without those institutions not only would large numbers of women have been unable to make contact with other women in order to form lesbian relationships, but also it would have been impossible to create lesbian communities."[21] Faderman points out that women risked a great deal to visit women's bars because they considered the gamble worth taking: "Although the gay bars posed various dangers, many young and working-class women were thankful for their existence. They represented the one public place where those who had accepted a lesbian sociosexual identity did not have to hide who they were. They offered companionship and the possibilities of romantic contacts. They often bristled with the excitement of women together, defying their outlaw status and creating their own rules and their own worlds."[22] Despite knowing that bars might be raided, that their names could be printed in local newspapers, that there was the potential for harassment and physical attacks as they entered and left the establishments, women who went to the bars did so because the community that the spaces offered was so valuable.

Marie Cartier argues that "bars served as cultural community centers or institutional foundations for gay women"[23] and "the bar was the only space in which these women could actually *be,* in the most literal sense. For many of these women these four walls were the space in which they could actually have an identity that felt natural to them."[24] This was particularly important when women attending the bars flouted societal rules governing their behavior, speech, and appearance. The fullness of the lesbian bar's function is best illustrated by one of Cartier's interviewees who told her, "Everything happened here. It was the only place."[25] Many women felt intensely lonely when unable to visit the bars. This is demonstrated by Myrna, an informant who told Cartier the story of her life in the middle of the twentieth century. Married, deeply closeted, and lonely, Myrna called gay bars in the middle of the night several times a week just to hear the sounds of the bar. When someone at one bar hung up, she called another and listened. She told Cartier the calls were her "lifeline," because they proved "there was a place somewhere—even if I couldn't go there—that place was out there. I could hear it. Freedom."[26]

Indeed, lesbian bars are often considered important even by the women who no longer frequent them or never did. Faderman explains that, though middle-class women did not often frequent early lesbian bars for fear of raids and because they had the means to entertain women in their homes, when they did venture into them they did so because "the bars were almost the only place, outside of their circle of friends, where they could see large groups of lesbians. The bars offered them the assurance of numbers that they could not get elsewhere."[27] Cartier argues that mid-century gay bars functioned in the lives of queer people as churches do in broader society, as places to commune, organize, and celebrate shared experiences: "While many people do not go to church *per se*, if they belong to the religion the church symbolizes and houses, the structure of the church will also provide a structure to their own lives—for the occasional visit, for the identification it provides, for the knowledge of a community they could enter into."[28] Some of those involved in the fight to save Hershee were not regular patrons, yet we understood the value of the bar. It provided the structure that Cartier describes, and its existence served as a reminder that a lesbian space continued to provide opportunities for community and shared identity.

Grahn says that, even when lesbian bars were critiqued by lesbian feminists in the 1970s and some women began creating alternative spaces where women could gather, "The bars remained, along with 'the Movement,' one of our two primary mother-places."[29] Bars continue to play an important—though diminished—role in many lesbians' coming out experiences today, and though lesbian bars have certainly changed, some of their original functions remain. Many of the women who publicly addressed Norfolk City Council in the fight to save Hershee Bar mentioned community, safety, and companionship as primary reasons for going to the bar. They identified it many times over as a "safe space" for exploring and inhabiting lesbian and queer identities in a world that still exhibited hostility toward queer-identified women. Though the lesbian bar has changed, it remains connected to its origins as a liberatory, sheltering space.

HISTORY AND SIGNIFICANCE
OF HERSHEE BAR

Hershee's first night in operation, March 4, 1983, was a celebratory one marred by the arrest of a patron. According to a report in *Our Own Community Press*, the local lesbian and gay newspaper, a woman "was seated in the bar with a group of friends when she noticed a man staring and laughing at her. When he continued to do so, she got annoyed and made an obscene gesture. 'I thought he was just some ignorant straight guy,' she said."[30] The woman said the man grabbed her by the arm and wanted her to go outside, and she was arrested after calling him an "obscene name." She had not realized he was a plainclothes officer. She recounted to the paper that a witness heard him call her a "lesbian bitch," and she described being handled roughly. It might seem like an inauspicious start, but it was not a particularly unusual incident for a lesbian bar in the 1980s, and it would define the struggle to keep Hershee open and safe over the years.

The 1970s, '80s, and '90s were the height of the lesbian bar scene in Norfolk. Between 1978 and 2000, seven women's bars operated in the city, and when Hershee opened in 1983, it became the city's third lesbian bar in simultaneous operation. These spaces were enthusiastically supported by queer women in the surrounding communities. For more than four and a half years, "Lesbians Front and Center," a women-only space in *Our Own*, had lovingly celebrated milestones at the local women's bars, and four months before Hershee opened, the section (by then renamed "Wommon's Wings") mourned the loss of the Spectacle, a short-lived lesbian bar that had recently closed, in an "obituary." Clearly, women writing for the paper did not think that Norfolk had too many women's bars, and the other bars' continued success indicates that the larger community did not think so either. Throughout the 1980s and '90s, there was never a time when the city had fewer than two lesbian bars operating simultaneously, and it often had as many as three.[31] During a 2015 interview with Marge Reed, a longtime resident, I asked why she thought there were so many lesbian bars concentrated in one small part of the city. "Because there were so many of us—they could fill 'em up!" she exclaimed.[32]

Hershee would be the longest running of all these bars, celebrating its thirty-fifth anniversary just seven months before being forced to close its

1980
Bogey's Lounge
3615 Tidewater Drive

1986
Stella Street
6425 Tidewater Drive

1994
Ms. P's
6401 Tidewater Dr

79   81   82   84   85   87   88   89   90   91   92   95   96

1978
Shirley's
811-813 Colley Ave

1983
Hershee Bar
6117-9 Sewell's Point Road

1982
The Spectacle
2742 Azalea Garden Road

1993
Charlotte's Web
6425 Tidewater Drive

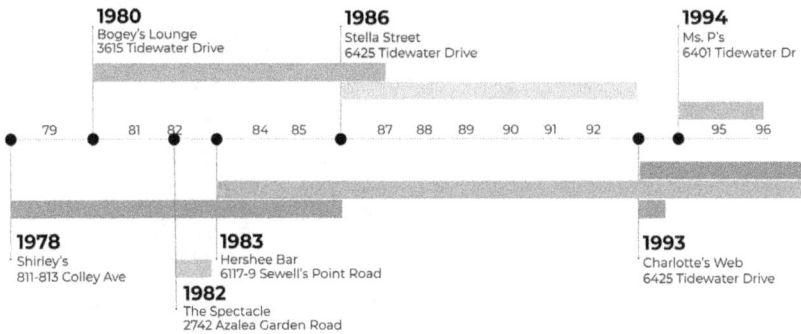

A chart of lesbian bars in Norfolk, Virginia, from 1978 to 1997. The city never had fewer than two lesbian bars operating simultaneously between 1980 and 1997.

doors for the last time. The bar was opened by Annette Stone and Bill Tyndall, but Stone was the powerhouse behind it. Her vision for the bar drove renovation and decorating choices, she designed and drew many of the bar's ads, and she made entertainment decisions.

The bar's identity was immediately established. The April 1983 issue of *Our Own* introduced Hershee to the local gay community, and a full-page ad on the back page declared Hershee to be "Where the Women Are," a tagline that would appear on Hershee ads for years. Soon after, Hershee ads borrowed "Free To Be Me" from Marlo Thomas's 1972 album *Free to Be . . . You and Me*. Thomas encouraged young children, particularly girls, to aspire to anything they wanted regardless of gender, and though the ads lacked the more overtly feminist overtones of Shirley's, another lesbian bar in town that opened five years before, they established Hershee specifically as a lesbian bar. The humor of "We Eat It Right!," presumably a reference to the bar's menu, but a phrase with a double meaning that landed Stone in hot water with ABC authorities,[33] also nodded to the bar's intended audience. Later ads became more explicitly lesbian when embracing mermaids appeared, urging patrons to "Explore [their] fantasies in the mystical land of HERSHEE'S."

By its second year the bar was booking nationally recognized performers like Alix Dobkin and Kate Clinton, and a constant in Hershee's advertising was its references to women. Many ads exclaimed that Hershee Bar was "Where the ♀ Are!!!," and a February 1986 ad showcasing the bar's new menu proclaimed, "Hershee's Is The Great American Women's Bar!"

HERSHEE'S

FREE TO BE ME

NEAR AND FAR
WHERE THE WOMEN ARE!

DJ 7 NITES A WEEK

6117 Sewells Point Road Norfolk, VA
(804) 853-9842

A 1983 advertisement for Hershee Bar reminiscent of the legend of Lady Godiva's naked horse ride. (*Our Own Community Press*, December 1983, p. 13; Special Collections and University Archives, Patricia W. and J. Douglas Perry Library, Old Dominion University Libraries)

In 1993, the bar expanded, knocking out a wall between it and the empty space next door. The expansion was met with opposition from some members of the Norfolk City Planning Commission (though it would ultimately vote 4–2 in favor of the expansion) and members of nearby Norview Baptist Church.[34] Most opposition cited alcohol sales as the primary reason for opposing the expansion, but during a public hearing there were also references to "a poster of the singer Melissa Etheridge, which one speaker described as a 'half-nude woman,' on the club's exterior wall."[35] Some objections obviously had as much to do with who was drinking as the alcohol itself.

In 1994, Hershee opened the new space. The much larger bar featured a women's bookstore in a side room. Over the next two decades, Hershee continued to reinvent itself. He Bar eventually opened in the bar's back room—the space once occupied by the women's bookstore. He Bar, with its male-specific branding and separate space, appealed to gay men without giving up the main bar's lesbian identity. These reimaginings of Hershee likely helped it remain open when many other bars found it difficult to survive.

Hershee also served as an important community space at a time when it was difficult to be out. Stone made free turkey sandwiches for Thanksgiving the first year the bar was open because so many of her customers could not go home for the holiday. The next year she served a full Thanksgiving meal as she did every November for more than three decades until the bar closed. In an interview with the *Virginian-Pilot,* Stone indicated that the event was always open to anyone who needed a meal "or just in need of companionship,"[36] and while most attendees were usually from the gay community, she also saw it as an opportunity to reach out to the struggling Five Points neighborhood that surrounded Hershee: "When the event first started, many people in the area who were disabled or didn't have transportation would come too. 'Everybody from that community at Five Points knew they could come there,' she said."[37]

Hershee was a hub for community organizing, hosting events and fundraisers for groups like the Moms & Kids Defense Fund, a local organization that assisted lesbian women embroiled in custody cases, and the Sharon Bottoms' Defense Fund.[38] In December 1983, the bar hosted a campaign speech and town-hall type question and answer event with Deborah Lass, who was running as the first openly gay candidate for Norfolk City Council, during which Lass addressed the anti-gay ABC laws targeting gay bars. Hershee hosted countless memorial services, weddings, and consciousness-raising and fundraising events for local AIDS organizations, recovery groups, and women's sports teams.

Like many gay bars, Hershee served a larger community purpose. In addition to providing a place for women to meet one another, it also built and maintained lesbian community by cultivating a space for celebrations, mourning, and community organizing.

THE FIGHT TO SAVE HERSHEE BAR

In 2018, just before Hershee Bar celebrated its thirty-fifth anniversary, Stone was informed that her lease would be terminated later that year. The bar occupied a lot in a desirable, high-traffic area centrally located at a compli-cated and busy intersection of Chesapeake Boulevard, Norview Avenue, and Sewells Point Road. Stone owned the bar but not the building it was in and has said repeatedly that she tried to buy the property in the early 2000s but was unsuccessful because the deal fell through when lenders learned of possible environmental issues.[39] She leased the space for many years from Five Points, LLC., and that company had recently negotiated a deal with the City of Norfolk. In February of 2018 the city agreed to purchase the land that Hershee and several adjacent buildings occupied for $1.5 million. The bar's lease was set to expire at midnight on October 31, and once leases ran out on other businesses on the property, the buildings would be razed so the city could take possession of an empty lot.[40] Long-term plans for the lot were unclear, but Five Points, LLC., had been trying to sell the property for a decade without success, so the city's dogged pursuit of the deal caused spec-ulation among the public and activists. In March 2018, Stone announced that the bar would be forced to close, and in the months that followed rumors ran wild about why the city was so interested in the property.

Stone complained that city officials did not adequately communicate with business owners and that their fate was never considered during sales nego-tiations. Hershee had occupied the space as a profitable business for thirty-five years, and Stone argued that she was entitled to direct communication from the city before it brokered a deal that would close her bar. Patrons and LGBTQ citizens were angered, too. Hershee was not just another bar. It was Virginia's oldest lesbian bar and one of the few remaining lesbian bars in the country. Hershee supporters argued that its service to the LGBTQ commu-nity and the neighborhood that surrounded it should have ensured that it was part of the initial deal between landowners and the city, and they demanded, through a series of visits to city council meetings, that the city amend the deal and preserve Hershee in its original and historically significant location.

What would become clear over the next few months is that Norfolk City Council had not considered the impact of closing a longstanding queer busi-ness and demolishing the building. Moreover, this oversight reached beyond the original sale of the property as the city offered little help to Stone. She was provided a list of spaces available for lease in the city, but this assistance, as meager as it was, ignored the significance of the physical space to the area's LGBTQ history and culture.

On June 5, 2018, Mamie Johnson, the Ward 3 Norfolk City Council representative, led a tour of her ward. In attendance were Norfolk city council members, residents, and business owners. When the group stopped at Five Points, Johnson told those present that the Greater Norview Task Force had spent the previous eight to nine months discussing plans for the Sewells Point Road property. She called the deal "opportunity purchasing," which she described as meaning "you don't always have a master plan, but what we see throughout the city that's very important is that when there's an opportunity you have to jump on it; you have to take advantage of it because people know that great things are happening in the city of Norfolk."[41] Councilmember Andria McClellan asked, "So, Mamie, are we going to do anything to commemorate the Hershee bar?"[42] Johnson assured McClellan that she was helping find a new location for the bar "because the Hershee Bar has been a part of this community for thirty-plus years, and they have become a family. It's not just a place of business; they do a lot of outreach to the communities; they've been great partners."[43] Johnson's answer to McClellan's question, a question that argued the bar deserved *commemoration,* ignored Hershee's historical and cultural importance and focused instead on getting Hershee into a new lease agreement in a new location. Councilmember Angelia Williams Graves added, "And if they want to have something to commemorate their thirty years, they're more than welcome to do so."[44] McClellan's use of "we" in the original question indicated she was asking what the city planned to do—not whether citizens were free to plan their own commemoration activities. The latter seems obvious. The hostility of Graves's answer was further revealed when she and Johnson pointed the blame at Stone for not buying the building. When McClellan asked about the termination of the lease Johnson told her, "We made sure that she had plenty of time to be notified exactly what was happening and also through the thirty years, Miss Annette Stone has had great opportunity to purchase the land herself, the building herself, so there was opportunity for her." Graves interrupted to add, "They weren't just kicked out on the street but they had plenty of time to find a new location, get themselves situated so that their businesses could continue to thrive."[45] Johnson replied, "Yep." The exchange was telling in that it closely resembled the ways the council repeatedly downplayed the bar's significance, focusing instead on what they saw as Stone's personal accountability for Hershee's closure.

In the same month as the Ward 3 tour, Jennifer Alomari, a longtime friend of Annette Stone and a fierce supporter of Hershee Bar, organized an "LGBTQ Community Takeover at Norfolk City Hall" on Facebook. She chose June because it coincided with Pride month and the anniversary of the Stonewall Riots. She saw the city council meeting as an opportunity to educate council members about "what they were doing and how it was impacting a whole community," and she believed that if council heard from members of the community about how much the bar meant to them that city leadership would change its plans and save Hershee.[46]

Fifteen people spoke in favor of Hershee Bar during the new business portion of the June 26 Norfolk City Council meeting.[47] It was a large turnout for a city council meeting, with several additional supporters in attendance who did not sign up to speak.[48] While some speakers were clearly angry about Hershee's closure, the exchanges were cordial, but later meetings would grow more tense.

The comments from the first city council meeting are particularly important in that it was the first time that many council members heard directly from the community about the decision to buy the property. They are also representative of many of the comments that would come during subsequent council meetings. Speakers repeatedly emphasized the bar as a safe space and a second home.

JENNIE MCCORMACK: What I would like to ask is that you think about this group of people, all of us who need this place, who love this place, who find comfort and home in this place, who find family when you've moved away from the family that you've always been with.

NINA BLOWE: Hershee Bar is not just a lounge. It's not just a place to come to party and have a good time. It's like everybody's like family. They're like family, and it just hurts me. It hurts me and saddens me deeply that this is happening. And I just want to say please, if you could just reconsider because it feels good to be able to walk in a place and feel love and feel comfort.[49]

There were also several references to Hershee as a refuge from homophobic violence experienced in the community and at the hands of family.

FRANKIE BUSITZKY: I have a scar on my forehead right here from being gay bashed. I was put in a mental hospital because my mom wanted to fix me at fifteen years old, so imagine when I find there's a gay bar called the Hershee Bar, you know, and I walk in and safety, the love that I felt immediately. You guys are gonna take away a very big part of my community. Everything I am is in that place. It's my home.

JENNIFER ALOMARI: The Hershee Bar is more than a bar to me and everybody else in this room. It's a community center. It's where we go to have our birthday parties. It's where we go to raise money for our friends. It's where we go to bury our friends. So, I understand to you this may just be a building but not to us. You're not just tearing down the building, you're tearing down a piece of our history, and you're tearing down a piece of our hearts.

SISSY BOTTOMLY: I've lived here for thirty years, and I've been going to the Hershee Bar for thirty-five years. I guess I could tell you the same story. My parents, they didn't care. They didn't accept me, and they wanted me gone. And I left. I came here where I was accepted. I found a place. . . . My church when I was growing up, said, "You're not good enough. You're gay, you'll go to hell." You know, that was the thing. Parents said, you know, you didn't look the part. You don't look like a girl. I don't want you around. So I left. I said, I don't want to be like that. I want to be me. I came here, and I was kind of lost. And then I found this community.

CISSY ELKINS: From the time I walked in the door, there were t-shirts that said "Free to Be Me." This is your place, feel at home. . . . Because in a time when people hated homosexuals, when you were shamed to be one, when your churches disowned you, your family disowned you, it was something else. And I was one of those people. My family turned on me so fast with their Southern Baptist stuff. . . . But there's a lot of ghosts in that building, because a lot of our friends have died, and I do not want to walk away from that building, and y'all are breaking our hearts. You really are.

Many, like Mary James, bristled at the lack of a plan for the property after demolition: "This is our family. This is our home. These are our lives. To tear it down without a second thought and without a plan is reckless."[50]

Others mentioned Annette Stone's service in the surrounding community. William Kesling, two-term president of the civic league in Hershee's neighborhood, spoke of his two decade working relationship with Stone and her civic engagement:

> When I was president of the civic league, I attended the Five Points Partnership meetings, and across the table many a night was Annette Stone. When the Five Points Partnership was wanting to put together different events, Annette always participated in it. Years ago, they were held at the Methodist Church. One time the church member didn't show up to open the door and let us in there; it just happens to be adjacent to the Hershee Lounge. I ran over there. Billy Tyndall opened the door, and I was very proud one evening because I had [Councilmember] Anthony Burfoot in a wonderful gay bar lounge with overstuffed chairs sitting under a picture of Melissa Etheridge. It was a very proud moment for me.[51]

Community members spoke for thirty-seven minutes about the importance of Hershee. At the end of the new business portion of the meeting, Mayor Kenny Alexander broke protocol and addressed the Hershee speakers directly for a minute and a half. He thanked the speakers, commended Stone and Tyndall for their contributions to life in the city over the years, and assured the audience that the city's economic development team was aware of the situation and that Five Points, LLC., the property owners, would likely help find a new location for the bar. These remarks did not address the importance of the bar in its original location—a point that activists would continue to address in upcoming meetings. He ended his statement by highlighting the city council's diversity.[52]

Mayor Alexander invited councilmembers to speak, and Councilmember Paul Riddick, who resides in the Hershee neighborhood and called the bar and its owners good neighbors, asked for clarification about the intended use of the property by the city. City Manager Doug Smith responded that the property was an investment for the city for which they had no specific plans.

Councilmember McClellan spoke next. She acknowledged that council had inadequate information when they made the original decision to purchase the property, noting that "for as inclusive as we are and diverse as we are, we have not done enough to reach out to the LGBTQ community to involve you in our economic development decisions. And we need to do a better job."[53] She urged LGBTQ community members to come to more of the city's open meetings.

The last person to speak was Councilmember Angelia Williams Graves, the representative from Superward 7, which includes the Five Points area. She expressed sympathy but noted that changing the terms of the agreement could set an unpleasant precedent for the city and reminded the audience that "the business owner is responsible in their part of being amenable to other locations."[54] She stopped just short of publicly accusing Stone and Tyndall of refusing to cooperate, saying, "Sometimes we just want what we want, and that may not be possible to stay where you are."[55] She did not understand that the location was important to those in attendance: "I cannot imagine that in this entire city, in all of the retail locations, and all of the commercial space that we have, that there is nowhere that a community of people can gather and make it a new home."[56] Someone from the audience shouted out, "Our ghosts are there. Our people who passed in the last thirty-five years that we'd loved are still there." Graves responded, "I appreciate that. But again, things do change, times do change."[57]

These initial exchanges demonstrate how many nonqueer people believe that a longstanding lesbian bar can simply be moved to a new location—that what happens inside that place is divorced from the place itself. Acknowledging the historical significance of physical spaces is not simply about their architectural importance, however. Those spaces hold the history of what happened in them, and people visit historical sites not just to see artifacts but also to stand in the same places that people before them stood. Doing so literally and figuratively grounds one in individual and collective histories. Queer people have very few opportunities to do that. The places that have been important to queer people before us are all too often unknown or destroyed. The city council's insistence that Hershee simply relocate ignored not only the huge financial costs involved but also the loss to the Five Points neighborhood and the historical loss. In finalizing this deal, council members did not differentiate between Hershee Bar and the check cashing business two doors down, believing that both could easily move to a new location and that the walls surrounding those businesses were interchangeable. Over the next several months, community members would try to help council members understand that the building itself was important in preserving the bar's thirty-five-year history and that demolishing it sent a powerful message about the city's lack of commitment to LGBTQ history.

Hershee supporters attended seven city council meetings between June and October, appearing nearly every two weeks. Many reiterated the importance of the physical structure. Beth Brooker said the Hershee Bar "is a gay icon, an iconic building," and Sandra Pryor, a professor of history at Old Dominion University, urged council "to consider the historical value of the Hershee Bar as a potential future historical landmark."[58] Melissa Friedrichs, a former student in one of my Old Dominion University courses and a Navy veteran, described her experiences on an LGBTQ walking tour that my students design each fall: "We stood in spaces that used to house old gay bars, and many of those spaces are now extremely expensive lofts, overpriced restaurants, or, most importantly, vacant lots. Those spaces are gone, torn down. What were safe places for the LGBTQ community are completely wiped from their spots, places that have physically fed and held fundraisers for those in need. Places my fellow sailors visited and felt at home in."[59]

Robbin Love read a portion of the city's vision statement that touts Norfolk as "a national leader in the quality of life offered to all its citizens" and argued that "in pushing out the Hershee Bar, City Council, whether it intends to or not, is signaling to its LGBT citizens that we are not included in the city's vision of community."[60]

I addressed Norfolk's history of homophobia. As the home of the world's largest naval base, the city has its own particular connection to the surveillance and disciplining of queer people. I told council, "Military police have parked outside bars, recording license plate numbers, and cities like Norfolk—including Norfolk—have raided those spaces."[61]

Several speakers described the kinds of homophobic harassment that LGBTQ people still encounter. ODU student Kira Kindley talked about her experience with protestors who used large signs and bullhorns to interrupt students' presentations during one of our queer history walking tours. She explained how unnerving it felt for our group to be followed back to campus where she and other students studied and lived, and she argued that these kinds of experiences are why places like Hershee Bar are so important.[62]

Robin Shelton, a psychotherapist in private practice, told a story about a fourteen-year-old client with whom she once worked. Her story echoed others that spoke to the ways that lesbian bars like Hershee can literally save lives and how they stand as visible markers of lesbian history:

> I was participating in a family therapy meeting in which she came out to her parents. And her parents were both educated people; they were professional people. And they told her that she should have never been born, and that they were sorry that she'd been born. So she ran out and she had been admitted because she tried to hang herself. So obviously, the staff were quite worried that she was running out of the building down Colley Avenue, I guess at seven, eight o'clock at night, and was going to go hurt herself. So the cops were called and everything. About an hour and a half, two hours later, she came back, and she was brought by these two women. She had run to Shirley's [a lesbian bar], and they talked to her about how even though her family wasn't accepting of her that she still had value, and she had a reason to live.[63]

SUPPORT FOR THE CITY

Though most of those at the meetings spoke in favor of Hershee, a small number supported the city's deal to buy the property. The most vocal was Jackie Rochelle, a resident of the neighborhood and a member of the Greater Norview Task Force, a group composed of Norfolk City Council members, other city representatives, and residents from the area. Rochelle first appeared at the third council meeting attended by Hershee supporters. As several council members had done previously, Rochelle shifted responsibility for Hershee's troubles back to Stone and the community. Rochelle told council, "We would like very much for the Hershee Bar, because they did not avail themselves of opportunities to purchase the land, in the eight months that they have, to find another [location]." She urged community members to assist Hershee's owners: "Our wish is that the people who have been the beneficiaries of their kindness over the years come forward, help them, as we have helped, and pointed places out that we would like to see them move to."[64] The help that Rochelle is indicating was meager—a list of possible spaces for lease in the city—and it was the city, not the community, who was in a position to best help Stone and Tyndall. Though Rochelle and council members who made similar statements never explicitly stated what kind of assistance they were suggesting, many of those attending city council meetings assumed they meant that the community should crowdfund the move. Such a request seemed unreasonable since it was the city's ill-informed decision that created the situation and because the local queer community, though not small, was not large enough to raise the money necessary for a move.

Before ending her speech, Rochelle suggested that people displaced by Hershee's closure take advantage of LGBTQ nights at two local straight bars and promised that "people who choose to avail themselves of these opportunities can be assured that they will be in a friendly, welcoming and safe environment."[65] Rochelle's suggestion that queer patrons "avail themselves" of queer-themed nights at otherwise nonqueer bars grossly underestimated the safety concerns of Hershee patrons and trivialized the importance of queer-run queer spaces.

ACCUSATIONS OF HOMOPHOBIA

In the third city council meeting, held on July 24, there were more pointed accusations of homophobia, such as Julia Edwards-McDaniel's comment: "Some of you may not agree with our lifestyle, but . . . it is not your job to judge us or any member in the community. It's your job to act on behalf of the community, to be the voices of those who elected you."[66]

It is impossible to pinpoint exactly why suspicions of homophobia surfaced at this point, but it was likely a combination of factors. Many of those attending council meetings and those streaming them from home felt their concerns were not being heard. Though it is customary to end the new business portion of council meetings without comment, the process nevertheless left participants and viewers feeling that concerns were going into a void. Nothing was changing in terms of the sale, no one from the council reached out to organizers, and emotional pleas were repeatedly made with few signals that they had really been heard. An incident on Councilmember Johnson's facebook page a few weeks earlier, in which she replied to a comment about saving Hershee Bar with a laughing-crying emoji,[67] also continued to damage relations, as did some councilmembers' inattention during the new business portion of meetings. In several meetings, council members left just as new business began or checked cellphones while citizens made their appeals on behalf of Hershee.

The absence of a plan likely also led to suspicions of homophobia. In my own remarks at one meeting I asked council to imagine a queer walking tour developed by students ten years in the future. My goal was to motivate council to think about how we might look back on this decision in the future. I provided a historical overview of Hershee Bar before asking them to imagine standing in front of a CVS. I had no reliable information about the possibility of a big box pharmacy moving onto the property. Rather, I wanted to point out that, without specific plans, the city had entered into a deal with taxpayer money that would demolish a longstanding small business for any number of future development possibilities. Had residents known the city's plans for the lot, they might have been more likely to oppose the city's deal with the owners. Instead, they would not know the plans until well after the deal was settled and the bar was demolished, and by then it would be too late. The sterile nature of a big box pharmacy in the scenario I described stood in contrast to the history, less pristine but much more real, of a thirty-five-year-old lesbian bar.[68] McClellan addressed the CVS comment saying, "That property was going to be purchased. It could be the city that owns it and manages it, or it could have been the CVS, so I think the idea was to purchase the property, and to imagine it [in]to something for the future."[69] Thus, she saw council as protecting a valuable piece of property, but many of those who came to speak at the meetings were clearly uncomfortable with the idea of demolishing Hershee without knowing what would replace it. Though McClellan could suggest that the city's deal protected against a big box pharmacy replacing Hershee Bar, she could not promise that it would not happen.

This uncertainty gave rise to many other ideas about what the corner occupied by Hershee might become. At many of the meetings people mentioned a parking lot or green space, and rumors about a dog park would play a prominent role in upcoming meetings. Council attempted to reassure the community that there were no plans for a parking lot, and task force member Jackie Rochelle admonished Hershee supporters for mentioning parking lots and dog parks for "effect,"[70] but these were legitimate concerns. Many queer bars in Norfolk have been replaced by parking lots and garages in the name of revitalization. A November 1982 article in *Our Own* about the closing of the Paddock, a downtown gay bar, noted that the business would be replaced by a parking lot, and the article identified four gay bars in as many years with the same fate—the Paddock, the Nickelodeon, Mickey's, and the Ritz.[71] Historian Samantha Rosenthal argues that urban renewal efforts have often been antiqueer. In the case of downtown Roanoke, Virginia, she notes that officials expanded efforts to clean up the city by targeting gay male cruising and sex work and by banning cross-dressing.[72] Roanoke's gentrification efforts thus "imagined historic urban centers preserved of architectural history yet scrubbed of social history, all in the service of promoting family-friendly urban spaces for shopping and entertainment."[73] Echoes of this can be heard in Councilmember Johnson's June 5 tour of Ward 3 when she praised Norfolk Pawn Shop owner Austin Loney and his business: "It's something to see once you go over to the pawn shop because once you visit it, you don't think that you're at a pawn shop. Austin retained a lot of the original fixtures, and they hand carved many of the fixtures that are in the pawn shop, and it is really nice. That was one of my first attractions to visit when I came to the Five Points area."[74]

Rosenthal also notes that demolition became a method for ensuring the "safety" of the city as many locations demolished in the 1980s were associated with gay male cruising.[75] It was not uncommon for "safety" and "crime reduction" to be brought up as reasons for redeveloping Five Points, and while Hershee was never accused of contributing to these problems, demolishing the building it occupied was often discussed as the only or best solution. During the Ward 3 tour Johnson invited Loney to speak about the city's plans for the area. Loney highlighted vacancies, using the word four times in his forty-second-long statement. Hershee Bar was not vacant, however. It was an established anchor business on the corner of the property. Stone was active in the neighborhood in both formal and informal ways, engaging with the civic league and participating in discussions about revitalization. Loney specifically mentioned the effects of vacant buildings on his own property, happy for the city to do "anything that doesn't leave vacant properties where, you know, crime could happen or just things get run down, look bad. It makes my business look bad being next to a vacant building."[76] Of the buildings slated for demolition, however, the one closest to Norfolk Pawn was actually occupied by Hershee Bar. Though it was not targeted for demolition because it was a queer business, Hershee was considered acceptable collateral damage in efforts to clean up the area.

Community members were frustrated by the council's inaction, and some interpreted that inaction, as well as the original sale, as potentially influenced by homophobia. It seems unlikely that the city's decision to purchase the property was solely motivated by homophobia, but the council's refusal, with some small exceptions, to publicly and strongly acknowledge the building's historical relevance,[77] its insistence that the community assume responsibility for helping the bar relocate, and its repeated references to Stone's failure to buy the building, demonstrate that they were out of touch with many of the issues important to LGBTQ people in the city.

LAST CALL

Two weeks before Hershee's last night Dr. Marie Cartier, performance artist and scholar of pre-Stonewall lesbian bar history, visited Norfolk. A community event was held in Norfolk's Park Place neighborhood, and city council members were invited to participate in the kind of open dialog that council meeting procedures did not allow for. Only Councilmember McClellan attended the event. She expressed regret that council did not realize the importance of Hershee Bar when they made the initial agreement to buy the property. Dr. Cartier moderated the discussion, and McClellan listened as community members told her why the bar was important to them individually and to the community. It was an important opportunity for city leaders and citizens to connect, and many were disappointed that more council members did not attend.

The October 23, 2018, city council meeting was the last before the bar's scheduled closure. Hershee supporters filled council chambers, and many wore stark white, handwritten "Save Hershee Bar" stickers on their shirts. With the bar scheduled to close in just over a week, organizers intensified efforts to bring community members to the meeting. In previous weeks, several of those leading the effort to save the bar formed the Hershee Action Coalition (HAC). The small group, made up of Robbin Love, Sarah Hustead, Hunter Noffsinger, Kathleen Casey, Barb James, Mary James, and myself,

Hunter Noffsinger addresses Norfolk City Council on October 23, 2018. It was standing room only in council chambers, with most of those attending in opposition to the sale that would close Hershee and demolish the building. (City of Norfolk, https://www.youtube.com/watch?v=W1YDMwXdWEM)

worked to better organize those attending this crucial meeting. As in previous months, some people who came to show support felt uncomfortable preparing their own statements, so HAC prepared relevant statistics and statements and distributed them. HAC designed large postcards for those unable to attend the meeting and delivered more than a hundred of these cards, addressed to the city council with handwritten messages in support of the bar.

The messages from those who spoke were not unlike at previous meetings, but there was an increased sense of urgency. Many focused on how city council could address its previous missteps by asking that it talk openly about the sale of the property, acknowledge its mistakes in entering into a deal without realizing the impact on the LGBT community, and create an LGBTQ advisory board.

Two young people discussed suicide attempts and abuse from family, emphasizing how vital spaces like Hershee Bar still are to young queer people. Others mentioned recent changes initiated by the Trump administration that affected the lives of many LGBTQ people—particularly transgender people. Dominic Melito, known personally and professionally by some council members, was representative of several speakers that night who were nervous to publicly align themselves with such an obviously queer cause but did so because they believed it to be so important: "I am a member of the Hampton Roads LGBTQ community. For those of you, a few of you, know me on the board, that's not something I go around saying all the time, so this is hard for me, but I feel like it's important at this point. For me, gay bars were the first place where I felt safe and secure to be myself before I was ready to come out. . . . Without the support of my friends and adoptive family that I had at the gay bars, I may never have had the courage to speak my truth and be myself."[78]

Speakers also focused even more intensely on the historic value of the bar. Melito said, "As a former history teacher, I can tell you that historical sites matter. At this point, the Hershee Bar is the last bar that I can say was part of my support, where I got my courage and confidence to be myself."[79] I passed Polaroids to the council that showed what became of former lesbian bar sites in Norfolk—a parking garage, a Chinese takeout restaurant, a grassy lot, and an empty storefront in an empty strip mall—as I told them, "These photos attest to the lack of a visible, recognizable lesbian existence in Norfolk. . . . Lesbians are invisible without Hershee Bar. We are barely reflected in local historical accounts of LGBTQ Norfolk; we are largely absent from the city leadership. But we have been here, we have made a difference here. It matters that we be remembered, that we be acknowledged, and that our lives be celebrated." I and others wanted part of the official record to reflect that Hershee Bar was the last remaining visible link to a lesbian past in Norfolk.

In all, thirty-eight people urged the city council to save Hershee Bar that night. They spoke for nearly an hour and a half, more than three times longer than the regular session. At the end of the new business section, Mayor Alexander and Councilmember McClellan again addressed the group. The mayor assured the audience that council had been listening intently since June and indicated, "You don't know our story, and if you have a chance to meet with us individually, you would be shocked about our story."[80] He seemed to be trying to decide how much to share as he continued:

I could go on and tell you my story, but I won't tell you my story tonight. But I will say this. In 1949, a young woman was born in Norfolk, Virginia, and in 1966, she got pregnant, but she had to leave because she was a lesbian. She went to New York City where she lived. She had to come back to register her son in public schools in Norfolk. Her mother was a secretary of a church; her father was a clerk of the church, but she could not live here in the City of Norfolk because she was gay. She died at age thirty-six. Today, her son is the mayor of the City of Norfolk.[81]

The mayor's story received some applause from the audience and moved McClellan to tears. It is important to acknowledge the pain inherent in that story—the pain of a woman unable to live her life openly and fully and the pain of a child grown into adulthood who was separated from his mother. It is also important, however, to consider how well it illustrates so many of the arguments made over the previous five months. In an effort to demonstrate that council was not the opposition, Mayor Alexander confirmed the importance of affirming spaces for queer people and for lesbians in particular.

THE END OF AN ERA

Hershee Bar's last night was similar to its first in some ways—full of queer women, dancing, and police. On October 31, 2018, Hershee's closing night, the small area around the bar was heavily patrolled by Norfolk Police Department cruisers. Between midnight and the bar's 2 a.m. closing time, patrols increased, and by 1 a.m. nearly a half dozen cruisers lined up along the fence in the church parking lot next door. The cars were pointed toward Hershee Bar in anticipation of trouble. At least two other cruisers were parked on the street near the side of the bar, and others patrolled the perimeter. The police presence was ominous, and patrons and bar supporters assumed that it signaled the city's concern that the bar's long fight with the city would end with violence and destruction of property. What it did was inflame the otherwise peaceful crowd outside the bar. Throughout the night, people had been adding to the hundreds of messages written on the bar's white cinder block exterior. Small groups gathered to tell stories about the first time they had been to the bar or spin tales about something outrageous they had seen or done there. As the night grew later, people met outside to say their goodbyes and to make plans to find one another. The group was grieving, and the police presence felt like an invasion. Many interpreted it as the City of Norfolk's final attempt to punish Hershee supporters. More likely, it was an overzealous response to what city leaders considered an unpredictable group agitated by months of protests against the city's refusal to do more to save Hershee Bar. It is not insignificant to note, though, that the bar's crowd that night was largely made up of Black queer people, and the very visible police presence was even more striking given the kind of violence that queer people of color have experienced at the hands of police in this country. The police presence also made it clear that a small but persistent group of supporters had been taken very seriously by city leadership. The group might not have had the political or financial clout to stop the city's plans, but it did make leaders nervous, and though no one was arrested on Hershee's last night, the fact that police were part of both the bar's opening and closing reminds us that while much has changed for the better over the last thirty-five years, some things have remained the same. Queer women, particularly queer women of color and queer working-class women, are still often seen as unpredictable and volatile. When Hershee closed its doors for the last time in the early morning hours of November 1, 2018, it was the first time since at least 1978 that the city of Norfolk did not have a space specifically for lesbians.

Over the next few weeks, the bar was quietly packed up. In November 2018, I took students and community members on a tour of the bar as part of that fall's queer history walking tour. Before we went inside some students read and added to the messages written on the exterior walls of Hershee. The messages memorialized friends and family, passed along goodbyes from regulars and employees, expressed grief at losing a longstanding queer space, and revealed anger, some of it quite intense, toward Norfolk City Council. Inside, tables, bar stools, and pool tables were piled high with boxes and items ready to be moved into storage. The celebratory tone of the walking tour shifted as participants snaked their way through thirty-five years of paperwork, memorabilia, and decorations. One of my students stopped to look at items near the front bar and told me, "I feel like I'm walking through a funeral." We were. The bar was dead, and we were witnessing the preparation of the body. The entire funeral process would take a month.

Demolition began in August 2019, and for nearly two years, the lot was underused and mostly empty. An October 24, 2020, update on the city's

Robbin Love adds a message to one of Hershee's exterior walls on the bar's last night. (Photo by author)

website described the area as follows: "The Five Points Neighborhood Spot is a temporary, flexible public park which provides safe, healthy, fun and educational pop-up programming during the COVID-19 pandemic."[82] It remained unclear what the city's long-term goals were for the area until an October 23, 2021, dedication ceremony and groundbreaking. That ceremony, exactly three years to the day after the last city council meeting before Hershee's closure, served as the official announcement that the space would become a park. The week before the ceremony I contacted Councilmember McClellan to ask if there were plans to commemorate Hershee. She passed my question to Danica Royster, the new representative for Superward 7. Two days before the ceremony I contacted Councilmember Royster to ask again, but she did not respond. Six community members protested the event. Some were draped in rainbow flags, and others of us held signs referencing Hershee bar and lesbian history. After the event, I spoke to both Royster and Johnson about plans to commemorate Hershee or local lesbian history. Royster told me the Hershee protests "predated" her time on council and that she had not heard from the community before that day. Johnson said she had not "thought that far ahead." Neither responded to email requests I sent after that event asking about commemoration of Hershee. Other members of the crowd had a very different response, however. Several candidates for the Superward 7 seat, the Norfolk sheriff, and many others thanked us for being there and expressed support for Hershee.

HERSHEE'S LEGACY

In some ways queerness is more visible than ever as many cities host elaborate Pride parades and festivals and queer people become increasingly present in advertising, on film, and in politics. One of the biggest complaints lodged against these forms of visibility is their superficiality, however. Pride festivals, for example, frequently rely on and court corporate sponsorships in exchange for blanketing events with branded advertising swag. Increased visibility in television and film often comes at the expense of more marginalized groups, particularly queer people of color, who remain vastly underrepresented. This superficial visibility and inclusion can be contrary to queer liberation efforts when the visible remnants of actual queerness in cities are eliminated through a failure to protect queer bars as viable businesses and important contributors to cultural life. Lesbian bars have long been sites of political and social activism as well as places where queer people were affirmed in their difference, and they are visible reminders of lesbian and queer resistance that stand in stark contrast to the more assimilationist, sanitized, and depoliticized versions of queerness that exist in events like Pride festivals. Supporting large-scale Pride events enables cities to project an image of inclusivity and acceptance that their other actions might not back up. Local governments can reap the benefits of supporting Pride, partnering with host organizations and marketing depoliticized Pride events to local citizens, without the sustained political effort toward queer liberation that would require the political bravery of, say, saving an established and solvent lesbian bar.[83]

Pro-Hershee activists were faced with disbelief and misunderstanding from city leadership, those who spoke before council were out in very visible ways that some worried would affect their personal and work relationships, and they were abandoned by much of the mainstream LGBTQ community who refused, sometimes derisively, to participate in efforts to save the bar. Thus, efforts to save Hershee served as a reminder that LGBTQ communities still favor so-called respectable political organizing that usually aligns with the concerns of cis white gay men.

Kennedy and Davis argue that lesbian bars were a crucial part of "lesbian resistance"[84] in the first half of the twentieth century and that the communities lesbians created in those spaces were "testimony to their tenacity, their drive to find others like themselves, and their desire for erotic relations with other women."[85] Those working to save Hershee Bar built on and continued a tradition of lesbian resistance both inside and outside of Norfolk. Recently, the right for lesbian and queer spaces to exist is again being publicly and vocally challenged, and their importance is questioned when local governments and communities make decisions that prioritize revitalization efforts over preserving them. The fight to save Hershee signaled a refusal to accept the destruction of lesbian spaces. The stories shared during council meetings serve as an important reminder that the violence and shame described by narrators from the 1930s in Kennedy and Davis's oral history interviews are not exclusively in the past.[86] Several young queer people shared painful stories of being abused and disowned by family, of contemplating and attempting suicide,[87] and several speakers in their forties, fifties, and sixties recounted, in detail, their struggles to understand and cultivate a lesbian identity in a hostile world. When even LGBTQ-friendly spaces are still rife with misogyny that devalues and denigrates lesbian identity, the lesbian bar remains an important site for lesbians to explore and celebrate lesbian identity. The fight to save this one bar is a powerful reminder that queer spaces are still vitally important to the happiness and safety of queer people and that we must continue to pay particular attention to how and for whom queer spaces are constructed.

Hershee's story also serves as a warning that many of the conversations about the demise of the lesbian bar are too narrowly focused. Like so much of the work of queer history, these conversations tend to focus on the closing and opening of lesbian bars in large coastal cities and either assume that those studies also apply to bars in the South, the Midwest, or in less populous communities or simply ignore these areas altogether. In either case, because so much of the writing about queer lives focuses on just a few areas of the country, we have too little information about what queer lives are like in other places. This is magnified when we are looking specifically at lesbian lives and lesbian bars. A failure to widen the area of focus, coupled with narratives of the lesbian bar's demise at the hands of its very patrons, leaves us with a story that is as inaccurate and incomplete as my own understanding of lesbian bars when I made my way through the streets of Norfolk on that night in 2000, headed into the relative unknown of Hershee and my first lesbian bar experience.

NOTES

Cathleen Rhodes would like to extend her gratitude to the staff of Old Dominion University's Special Collections and University Archives for their assistance in conducting this research and to the many students, past and present, whose enthusiasm for local queer history research invigorate her work.

1. Ubiquitous in 1990s-era gay bookstores and novelty shops, pride rings were six cheaply made rings, each in a color of the ROYGBV rainbow, sold on inexpensive chains. At the time, pride rings were easily identified within the queer community as signaling queerness while not being recognized as such by others.

2. Charlotte's Web, opened in 1993, was the city's other lesbian bar.

3. Though the importance of representation is not infrequently written about or discussed, one can sometimes forget just *how* important it can be. As a latecomer to the HBO/BBC series *Gentleman Jack*, I was reminded of this when listening to *Shibden after Dark*, a fan podcast about the show. Listening to podcast episodes from 2019 when *Gentleman Jack* first aired, I was surprised by how intensely the hosts and their listeners responded to its lesbian representation. The hosts' preoccupation with physical intimacy between main characters Anne Lister and Ann Walker and podcast listeners' enthusiastic reception to these discussions attests to how starved young lesbians still are for these images.

4. Some of the more recent include Jack Jen Gieseking's *Dyke Bars*: *Queer-Trans Spaces for the End Times,* Mairead Sullivan's *Lesbian Death: Desire and Danger Between Feminist and Queer,* and Krista Burton's travelogue *Moby Dyke: An Obsessive Quest to Track Down the Last Remaining Lesbian Bars in America.*

5. Even during the writing of this essay there have been fluctuations, and from my initial writing to final revisions the number of lesbian bars increased slightly. The total number of all lesbian bars in the U.S. remains very small, however, and is far below the numbers in the 1980s and 1990s, so the phrase "dwindling numbers," still seems appropriate.

6. The Lesbian Bar Project, a fundraising campaign whose goal is to "celebrate, support, and amplify the remaining Lesbian bars" in the United States, identified twenty-one remaining bars on their website as of June 19, 2021, twenty-seven as of July 17, 2023, and thirty-three as of September 15, 2024 (https://www.lesbianbarproject.com/).

7. Babes, opened in Richmond, Virginia the year after Hershee and remains open in 2024. Though it opened and operated for many years as a lesbian bar, it later advertised itself as a queer bar and then as both. Its facebook page (https://www.facebook.com/babesofcarytown) in 2024 says it is "Richmond's Everybody's Bar."

8. Hershee was a lesbian bar inclusive of transgender and nonbinary people.

9. As a record, I believe it important to include very specific details, including much of what was said at Norfolk City Council meetings. Regretfully, I must also leave out many details and contributions of important players in Hershee's story due to space limitations.

10. Jack Jen Gieseking's discussion of financial solvency calls this particular argument into question, pointing out that couples made of two women make considerably less than heterosexual and gay male couples (an inequality compounded for people of color and trans and gender-nonconforming people), gay men are less likely to have custody of children than lesbians (and we might also look at caregiving for elderly family members), lesbians are more likely to be renters and take longer to realize home ownership, and trans and gender-nonconforming people face discrimination in housing and employment that disadvantage them financially. Jack Jen Gieseking, *A Queer New York: Geographies of Lesbians, Dykes, and Queers* (New York: New York UP, 2020), 27–29.

11. Simplistic explanations have also been used to explain what has happened to lesbian spaces more generally, including bookstores, coffee shops, and music events. A notable exception is Gieseking who offers a more nuanced explanation for "the decline of lgbtq spaces," saying that "my 2000s-generation participants' stories show it is not just the increased use of social media and mobile devices that has propelled the decline of lgbtq spaces, but other phenomena as well: the post-gay assimilation narrative, limited access to lgbtq history, policies and incentives that make the city welcome to landlords and not renters,"

and heterosexual people gentrifying lgbtq neighborhoods. Gieseking, *A Queer New York,* 25.

12. Gieseking makes a compelling argument about u-hauling (the supposed phenomenon of queer women moving in together after a very short time dating) that is relevant to this discussion, arguing that it is a radical queer practice that, in part, is related to the tenuousness of many women's existence as they face violence, financial hardships, and other difficulties. According to Gieseking, it is "an outcome of the precarity of lesbian-queer life. U-hauling and cruising can also be seen as queered responses to the hypermobility enforced by heteronormative state logics. . . . That U-hauling is also often considered a joke rather than a tactic of political economic survival speaks to the fragmented nature of lesbian-queer spaces and experiences that I show are tied together." Gieseking, *A Queer New York,* 225–28.

13. This, after all, is a primary reason for the existence of museums and historic houses.

14. My queer studies students and I take local residents on queer walking tours each year, and many of the sites we visit are empty not only of the queer organizations and businesses that once occupied them but also the buildings themselves. Several have been turned into parking garages, so neither the structures nor the address numbers exist any longer.

15. I founded and direct the Tidewater Queer History Project (https://sites.wp .odu.edu/tqhp/). TQHP preserves the LGBTQ history of southeastern Virginia through oral history interviews and the development and maintenance of digital and physical archives representing the area's queer past.

16. Judy Grahn, *Another Mother Tongue: Gay Words, Gay Worlds* (Boston: Beacon Press, 1984), 275.

17. Marie Cartier, *Baby, You Are My Religion: Women, Gay Bars, and Theology before Stonewall* (New York: Routledge, 2014), 5.

18. Elizabeth Lapovsky Kennedy and Madeline D. Davis, *Boots of Leather, Slippers of Gold: The History of a Lesbian Community* (New York: Routledge, 1993), 2.

19. Ibid., 3.

20. Lillian Faderman, *Odd Girls and Twilight Lovers: A History of Lesbian Life in Twentieth-Century America* (New York: Penguin Books, 1991), 80.

21. Ibid., 306.

22. Ibid., 162.

23. Cartier, *Baby, You Are My Religion,* 3.

24. Ibid., 4.

25. Ibid., 11.

26. Ibid., 172.

27. Faderman, *Odd Girls and Twilight Lovers*, 182.

28. Cartier, *Baby, You Are My Religion*, 1.

29. Grahn, *Another Mother Tongue*, 276.

30. "Local Womon Charges Harassment," *Our Own Community Press*, April 1983.

31. This is rather remarkable considering that Norfolk, Virginia is a midsized city whose lesbian bar representation rivaled that of much larger cities. For example, Gieseking notes, "At its Amazon apex in the late 1990s and early 2000s, there were as many as five dedicated lesbian bars open at the same time in [New York City]." Gieseking "On the Closing of the Last Lesbian Bar in San Francisco: What the Demise of the Lex Tells Us About Gentrification," *Huff-Post*, October 28, 2014, https://www.huffpost.com/entry/on-the-closing-of-the -las_b_6057122.

32. Marge Reed, interview by Cathleen Rhodes, Norfolk, Virginia, May 29, 2015, transcript.

33. Annette Stone in discussion with the author, March 10, 2021.

34. Norview Baptist Church had a history of antigay bigotry. In December of 1992 it and other local Southern Baptist churches placed a $6,000 antigay advertisement in the region's newspaper, the *Virginian-Pilot*. For a sense of the climate at the time for LGBT people, in 1993, just two months after the antigay ad, the *Virginian-Pilot* refused to print an advertisement for a winter pride festival to be held at nearby Old Dominion University.

35. Keith Maranger, "Commission OK's Expansion of Lesbian Bar," *Our Own Community Press*, December 1993.

36. Saleen Martin, "Former Hershee Bar Owners Carry on Thanksgiving Tradition at 37th and Zen," *Virginian-Pilot*, November 24, 2020, https://www.pilotonline .com/holidays/vp-nw-fz20-37th-and-zen-thanksgiving-20201124-wqrtswwlr5b jrjoufshjc5yy4a-story.html.

37. Martin, "Former Hershee Bar."

38. Sharon Bottoms was a Virginia woman who lost custody of her child because she was a lesbian. See *Our Own Community Press*, October 1993, 14.

39. Over the next several months, proponents of the city's purchase of the land repeatedly indicated that Stone should have bought it first. Many people who had not been participating in the work to save Hershee Bar also offered well-meaning advice about applying for historical status. It took valuable organizing time to repeatedly explain that we had been in touch with Virginia's Department of Historic Resources. DHR is very responsive to LGBTQ concerns, but Hershee was ineligible both for the Virginia Landmarks Register and the

National Register of Historic Places for two reasons: property owners must grant permission for a property to be listed and the property's historical significance must be at least fifty years old or the property must be "of exceptional importance." Contacts at DHR offered helpful advice about documenting the bar's interior and exterior, but there was little else they could do to help. Even if the property had been added to the registers, that would not necessarily prevent demolition and would not compel owners or government entities to preserve the structure. See https://www.dhr.virginia.gov/historic-register/.

40. The property was to be part of redevelopment in the area, and a condition of the agreement was that all buildings be razed before the sale was finalized. The *Virginian-Pilot* reported that this stipulation had recently become a regular practice for property purchased by the city. See Matthew Korfhage, "Hampton Roads' Only Lesbian Bar Is under Threat after Norfolk Buys Its Building," *Virginian-Pilot*, November 17, 2018.

41. NorfolkTV, "Norfolk City Council Tours Ward 3," June 7, 2018, YouTube Video, 1:09:39, https://www.youtube.com/watch?v=j7Aq1wj05Os&t=3s.

42. Ibid.

43. Ibid.

44. Ibid.

45. Ibid.

46. Jennifer Alomari, text message to author, June 15, 2021.

47. In comparison, only three Norfolk residents spoke that night about unrelated issues in the city. This was typical of the meetings Hershee Bar supporters attended. Hershee supporters almost always vastly outnumbered people speaking about other issues in the city, and often comments about Hershee were longer than the regular portion of the meeting.

48. Addressing council required signing up in advance. Norfolk's process opens sign up the evening of a council meeting and closes fifteen to twenty minutes before the meeting is scheduled to begin. Sign up requires full names and addresses. City council formal meetings are recorded and made publicly available on the city's website and on YouTube, and the minutes are available on the city's website. Minutes and recordings include names and addresses of all speakers. It is an intimidating process to many, but the public sharing of personal addresses made it even more intimidating for LGBTQ people.

49. NorfolkTV, "Formal Session—Norfolk City Council 6/26/18," June 27, 2018, YouTube Video, 1:48:33, https://www.youtube.com/watch?v=WinPRy8UeQo.

50. Ibid.

51. Ibid.

52. It should be noted that Norfolk City Council has had only one out gay member, Nicole Carry, who served a two-month temporary appointment. This would come up again in future meetings as some members of the LGBTQ community felt that the council's inaction on the Hershee issue was largely due to their misunderstanding of the queer community and the importance of long-standing queer spaces.

53. NorfolkTV, "Formal Session—Norfolk City Council 6/26/18."

54. Ibid.

55. Ibid.

56. Ibid.

57. Ibid.

58. NorfolkTV, "Formal Session—Norfolk City Council 7/10/18."

59. NorfolkTV, "Formal Session—Norfolk City Council 072418."

60. NorfolkTV, "Formal Session—Norfolk City Council 7/10/18."

61. Ibid., I drew on my own oral history work for these examples, but Norfolk is mentioned in others' work as well. Falcon, an informant for Marie Cartier's study of pre-Stonewall lesbian bars, recalled harrowing instances of violence at the hands of police and others while visiting bars in Roanoke, Richmond, and Norfolk. Cartier, *Baby, You Are My Religion,* 17.

62. NorfolkTV, "Formal Session—Norfolk City Council 072418."

63. Ibid.

64. Ibid.

65. Ibid.

66. Ibid.

67. Though some interpreted the response as insensitive, Johnson responded that her emojis were intended specifically for a commenter with whom she had a friendly working relationship.

68. The idea that a gay bar would become a CVS is also not a far-fetched one. In 2015, the owner of the Hippo, a popular gay club in Baltimore, closed the bar after forty three years and leased the building to CVS.

69. NorfolkTV, "Formal Session—Norfolk City Council 072418."

70. Ibid.

71. "Three Area Bars Close," *Our Own Community Press,* November 1982. Also on the front page of the same issue was news that the film *Taxi Zum Klo* had been seized for obscenity after being shown at the Naro Expanded Cinema on October 5. The city's "clean up" efforts were affecting queer people in multiple ways.

72. Gregory Samantha Rosenthal, "Make Roanoke Queer Again: Community History and Urban Change in a Southern City," *Public Historian* 39, no. 1 (February 2017): 44.

73. Rosenthal, "Make Roanoke Queer Again," 45.
74. NorfolkTV, "Norfolk City Council Tours Ward 3."
75. Rosenthal, "Make Roanoke Queer Again," 45.
76. NorfolkTV, "Norfolk City Council Tours Ward 3."
77. One of those exceptions came from McClellan in her address to speakers at the end of the July 24 council meeting when she remarked, "I believe, and this is Andrea McClellan speaking only, that we should move and help Hershee Bar find a new location, and I know that will make some of you unhappy because you want it to remain where it is. I believe it's a historic and relevant and important piece of Norfolk's history" ("July 24").
78. Ibid.
79. Ibid.
80. Ibid.
81. Ibid.
82. "OpenNorfolk Presents the 757 Market at Five Points," City of Norfolk, accessed November 1, 2021, https://norfolk.gov/Calendar.aspx?EID=11665#:~: text=The%20Five%20Points%20Neighborhood%20Spot%20is%20a %20temporary%2C%20flexible%20public,during%20the%20COVID%2 D19%20pandemic.
83. La Shonda Mims's study of lesbian communities in Charlotte, NC, and Atlanta, GA, is helpful in understanding this. Once Pride events became more corporate, they became both a cost-effective and safer strategy for city leadership and businesses: "The temporary tattoos, bottle openers, plastic cups, highlighters, and other branded giveaways were wise and cost-effective investments when compared with a national, or even regional, advertising campaign. Pride sponsors did not risk a widely visible alliance with the local queer community, given Pride's limited and target advertising venue." Mims notes that this "opportunity to quietly support Pride was especially important for regional sponsors in the South." Noting Food Lion's sponsorship of Pride in Charlotte in 2012, she says, "Most people who did not attend were never aware." Food Lion's "support of Pride remained invisible on its company website and in broad-based advertising campaigns in the early years of the twenty-first century. Yet for queer revelers, corporate financing of Pride brought significant popularity and visibility to the festivals and offered a false sense of acceptance in the mainstream marketplace." Thus, Pride celebrations today offer corporate and governmental participants the opportunity to appear supportive of LGBTQ people and causes, but the depoliticized nature of Pride events calls into question their level of commitment beyond showing up and giving away cheap, branded merchandise. La Shonda Mims, *Drastic Dykes and Accidental Activists:*

Queer Women in the Urban South (Chapel Hill: UNC Press, 2022), 137–38.

84. Kennedy and Davis, *Boots of Leather,* 29.

85. Ibid., 31.

86. Patrick Sisson, writing after the shooting at Pulse Nightclub in Orlando, argued that the Pulse tragedy itself demonstrated the need for queer bars: "The shocking horror of the weekend's shootings made clear the continued relevance and importance of these bars and nightclubs. . . . Gay nightlife has always served as vital space for community building and escaping societal persecution." See *Curbed,* "How Gay Bars Have Been a Building Block of the LGBTQ Community," June 17 2016, archive.curbed.com/2016/6/17/11963066/gay-bar-history -stonewall-pulse-lgbtq.

87. Just months before Hershee closed, the Human Rights Campaign released results of a survey of teens in the U.S. that identified "persistent, serious challenges for LGBTQ youth" despite positive cultural and legislative shifts up to that point (2018 LGBTQ). See https://hrc-prod-requests.s3-us-west-2 .amazonaws.com/files/assets/resources/2018-YouthReport-NoVid.pdf?mtime =20200713131634&focal=none.

QUEER LIBERATION AND THE OBSCENITY DEBATE IN HAMPTON ROADS

—

Charles H. Ford and Jeffrey L. Littlejohn

N ational histories of the lesbian, gay, bisexual, transgender, and queer (LGBTQ) rights movement generally open with a set of well-known events that occurred between 1945 and 1970. There is good reason for this approach. At the end of World War II, most gay Americans lived a closeted lifestyle governed by fear and paranoia. As scholar Gregory Briker has argued, "a nationwide consensus held homosexuality to be perverse and even dangerous, and gays and lesbians faced harassment by public authorities and private citizens alike."[1] In the years after the war, however, LGBTQ activists and everyday citizens launched multiple challenges to the pervasive discrimination that they faced. The first gay men's national organization, the Mattachine Society, emerged in 1950, and five years later lesbian leaders created their own group, the Daughters of Bilitis. At the same time, activists in California founded the community's first national magazine, *ONE*, which aimed to "push the [gay rights] message outward, not only to gays and lesbians . . . but to heterosexuals throughout the country."[2] These advances in the 1950s gained further momentum during the next decade, as teenagers and young adults participated in a sexual revolution that challenged older, Victorian norms of behavior, and federal courts legalized the use of birth control by women. The Stonewall Uprising in New York City in June 1969 capped off this period of struggle, as an array of queer folks protested police raids on the Stonewall Inn, launching the modern queer rights movement.[3]

Despite these advances in the years following World War II, state officials and police departments around the country continued to use sodomy laws to outlaw same-sex relationships and condemn people who participated in them. In addition, governments at every level equated homosexuality with obscene, illegal behavior. In 1953, for example, President Dwight Eisenhower signed Executive Order 10450 on security requirements for government employment. The document classified homosexuality as "sexual perversion" and cited such conduct as grounds for dismissal from the federal workforce.[4] In fact, historian David K. Johnson has shown how the federal government investigated and purged hundreds of gay employees during the 1940s and 1950s in what he calls the Lavender Scare.[5]

The U.S. Supreme Court generally failed to address the widespread and varied forms of discrimination that members of the LGBTQ community faced. Although the court did rule in *One Inc. v. Olsen* (1958) that homosexuality was not, by definition, obscene, the Court's other rulings on obscenity during the period—*Roth v. United States* (1957), *Memoirs v. Massachusetts* (1966), *Miller v. California* (1973), *Paris Adult Theatre I v. Slaton* (1973)—allowed localities wide discretion in determining if same-sex magazines, movies, and other forms of expression were obscene. Put another way, federal wavering on homosexuality and obscenity led local officials, particularly in the South, to maintain more comprehensive definitions of obscenity than the U.S. Supreme Court likely intended.[6] The community standards test, which originated in *Roth*, allowed municipalities to define homosexuality as a deviant, illegal sexual act. By the 1970s, however, the initial *Roth* community standards test had become too complex and contradictory. Even Justice William Brennan, the author of the original test, abandoned any attempt at defining obscenity in *Miller* because it was impossible to do so. Despite the profound social and cultural changes that had occurred between *Roth* and *Miller*, the Court left decisions regarding obscenity up to local officials based on the vague rubric of prurient interests or lacking cultural value.[7]

This chapter examines three controversies over homosexuality and obscenity that erupted in Tidewater Virginia during the era of gay liberation. It opens with a brief discussion of the police raids that took place at local bars in the 1970s, highlighting, in particular, harassment by the Virginia Alcohol Beverage Control Authority (ABC) of law-abiding gay customers at the Cue Club, the Pantry, and other gay bars. Next, we turn to queer publications that emerged in the 1970s, including Norfolk's Unitarian-Universalist Gay Caucus newsletter, which eventually became *Our Own Community Press*. It offered a voice and community-building nexus for gays and lesbians in the area. Conservative Christians and opponents of homosexuality in Hampton Roads viewed *Our Own* and other gay newspapers as instruments of deviant behavior, however, and demanded that they be removed from public libraries. As this debate raged, the showing of Frank Ripploh's controversial 1981 film *Taxi Zum Klo* kicked off another fight. The film, a dark comedy about a Berlin school teacher who lives different public and private lives, proved too sexually explicit for many audiences. In 1982, authorities seized the film after it was shown at the Naro Expanded Cinema in Norfolk's Ghent neighborhood, but the movie soon achieved a cult status among queer audiences who considered its treatment of gay culture and sexuality groundbreaking.

By examining these three flashpoints, this chapter highlights the uneven and ambiguous nature of perceived progress in the 1970s and 1980s. While LGBTQ activists challenged harassment at local bars and libraries, the U.S. Supreme Court's failure to clearly articulate gay rights left many people in the community open to even more persecution. On the other hand, we suggest that official bullying—from ABC raids to library restrictions—represented increasingly desperate attempts to forestall gay liberation, limit First Amendment rights, and manage heteronormative hegemony. In fact, the last of the three controversies occurred at a well-known art-house cinema that made its name showing provocative and award-winning fare that was not generally featured in the region's commercial, mainstream theaters. One would think that this would have been a safe space for free expression, but that was not the case in 1982, when municipal authorities seized the rented reels of the allegedly offensive film and refused to return it to its rightful owners.

The gradual emergence of visible lesbian, gay, bisexual, and transgender communities and spaces after World War II challenged conventional mores and standards. Yet, punishment for violating those spoken and unspoken rules seemed to be accepted in Hampton Roads, Virginia, until the early

1970s, when one *Virginian-Pilot* staff writer noted, "Tidewater's homosexual community appears to be emerging from the closet in a militant mood."[8] Galvanizing this change in attitude was the suddenly robust enforcement of the ABC's stricture that the commission of an obscene act in a licensed restaurant or bar would be enough to revoke that establishment's business and liquor permit. The agency had always defined the word "obscene" quite loosely: from the official suspicion that one was gay or appeared to be a homosexual or transvestite to the mere self-identification of oneself as gay or sexually deviant in any way. These banned behaviors could include engaging in same-sex dancing or participating in explicitly homosexual acts in public or private. Nonetheless, as increasing numbers of people openly proclaimed their queer identities, the ABC's harassment of otherwise law-abiding and deferential citizens became more and more controversial.[9]

For example, in the spring of 1972, the Cue Club, a bar off Hampton Boulevard near Old Dominion College, hosted a performance by patrons of the critically acclaimed play *The Boys in the Band,* which had been showing as a feature-length film in many of Tidewater's and the nation's movie theaters for at least one and a half years without complaint. Unbeknownst to the bar, however, was the presence of an undercover ABC investigator in the audience, who found the whole production to be obscene because of the openly gay nature of its characters. He eventually recommended the revocation of the bar's liquor license, but not before gathering evidence on three separate situations of handholding and group singing among male customers at the bar. The ABC promptly revoked the Cue Club's license, but the club's attorney, Peter Babalas, who also happened to be a popular Democratic state senator, secured a temporary injunction allowing the bar to continue to serve beer until the case was resolved. Babalas pulled no punches in his vivid description of the ABC's activities: "It's just like the Gestapo. The ABC people say, 'We say you did it, so prove to us you didn't.'"[10]

In order to protect its customers from both the ABC detectives and plainclothes street cops, the Cue Club installed a warning light system to be flashed when their presence was expected or when they were believed to be in attendance. Flashing bulbs and bursts of accompanying sounds would inform patrons to vacate dance floors and to close out their tabs before exiting. But that was still not enough to deter police from arresting people—mainly gay men—whom they perceived as homosexual based on their dress, hand

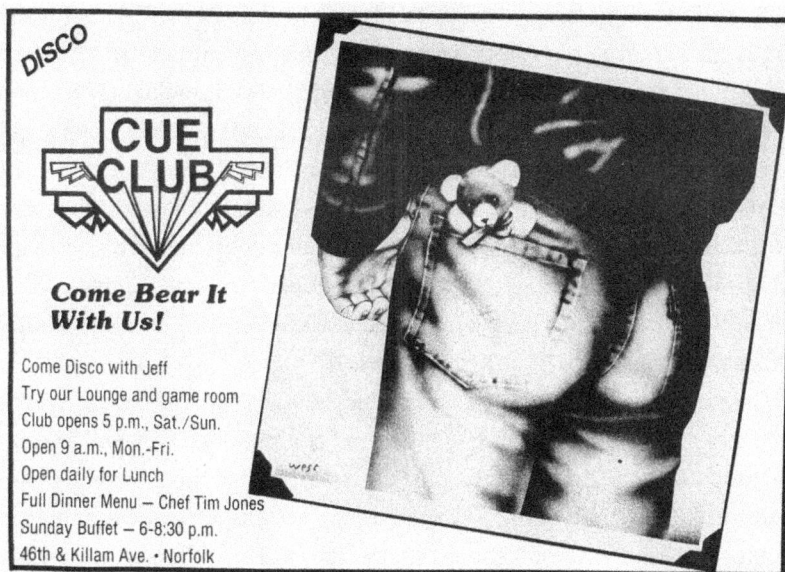

The Cue Club served as Norfolk's first openly gay bar. It was located near the campus of Old Dominion University. (Special Collections and University Archives, Old Dominion University Libraries)

gestures, posture, or ways of walking. *Virginian-Pilot* reporter Don Nunes detailed one instance in which undercover officers wearing athletic warm-up suits and tennis shoes arrested one young man literally for looking at them in the wrong way. The charge was for obstructing justice, but it was dropped a few minutes later after the officers let him go and gave the young man a warning about staring at other men and carrying himself in a masculine manner.[11]

This systemic harassment led to the birth of the Gay Freedom Movement of Tidewater, which attracted hundreds to meetings at Norfolk's Unitarian Church in August and September 1972.[12] Other meetings occurred at Mickey's, a bar in downtown Norfolk, which provided an internationally known respite for sailors and their friends during the height of the Cold War. It was adjacent to many small shops that catered to those in the Navy, and the Navy YMCA was right across the street. By the 1970s, however, it had acquired a largely gay male clientele, and, in 1972 with the emergence of the Gay Freedom Network of Tidewater, Mickey's even spawned the first local gay newspaper in the area, edited by Jerry Halliday and H. T. Kelly, Jr. The paper was

given the innocuous name *Friends* to please the majority of "nervous nel-
lies" at the bar, even if the relatively radical "gay-lib" editors had wanted it
to call it *Tidewater Gay Militant.* It lasted four issues in tabloid format and
featured ads for several prominent nearby businesses. While openly gay
and thus obscene by contemporary standards, neither the newsletter nor the
bar incurred the wrath of the ABC or the local police. Perhaps this was due
to the fact that the Cue Club was in a residential neighborhood by a college,
and Mickey's was located in a gritty part of downtown whose middle-class
residents had long left for what they considered to be oases of respectability
further west and north of the port city.[13]

The next local hightide of gay advocacy would spur the founding of a
much more formidable force for identity and community, *Our Own Community Press.* Beginning in 1975, two court cases accelerated the growth in mem-
bership and confidence of the Gay and Lesbian Caucus of the local Unitarian
church—first the case of Leonard Matlovich, the first person to declare
himself to be gay voluntarily in the military, and then that of the Pantry
Twelve. The case of the Pantry Twelve also reflected the lingering power of
the ABC's strictures on obscenity. In March 1976, Norfolk police raided Stephen Brown's bar, the Pantry (which would soon become the Nickelodeon)
at 118 West City Hall Avenue. They apprehended twelve people on an array
of charges from selling liquor by the glass to engaging in "lascivious" homosexual acts like holding hands with someone of the same sex or facilitating
a "house of ill repute." The Pantry Twelve stood up for themselves: in court
they donned suits and ties, and they hired a well-known and effective local
attorney and straight ally, the celebrated Pete Decker. As a result, the judge
dismissed all but one of the misdemeanors alleged against them. As in 1972,
the association with a well-connected star of the Democratic establishment
ultimately freed the victims of official harassment.[14]

Unlike the Democratic establishment as a whole, however, the Unitarian
Church in Norfolk had always stood up for social justice. During massive
resistance to school desegregation in the 1950s, its minister, the Reverend
James Brewer, led efforts to reopen a set of six public schools in Norfolk that
had been closed by the governor to prevent desegregation. Thus, in that tradition, the Unitarian Church was the launching pad for *Our Own Community
Press;* the first issue of this LGBT paper was a one-page newsletter of the Unitarian Universalist Gay Caucus in September 1976. Joseph McKay, Jayr Ellis,

Jim Early, and Garland Tillery, among other church members, were instrumental in establishing this monthly vehicle for awareness and advocacy.[15]

By October 1979, *Our Own Community Press* was disseminated for free at a variety of local restaurants, bars, beauty shops, universities, theaters, churches, and public libraries. Distribution in Norfolk seemed dominated by the port city's many gay bars, while the seemingly staid Virginia Beach, the "white flight" suburb to the east, had five branches of its public library system to take up the slack: Bayside, Great Neck, Kempsville, Virginia Beach Central, and Windsor Woods.[16] This public library emphasis may explain why Virginia Beach, not Norfolk, became the center of controversy over obscenity in the next year, but the rumblings and concerns over alleged breaches of community decorum began in the older port city.

In the first few months of 1978, the UUGC had distributed copies of *Our Own* for free at several Norfolk Public Library (NPL) branches. This was done apparently "with the permission of individual librarians." Someone then complained to the NPL trustees that this paper was openly gay and therefore obscene, and the board prohibited further distribution in May 1978. Two months later, Dr. Robert Melton, a member of the UUGC and a professor at Old Dominion University, requested that the NPL board reverse its

Norfolk's Unitarian Church served as home to *Our Own Community Press* and openly supported the LGBTQ community. (Sarah Bell Murphy)

ban on *Our Own,* noting the fact that other nonofficial publications were being given out by libraries. To him, *Our Own* was no different than a civic league's newsletter.[17] In September, a board member informed Jayr Ellis, a member of the UUGC, about the NPL board's decision in executive session not to allow the distribution of *Our Own* for the foreseeable future. Ellis promptly asked for a copy of the policy prohibiting the distribution of free, nonofficial materials, and he was told to issue a Freedom of Information Act (FOIA) request since the policy had been shaped in closed or executive session. This secret policy turned out to be a lie, and, in January 1979, the full NPL Board took up the question of whether *Our Own* could be distributed at its branches. Jim Early, a member of the Unitarian Universalist Gay Caucus and a founder of *Our Own,* had requested that a formal policy be adopted by Norfolk's system "governing the distribution of materials."[18] Accordingly, the NPL board formed a committee to draft such a policy by March 1979. At any rate, *Our Own* was still not available at any of the NPL branches.[19]

About a year later, in March 1980, controversy erupted in Virginia Beach over the alleged inclusion of obscene materials in the latest editions of *Our Own.* A news reporter from the *Virginia Beach Beacon,* the neighborhood supplement to the *Pilot,* criticized the content of three political or satirical cartoons and the background image on a women-oriented page. Especially egregious to this reporter was the republication of an original *National Lampoon* piece in which a child is portrayed sucking a thumb that was shaped to look like a penis. The background graphic went even farther—having real women wearing oversized sunglasses their breasts, with the saucy caption "What's up with those Foster Grants?"[20]

Official opinions varied. The library system's director, Marcie Sims, felt the materials were off-color and inappropriate, but she also thought these breaches of taste did not warrant pulling the copies. The city's vice mayor—dentist Henry McCoy—went further. He believed that sexuality in general, gay or straight, should not be addressed in a public library, and that *Our Own* was obscene because it broached the taboo topic. City manager George Hanbury agreed with McCoy; he ordered the removal of the remaining March issues from the libraries' premises. City councilman R. L. "Buddy" Riggs applauded the manager's action, saying that the libraries did not allow copies of *Playboy* to be lying around for anyone to pick up. Thus, the earnestly political *Our Own* was in the same category, to Virginia Beach officialdom, as the softcore heterosexual pornography in *Playboy:* it was inherently obscene.[21]

FREE

For information and help call
423-8291 or 499-3920

Sept. '76
1st issue

Unitarian Universalist Gay Caucus

P.O. Box 6184 Norfolk, VA.

not just another gay group is born...

In this first issue of our newsletter, we want to explain the philosophy of our group. Many gay groups have come and gone in the area without successfully motivating the community to action. Without a solid philosophic groundwork, we also could become sidetracked and divided, defeated from within as well as externally.

We devote ourselves to the improvement of gay life through increased positive visibility. Our minority is unique in that we are not outwardly visible unless we allow ourselves to be. We can be noticed in any number of ways, i.e. stereotypically, detrimentally, or productively. How can Tidewater continue to reject a group providing benefits not only to gays, but straights as well.

The gays who are confused, lack self-confidence, or question their unique life style are gays who must be reached. They must be helped to realize whatever decisions they make for themselves cannot be labeled "good" or "bad" by virtue of a simple sexual preference. Gay is good when we first accept it for ourselves, and better when we educate the pub-

SPAGHETTI FOR HELPLINE

In order to raise consciousness and support for the gay community at large, our group sponsored a spaghetti dinner. Approximately 70 men and women attended the buffet at the Unitarian Church, Yarmouth Street on the Hague on Tuesday, Aug. 2.

Discussion took place regarding the feasability of forming a gay help organization. A follow-up was slated for Aug. 10.

At the open-forum organizational meeting on that date, various means of awakening the Tidewater community to the needs of gays were discussed. We hope to petition for federal funds slated for minority groups in the near future. With these funds, the group will activate such programs as a gay helpline, a gay V.D. clinic, and counseling and legal aid for gays. Weekly meetings are open to the entire community and are held each Tuesday at 7:00 pm. We thank the Unitarian Church for the use of its facilities and would like

ADMISSION CHARGE: USED, BUT STILL USABLE CLOTHING TO BE GIVEN TO THE SALVATION ARMY (IN THE GROUP NAME) AT: UNITARIAN CHURCH ON THE HAGUE

BRUNCH SUNDAY SEPT 12 2 PM

In September 1976, *Our Own Community Press* published its first issue. (Special Collections and University Archives, Old Dominion University Libraries)

Norfolk's establishment, which took no action against the distribution of *Our Own* in its own libraries, advised Virginia Beach to allow distribution there as well. On March 29, 1980, the *Virginian-Pilot*'s editorial board weighed in. While criticizing *Our Own* for publishing the cartoons and background graphic in question, they urged Virginia Beach to allow distribution on the basis that *Our Own* was more than just these offending images. Indeed, they saw this gay newspaper as putting forth "a serious attempt to discuss an issue of social significance. For that reason, it deserves a place." They hoped that Tidewater would develop better and "more mature" mechanisms and processes in dealing with unpopular views and causes; banishment simply would not work in a diverse democracy.[22]

As a sop to those civil libertarians and to prevent potential litigation, the Virginia Beach Library Board voted 7–2 on April 7, 1980, to recommend to the city council a single, noncirculating copy of *Our Own* be available for patrons to view in the periodicals section of each of the system's five branches. Rightwing religious leaders had wanted the council to ban all copies from public libraries, arguing that the municipal government should not aid and abet violations of Virginia's Crimes against Nature Act of 1896.[23]

The Virginia Beach decision had unexpected ripple effects. Norfolk State University's Lyman Beecher Brooks Library abruptly removed its remaining March 1980 issues on March 25. The leadership there, including the library director Dr. Patricia Jordan, was "deeply saddened" to see Norfolk State's name on the distribution list for *Our Own* printed in the *Virginian-Pilot*. That open exposure was too much for the historically Black campus, whose officials worried about the negative consequences of being mired in such a hot-button issue.[24] Nevertheless, in February 1981, this earlier controversy probably did allow for the first mention of gay people in Norfolk State's student newspaper, the *Spartan Echo*—a front-page interview with Hal Carter, the founder and leader of Umoja, a local social network for African American gays and lesbians.[25]

Back in the white-flight suburb of Virginia Beach, because of the ACLU's promises to bring litigation, the city council delayed its final vote into the summer. It did not rubber-stamp the board's recommendation, as most had predicted. Officials soon grew dismayed that they would be sued no matter what they did—they had made their bed of controversy and now they had to lie in it.[26] While the council dithered, fundamentalist preachers went into action. Deeming *Our Own* as the equivalent of *Her Own*—a hypothetical how-to guide for prostitutes—Reverend Rodney Bell of the Tabernacle Baptist Church launched a petition drive to place this hot-button issue as a referendum on the 1980 presidential ballot. If the city council could not act because of legal technicalities, the voters should do so directly.[27]

This brought on a legal response. The Virginia Beach Friends of the Library, as well as the Freedom to Read Foundation, planned to sue to prevent the antigay referendum from being on the ballot. The Library Board's president, John H. Robertson, also backed this effort because the referendum set an inappropriate precedent for popular interference in library management. The referendum was not legally binding, but the city council had said they would do whatever the people wanted, even if it might technically violate the First and Fourteenth Amendments to the U. S. Constitution. The referendum lawsuit never materialized as its potential claimants fought among themselves, but at the same time, in September 1980, the ACLU brought forth a lawsuit to immediately restore distribution of *Our Own* at the libraries, citing discrimination and violations of expressive freedoms.[28]

Local voters, energized by the conservative presidential candidate Ronald Reagan, went overwhelmingly to the antigay side on November 4; all thirty-six precincts in Virginia Beach voted to ban the distribution of any publication that advocated or depicted homosexual acts in Virginia Beach libraries. *Our Own* said that since it did not do that directly, it was exempt.[29] At the same time, since the referendum was technically just advisory, it did not automatically generate opposing litigation. At any rate, it all became moot on February 9, 1981, when the ACLU and the UUGC dropped their lawsuit because the library board adopted a new standardized policy on the distribution of unsolicited, unofficial, free publications. The board now said that it would not allow any distribution, regardless of content.[30] The UUGC had apparently decided to call this new shell game a victory and go home. Meanwhile, the library board in neighboring Norfolk, allegedly the more cosmopolitan core city of Hampton Roads, refused to consider even the distribution of a didactic brochure entitled *A Message to You from the Unitarian Universalist Gay Community of Norfolk*. The pamphlet was not prurient at all but rather an intentionally dry treatise, but library board chair Charles E. Jenkins refused in writing to allow any free copies of this work to be given out at Norfolk libraries.[31]

In contrast to Norfolk's complete ban on the distribution of explicitly gay materials, Virginia Beach maintained its policy of one noncirculating copy per branch throughout this back-and-forth legal mess, but officials still wanted to show their politically correct contempt for gay people and cultures. Accordingly, right after the dropping of the lawsuit, the city sued the UUGC, hoping to recoup the costs of defending against the lawsuit. In August 1981, U.S. District Court judge John A. McKenzie ruled against the City of Virginia Beach, stating that "the public domain requires from time to

time that constitutional issues which affect a substantial portion of the population ought, without being threatened with attorney's fees ... to be aired."
Judge McKenzie maintained that a municipality should not discourage lawsuits brought on behalf of a significant number of citizens by making them
pay hefty legal fees incurred when there is a public debate and controversy
involved. In contrast, Assistant City Attorney R. J. Nutter had dismissed the
seriousness and credibility of the UUGC's original case; he surmised that it
had only been brought forward to raise money for and awareness of the especially opportunistic ACLU.[32]

On August 10, 1981, the City of Virginia Beach, which had been under
pressure from rightwing groups such as Citizens for the Family, appealed
Judge McKenzie's decision to deny awarding the municipality the dis-
puted attorney's fees. A single noncirculating copy of *Our Own* remained
available at each of Virginia Beach's libraries, and that limited access was still
angering certain Protestant ministers and their congregations who wanted
the paper banned permanently from the premises. Despite the popular support for the most draconian option, the city council and its lawyers took
their time in preparing their briefs, and it was not until July 12, 1982, that the
U.S. Fourth Circuit of Appeals met in Wilmington, Delaware, to hear oral
arguments, which sounded very similar to the ones heard by Judge McKenzie
nearly a year before. As expected based on the judges' line of questioning
during the trial, on August 26, 1982, the Court of Appeals unanimously
upheld Judge McKenzie's previous denial of attorney's fees. Religious groups
continued to lobby for a total ban, but the city council remained worried
about losing even more taxpayer money on endless lawsuits. Even the most
prim and proper council members seemed happy to maintain the current
policy, a compromise that activists on both sides hated. The 1980 referendum
had shown wide public support for a blanket prohibition, but the city council
made no efforts—privately or publicly—to comply with that explicitly homophobic sentiment.[33]

The legal definitions of obscenity changed dramatically during the late
twentieth century, and much of that change stemmed from test cases and
controversies in Tidewater Virginia. In the 1980s, the cities of Hampton
Roads and their surrounding counties still prosecuted adult bookstore

owners, pornography distributors, and theater owners for obscenity, which prosecutors increasingly defined as depictions of deviant sexual or nonheterosexual acts. The distribution of the gay newspaper *Our Own Community Press* was contested by certain public and university libraries as obscene, and entire state parks in eastern Virginia were closed for months to prevent what was considered obscene male cruising. A scholarly patina protected museums and universities from state laws delineating obscenity, but that respectable fig leaf was not there for cultural organizations with fewer resources. On the evening of October 5, 1982, the Naro Expanded Cinema in Norfolk's Ghent neighborhood screened the explicit if award-winning German film *Taxi Zum Klo* (Taxi to the toilet), which revolved around the love life of a young schoolteacher in Berlin and his fetishistic and sadomasochistic gay male encounters. The Norfolk police eventually charged the parent company of the Naro with obscenity, and the company and the Naro's owners had to plead guilty and pay a $250 fine. Although the Naro never again showed an X-rated film, the subsequent involvement of the ACLU and its legal briefs exposed the random and absurd application of the "community standards" at the heart of obscenity laws.

By 1982, the Naro had become what it is today: an iconic art house theater showing both camp and cult classics as well as cutting-edge fare. Just five years before, its owners Tench R. Phillips III and Thom Vourlas had transformed an aging vaudeville space built in the mid-1930s into a successful neighborhood anchor, resisting the headwinds of white flight and population loss that affected similar urban neighborhoods nationwide at that time. While its clientele remained largely middle-class and white until very recently, the Naro has always tried to expand the horizons of its audiences by sometimes shocking the bourgeois. But, in the case of the acclaimed movie *Taxi Zum Klo,* they thought they were catering to educated and elevated tastes. It was the first major work from the West German producer Frank Ripploh, and it was described as autobiographical by its promoters. One year before the Naro screening, the film had premiered at the New York Film Festival and went on to be included in a number of high-profile international events. It shared the Boston Society of Film Critics' award for best foreign film in 1981, and it went on to win an equally prestigious honor in Chicago. When it was screened at the Naro, an elaborate tour of college campuses for the film was planned to take place in the Christmas season and beyond. John Tilley, distributor of the film in New York, did admit that he was initially worried about the off-Broadway reaction to the film. Nevertheless, because it had attracted both critical acclaim and robust audiences, he was caught off guard by what then happened in Norfolk.[34]

Tench Phillips and Thom Vourlas also initially worried about the public reaction to the film's explicit sex scenes, but they had shown works with similar edgy content before without problems. Still, they only scheduled one screening of the film, worrying that its homosexual themes might turn off otherwise liberal straight patrons. To cover themselves, "a large sign at the ticket window warned patrons that the film was for adults only, and identifications were checked." Publicity reached the port city's gay community, however, who turned out in force; the theater was packed on a school night with even its balconies filled by over five hundred people. Jerry Halliday, a local gay puppeteer and showman, entertained those in line outside the theater with his erotic marionettes, providing a celebratory, carnival-like reception. This impromptu decadence must have angered Corporal L. R. Barnard of the city's vice squad as well as Chief Magistrate R. H. Carawan, who were in the audience, too. They apparently were not amused by the movie itself either, and they typed up an affidavit for the search warrant that was deployed to seize the Naro's copy of the film from Thom Vourlas's apartment just behind the theater in the wee hours of the night. Married with young children at the time, Vourlas described how frightening it was to have uniformed police banging on his door at 1 a.m. Thom was taken to the local station for questioning and was only released near dawn. The copy of the film remained in official hands, however, until years after the charges were brought.[35] Barnard and Carawan stated in the affidavit that the film was "graphically obscene" by community standards and that its content showed a "shameful, morbid interest in homosexual love affairs" that had "no serious medical, artistic, or literary material and went beyond the limits and candor of social acceptability."[36]

Almost a month later, on November 3, 1982, a circuit court grand jury indicted the Naro's parent company, Art Repository Films, Inc., for showing a "graphically obscene" film. The grand jury had met the week before to view the whole movie at the famed Granby Theater. Grand jury members included Sam Barfield, the owner and president of Hagan Plumbing Supplies, a former city councilman, and the current Commissioner of the Revenue;

other courthouse crowd members included Barfield's relatively liberal colleague on the city council Betty Howell. The Naro had retained the famed defense attorney Peter Decker, who had defended the Pantry Twelve six years before and obviously knew everyone in the room. Decker was quite the showman and man-about-town, and he cared deeply about the exercise of civil liberties. When the presiding judge for the Pantry Twelve trial saw Decker entering the room, he promptly dismissed the case saying these men could not have done this kind of obscene behavior if they knew Peter Decker. That kind of chumminess must have been present at the Granby Theater but it could not help his clients this time around—as the movie progressed into its "golden shower" scene, Decker allegedly exclaimed, "Well, there goes our case."

Indeed, Decker was more concerned about the liberty and reputation of his clients than about using this situation as a test case for civil liberties. His friend, City Attorney Philip R. Trapani, had informed him that "the two owners and their corporation could have been indicted on five counts of obscenity." Thus, Decker was convinced that Phillips and Vourlas should have their parent corporation plead guilty to a misdemeanor charge, which would be much better than losing far more before a jury not used to seeing graphic homosexual acts. Decker noted that explicit sex "was not the main theme of the movie, but according to Norfolk's community standards, it was close enough to the line that he felt comfortable to plead guilty to one charge and to pay a relatively small fine." He defensively went on to say: "I can guarantee there will be lots of freedom-of-speech scholars who are going to second-guess me, but I don't give a damn about them. I care about my clients."[37] In addition, Phillip and Vourlas were worried about the effects of the publicity on their box office, declining to screen the film *Insatiable,* which featured pornographic actress Marilyn Chambers, because they were not sure that the softcore version of the film would be legal in Norfolk. And, despite their private sympathy for local gays and their struggle for acceptance, they did not want to be seen as a gay couple. Given all these reasons, they took Decker's advice and pleaded guilty.[38]

Phillips told a *Virginian-Pilot* reporter that he did not want to be alone in any fight with the city, but there were others willing to help their cause. In particular, the director of the ACLU, Shan Kendrick, worried about "a significant chilling effect in Norfolk," as theaters would choose not to show a film with any controversial content rather than face steep legal fees from drawn-out litigation. Dr. Gordon Ball, assistant professor of English at Old Dominion University and an editor of Alan Ginsberg's journals, was also concerned that the settlement of the case might begin a national campaign of censoring anything that pushed the envelope culturally.[39]

Supportive letters to the editor of the *Virginian-Pilot* followed, sometimes coming from unexpected quarters. For example, Father John T. Cummings of Saint Mary's Catholic Church in Norfolk, a predominately African American congregation, admitted that he had seen *Taxi Zum Klo* in London and felt it was "not an attractive film." Nevertheless, he discerned some cultural or sociological value in its "realistic" look at compulsive behaviors such as sexual addiction. This case just happened to feature a homosexual. No one, he believed, in the audience would try to copy the main character's sexual addiction, but rather he suggested that they might reflect upon their own unhealthy choices in sexual behaviors or partners. In accompanying letters to the editor, concerned citizens Morris D. Smith and Chris Renner agreed with Father Cummings. Smith criticized the arbitrary community standards that had ushered in the controversy here, characterizing them as "fear, ignorance, and hypocrisy." Renner, a self-described "educated taxpayer," wanted the city to stop making moral decisions for him, noting that the ban on sexually explicit materials such as in *Taxi Zum Klo* was woefully out of step with contemporary cultural mores.[40]

More supportive letters followed. About a week later, Zachary Loesch, president of the Old Dominion University (ODU) Literary Club, wrote that he was shocked and dismayed at the city's seizure of *Taxi Zum Klo;* he pled for "every thinking individual to let our public officials know that we cannot accept esthetic standards by decree."[41] In a letter published the next day, Thomas W. Poynor was concerned about the lack of municipal priorities—comparing the seizure of the film's rented reel with the recent over-the-top arrest of an exiled prostitute by twelve city detectives. Insisting he was "neither a homo nor a customer of the exiled hooker," Poynor lamented the obvious waste of scarce municipal resources in pursuing these petty matters.[42]

Norfolk's leaders were rather petty and spiteful here. It would take nearly two more years of legal wrangling to return the seized reel to its rightful owner. While the local owners had felt pressured to settle, in January 1983 the New York distributor of the film, Promovision, teamed with the ACLU to file suit against three Norfolk notables—City Attorney Philip Trapani, Assistant City Attorney Lydia Taylor, and Clerk of the Circuit Court of Norfolk Hugh Stovall—seeking the return of their copy of the film.[43] Stovall was named because the seized copy was in his custody. In its complaint, Promovision emphasized that *Taxi Zum Klo* had never been found obscene by any court in the United States, including in Norfolk itself. Using the nuanced and fluid language of the community standards rubric, Promovision also showed how *Taxi* was not obscene by the federally sanctioned definitions. Thus, it requested that the court issue an unequivocal statement that the film was definitely not obscene. Finally, the company wanted compensatory damages and attorney's fees in the amount of $150,000 from the defendants.[44] Trapani and company sought dismissal of this suit on the grounds that, as government officials, they had immunity, and that none of the named three had the authority to release a film deemed "contraband" by the judge presiding over the Naro's settlement. They cited *Younger v. Harris* to argue that federal courts should stay out of state court criminal cases unless the localities and state had acted completely and intentionally out of bounds.[45]

It would take Norfolk's U.S. District Court Judge Robert Doumar until August 1983 to rule unequivocally against Promovision. He denied its recovery of the seized reel and further decided that Promovision had exhausted its opportunities to have the film returned. Promovision appealed and, on October 4, 1984, the Fourth Circuit Court of Appeals overruled Doumar and remanded the case back to him for reconsideration on the basis of failing to give the distributor a hearing on First Amendment grounds. The appellate court, however, made no mention of the film's legal obscenity. A few months later, Promovision and the city attorneys settled the case, with the distributor getting their reel back without any definitive judgment on the film's obscenity or any money. The *Taxi Zum Klo* case in Norfolk died with a whimper and not a bang.[46]

Much more satisfying to gay activists and civil libertarians, nevertheless, was the outcome of an impromptu controversy over the showing of *Taxi Zum Klo* in nearby Richmond, the Old Dominion's capital, in 1983. Here a Virginia Commonwealth University (VCU) student group of self-described "film buffs" planned and advertised to screen *Taxi Zum Klo* to their members and the general public on April 2. Somehow, this screening came to the attention of Richmond Circuit Court Judge James B. Wilkinson, who viewed the film in its entirety the day before the planned screening. Disgusted by its content, Judge Wilkinson immediately issued an initially permanent (revised later to forty-five day) injunction against it being shown in Richmond. The judge warned that if *Taxi Zum Klo* was to be shown by the student club in defiance of the injunction, club members present would be arrested and the physical copy of the film would be seized. The university administration agreed with the judge, further insisting that full-time faculty members from VCU vet the club's public screenings in the future.[47] The ACLU then stepped in to aid the students; it appealed the injunction, which expired before any court could act. The ACLU went back to court for the students in late summer before a different Richmond Circuit Court judge, Marvin F. Cole, who reversed his colleague after a two-day trial. Judge Cole found the film categorically "not obscene" by the *Roth* test and revised community standards of the day. The students were given the green light to screen the film, which they did to a record audience of eight hundred people on September 11, 1983. This was the decisive victory for expressive freedoms and gay rights that had not and would not happen in Norfolk. Only the ACLU's strategic decision to rely exclusively on straight experts and witnesses rather than including the testimony of a leading and openly gay student member of the club rankled Jim Early, *Our Own*'s reporter from the port city.[48]

The application of *Roth* community standards and their tailored revisions in reference to obscenity was supposed to be transparent, clear, and fair. In actuality, as we have seen in Hampton Roads during the 1970s and 1980s, the local, state, and federal courts were often in disagreement, reflecting personal bias more than objective argument. As late as the Reagan era, many municipal officials in eastern Virginia still viewed homosexuality as inherently obscene under the laws—something that the Warren Court had abandoned in 1958. The murkiness of this legal landscape could lead to dramatic moments and the eventual extension of civil rights, but it only underscored the precariousness of citizenship for openly queer individuals in the Old Dominion during and immediately after gay liberation.

NOTES

1. Gregory Briker, "The Right to Be Heard: ONE Magazine, Obscenity Law, and the Battle over Homosexual Speech," *Yale Journal of Law and the Humanities* vol. 31, no. 1 (2020): 66. Also important during this period was Alfred Kinsey's report *Sexual Behavior in the Human Male* (1948), which challenged previous academic studies that estimated homosexual people to be no more than 3 percent of the population. Kinsey reported that "thirty-seven percent of his subjects had experienced some kind of homosexual conduct between adolescence and old age." Indeed, Kinsey suggested that over six million American men were predominantly homosexual.

2. Briker, "The Right to Be Heard," 80.

3. Michael Bronski, *A Queer History of the United States* (Boston: Beacon Press, 2011).

4. Bricker, "The Right to Be Heard," 106.

5. David K. Johnson, *The Lavender Scare: The Cold War Persecution of Gays and Lesbians in the Federal Government* (Chicago: University of Chicago Press, 2004).

6. The U.S. Supreme Court first sought to define the relationship between sexuality and obscenity in *Roth v. United States* (1957). In that case, regarding the mailing of pornographic material in violation of the 1873 Comstock Act, Justice William Brennan argued that there were limits to the First Amendment's protection to free speech. Brennan discerned that those limits might best be decided by "the average person, applying contemporary community standards." If such a person found that "the dominant theme of the material, taken as a whole, appeals to prurient interest," then it would be obscene. In contrast, however, Brennan also wrote that material with "the slightest redeeming social importance" could not be considered obscene. "Sex and obscenity," he said, "are not synonymous." The Court followed this complicated ruling in 1966 by refining its definition of obscenity in *Memoirs v. Massachusetts,* adding that obscene material must not only appeal to prurient interest and lack social value, but must also be "patently offensive." Later, in 1973, the Court ruled in *Miller v. California* that obscene content "lacks serious literary, artistic, political, or scientific value." Yet, in *Paris Adult Theatre I v. Slaton,* the court narrowly ruled that community standards could be used to limit the showing of adult films in rural Georgia.

7. Bricker, "The Right to Be Heard."

8. Don Nunes, "Gay Movement in Tidewater Mildly Militant," *Virginian-Pilot,* October 29, 1972.

9. Ibid.

10. Ibid.

11. Ibid.

12. Ibid.

13. Charles H. Ford interview with Jerry Halliday, October 15, 2016.

14. James Sears, *Rebels, Rubyfruit, and Rhinestones: Queering Space in the Stonewall South* (New Brunswick, New Jersey: Rutgers University Press, 2001), 208–9.

15. *Our Own Community Press*, September 1976.

16. *Our Own Community Press*, October 1979.

17. Ibid.

18. *Our Own Community Press*, February 1979.

19. Ibid.; J. D. (Doyle), "*Our Own* Has Its Own History," *Our Own Community Press*, August 1979, 10.

20. "*Our Own* Distribution at Beach Libraries Halted," *Our Own Community Press*, April 1980, 1.

21. Ibid.

22. "No to Censorship," *Virginian-Pilot*, March 29, 1980.

23. Gary Hankins, "Library Board Axes Paper; Council to Decide Final Fate," *Our Own Community Press*, May 1980.

24. "Distribution," *Our Own Community Press*, April 1980; Stephen Heninger, "Opinion: Norfolk State Crisis," *Our Own Community Press*, May 1980.

25. "First Gay Story in Spartan Echo," *Our Own Community Press*, March 1981.

26. Jim Early, "*Our Own* Decision Due June 16," *Our Own Community Press*, June 1980; Gary Hankins, "Council Ineffective in Gay Controversy," *Our Own Community Press*, July 1980.

27. "Bell Launches Anti-Gay Referendum," *Our Own Community Press*, July 1980; Gary Hankins, "Referendum Likely to Be on Ballot," *Our Own Community Press*, August 1980.

28. Gary Hankins, "Suit Announced to Halt Anti-Gay Referendum," *Our Own Community Press*, September 1980; Gary Hankins, "ACLU Files Suit against Beach," *Our Own Community Press*, October 1980.

29. Gary Hankins, "Beach Votes 'No' on Referendum," *Our Own Community Press*, November 1980.

30. "UUGC ENDS LAWSUIT," *Our Own Community Press*, February 1982.

31. Jim Early, "Men Address Library Board," *Our Own Community Press*, December 1980–January 1981.

32. Jim Early, "Final Court Order in *Our Own* Suit," *Our Own Community Press*, August 1981. See also "Beacon Misleads Readers, Negotiation Claim Untrue," *Our Own Community Press*, July 1981.

33. "City Appeals *Our Own* Ruling," *Our Own Community Press*, October 1981; "City Files Brief in Our Own Case," *Our Own Community Press*, May 1982, 1,7; "Our Own Case Argued," *Our Own Community Press*, August 1982; "UUGC's Claim 'Far from Frivolous, Unreasonable, or Groundless': Virginia Beach Loses Case Against UUGC," *Our Own Community Press*, October 1982.
34. Steve Stone, "Police Seize German Film from Theater," *Virginian-Pilot*, October 8, 1982. See also *"Taxi Zum Klo* Confiscated," *Our Own Community Press*, November 1982, 1.
35. Stone, "Police Seize German Film from Theater"; Daniel Rubin, "Naro Pleads Guilty to Obscenity Charge," *Virginian-Pilot*, November 13, 1982.
36. *"Taxi Zum Klo* Confiscated," *Our Own*, 1.
37. Rubin, "Naro Pleads Guilty to Obscenity Charge."
38. Ibid; Charles H. Ford interview with Tench R. Phillips III, February 2017.
39. Rubin, "Naro Pleads Guilty to Obscenity Charge."
40. "'Taxi Zum Klo' Definitely Not Obscene," *Virginian-Pilot*, November 19, 1982.
41. "Public Morality Decree," *Virginian-Pilot*, November 25, 1982.
42. "12 to 1 Ridiculous," *Virginian-Pilot*, November 26, 1982.
43. "German Film's Seizure Prompts Lawsuit," *Our Own Community Press*, February 1983.
44. Ibid.
45. Ibid.
46. Jim Early, *"Taxi Zum Klo* Returns to District Court," *Our Own Community Press*, November 1984. See also *"Taxi* Stalled Again," *Our Own Community Press*, May 1983; *"Taxi* Decision Expected Soon in Norfolk," *Our Own Community Press*, August 1983; *"Taxi Zum Klo* Case To Be Heard," *Our Own Community Press*, March 1984.
47. "Richmond Judge Forbids Taxi Showing," *Our Own Community Press*, May 1983.
48. Jim Early, "View from the Gallery," *Our Own Community Press*, October 1983. See also, "'Taxi' Draws Big Crowd in Richmond," *Our Own Community Press*.

SELECTED RESOURCES
ON LGBTQ HISTORY
IN VIRGINIA

Over the last generation, Virginia's state agencies and major institutions have provided digital access to queer history and cultural sites that show-case relevant and needed information for state residents and tourists alike. Most significantly, the Virginia Tourism Corporation (VTC) offers an array of such sites. The most comprehensive is by long-time VTC employee Wirt Confroy, who has deftly matched LGBTQ+ content to the famous slogan of Virginia tourism: "Virginia is for Lovers" (https://www.virginia.org/blog/post /lgbtq-virginia-history/). A stunning 2020 portrait of Thomas(ine) Hall, the gender outlaw of 1629 Jamestown, starts the story, as Confroy mixes histori-cal tidbits with current programming for the various Pridefests around the state. After going through events in Hampton Roads, Blacksburg, Arlington, Richmond, Bristol, and other towns in southwest Virginia, Confroy mentions the visit of author JD Doyle, whose book 1981: *My Gay American Road Trip* chronicles his travels as a young man from Norfolk throughout the rest of the country. Links to Doyle's array of online queer resources and content are given in this description. Finally, Confroy ends with a glimpse at regional filmmaker Angela Harvey and her *Black Rainbow Love*. At a linked and related site (https://www.virginia.org/blog/post/historian-jd-doyleguardian-of-queer -music-history-and-advocacy/), Confroy offers extended interviews of Doyle, Harvey, business owners, and other queer notables and experts from around the Commonwealth.

Similarly, the Virginia Department of Historical Resources maintains its LGBTQ Heritage in Virginia site (https://www.dhr.virginia.gov/blog -posts/lgbtq-heritage-in-virginia) with interactive maps focused on the metropolitan Richmond area. This site also features an architectural survey of historic LGBTQ spots in Richmond with valuable context on the evolution of queer culture in the former capital of the Confederacy. It also has links to self-guided walking tours of queer places on the campus of Virginia Commonwealth University as well as in downtown Richmond, accompanied by relevant context.

The Virginia Museum of History and Culture also has a queer history site of its own (https://virginiahistory.org/topics/lgbtq-history) that delves into the local Richmond scene. Correspondence between queer artist Andy Warhol and Richmond socialites is highlighted, along with lectures by historians of queer culture about various aspects of sexual identity.

At its official website, Hampton Roads Pride features two pioneering films on local LGBTQ+ history—one on the City of Hampton, and the other on the neighborhood of Ghent in Norfolk (https://hamptonroadspride.org/rlcr). In these films, Charles H. Ford, a coeditor of this volume, describes a medley of queer spaces and conventional spaces launched or shaped by LGBTQ+ people that reflect this film series' title, "Red Lights and Civil Rights." Local controversies that got national coverage are included, such as the ejection of the Catholic LGBTQ+ advocacy group Dignity from Sacred Heart Church in Ghent and the story of Leonard Matlovich, who became the first voluntarily out member of the U.S. armed forces while stationed at Langley Air Force Base in Hampton.

The Tidewater Queer History Project at Old Dominion University (https://sites.wp.odu.edu/tqhp/) offers oral history interviews, commemorations, podcasts, and timelines about queer history and culture in Hampton Roads. Cathleen Rhodes, a contributor to this collection, launched this effort in the mid-2010s to interview long-time residents who were able to reveal aspects of queer history and culture during the heyday of gay liberation and beyond.

The College of William and Mary has launched its new Archive of American LGBTQ Political and Legal History (https://libraries.wm.edu/news/2022 /05/william-mary-libraries-announces-new-archive-american-lgbtq-political -and-legal-history) at Swem Library in honor of eminent historian and William and Mary alum John Boswell, whose brother, a straight ally, served as a Virginia Beach policeman managing the official response to queer protests at the Founders Inn.

For updates on more current events, Equality Virginia, the leading advocacy group for queer people in the state (https://equalityvirginia.org/), has links to the progress of pending legislation as well as to the origins and provisions of legal and political rights extended recently to all the Commonwealth's citizens, regardless of sexual orientation or gender identity.

CONTRIBUTORS

AMY BERTSCH (she/her) is an independent scholar with a focus on African American and Virginia history. Her published work includes essays in *African American Emancipation in an Occupied City* and the *Journal of Early Southern Decorative Arts*.

CHARLES H. FORD (he/him) is a professor of history at Norfolk State University in Norfolk, Virginia. With Jeffrey L. Littlejohn, he has published a number of works, including *Elusive Equality: Desegregation and Resegregation in Norfolk's Public Schools*, as well as essays in the *Journal of African American History* and *Southwestern Historical Quarterly*.

JEFFREY L. LITTLEJOHN (he/him) is a professor of history at Sam Houston State University in Huntsville, Texas. With Charles H. Ford, he has coedited *"The Enemy Within Never Did Without": German and Japanese Prisoners of War at Camp Huntsville, Texas, 1942–1945*, as well as authoring an array of books and articles including essays in *American Journalism* and the *Virginia Magazine of History and Biography*.

SENLIN MEANS (she/her) is coowner of The Beautiful Idea, an antifascist bookstore, queer art market, and radical community space in Charlottesville, Virginia. Before that she was Writer at Large for *C-VILLE Weekly* for many years, covering everything from art and wine to crime and politics. She is a trans woman and native of Charlottesville.

CATHLEEN RHODES (she/her) is a master lecturer and University Distinguished Teacher in the Department of Women's and Gender Studies at Old Dominion University in Norfolk, Virginia. In 2015, Rhodes founded the Tidewater Queer History

Project, a community-based organization dedicated to collecting, preserving, and documenting LGBTQ history in southeastern Virginia. Under her leadership, TQHP has built the Tidewater region's largest digital repository of local queer history and physical archive of historical objects. Having grown up in rural Virginia, she is particularly interested in queer stories and experiences in the rural South.

G. SAMANTHA ROSENTHAL (she/her) is Associate Professor of History at Roanoke College and Visiting Assistant Professor of American History at Washington & Lee University. She is the author of two books, most recently *Living Queer History: Remembrance and Belonging in a Southern City.* She is cofounder of the Southwest Virginia LGBTQ+ History Project, a nationally recognized queer public history initiative.

JAY WATKINS (any pronouns) is a Teaching Professor of history at William & Mary. Watkins has published *Queering the Redneck Riviera: Sexuality and the Rise of Florida Tourism.* Watkins is also cochair of the LGBTQ+ History Association.

INDEX

www.ingramcontent.com/pod-product-compliance
Lightning Source LLC
Chambersburg PA
CBHW030826270326
41928CB00007B/923